JACOB BOEHME
THE WAY TO CHRIST

TRANSLATION AND INTRODUCTION
BY
PETER ERB

PREFACE
BY
WINFRIED ZELLER

PAULIST PRESS
NEW YORK • RAMSEY • TORONTO

Cover Art:
The artist WILLIAM RABINOVITCH is a painter and sculptor who since 1973 together with artist partner Arthur Guerra has directed the Rabinovitch and Guerra Gallery in New York City's SoHo. He has studied at the San Francisco Art Institute, Whitney Museum Program, Boston Museum School of Fine Arts and a number of European schools. He has exhibited at the Allan Stone Gallery in New York City and the Monterey Peninsula Museum of Art in Monterey, California; he has also had a one-man show at the Casa Americana in Madrid and other galleries. Of his cover painting he says, "Boehme perceived God as having two faces, the face of love and the face of darkness. For Boehme, all life is fire. . . . This is the fire of God's love and the fire of his wrath . . . one fire divided into two principles. God's interior life manifests itself in this dynamic process, in the battle between contrary principles. Only through these contraries, this fiery movement, is love made manifest. The Trinity is not static, but living and animated. Hence, the image of the dark face . . . the light face . . . and the fire of love, existence, blazing forth."

Design: Barbini Pesce & Noble, Inc.

Library of Congress
Catalog Card Number: 77-95117

ISBN: 0-8091-2102-6 (Paper)
ISBN: 0-8091-0237-4 (Cloth)

Published by Paulist Press
Editorial Office: 1865 Broadway, New York, N.Y. 10023
Business Office: 545 Island Road, Ramsey, N.J. 07446

Printed and bound in the
United States of America

CONTENTS

The Editors of this Volume:

PETER ERB was born in 1943 in Tavistock, Ontario, Canada. He is presently Assistant Professor of English and Religion and Culture at Wilfrid Laurier University, Waterloo, Ontario, Canada. Dr. Erb's specialization is in late medieval spirituality. After serving as pastor of the Amish Mennonite Church in Tavistock, he re-entered the academic world, completing his M.S.L. at the Pontifical Institute of Medieval Studies, and his Ph.D. at the University of Toronto. He has published numerous articles, reviews and papers on Protestant spirituality. His books include *Schwenkfeld in His Reformation Setting* and *The Spiritual Diary of Christopher Wiegner*, and he is now working on a book entitled *Toward a Definition of the Contemplative Life*. He is the recent recipient of a Canada Council Grant to complete a book on Gotfried Arnold. Professor Erb has combined teaching and writing with an active career in research on Protestant monastic communities in North America, and Patristic scholarship among the Radical Reformers. Dr. Erb is Director of Library and Archives at Conrad Grebel College, University of Waterloo, Ontario, and Associate Director of the Schwenkfeld Library, Pennsburg, Pennsylvania. He has supervised doctoral and masters students at various universities in Canada and the United States. He resides in Waterloo, Ontario with his wife, Betty, and their two children, Catherine and Suzanne. Dr. Erb is a member of the Ostdeutscher Kulturrat, Kulterwerk Schlesiens, American Society of Reformation Research, American Society of Church History and the American Theological Library Association.

WINFRIED ZELLER, one of the most distinguished authorities on Protestant Spirituality alive today, was born in Berlin in 1911. He completed his graduate studies at the University of Berlin in 1946. He has been associated with the

University of Marburg since the early 1950's where he became a full professor of Church History in 1971. Dr. Zeller has published extensively, particularly on Protestant Spirituality of the 17th Century. Some of his more significant books include *Protestantism of the 17th Century* (1962), *German Mysticism* (1967), *Spirituality in Hesse* (1970), and *Theology and Spirituality* (1971). Since 1966 he has been a member of the Historical Commission for Research in Pietism. He serves in an editorial capacity with Will-Erich Peuckert on the edition of *The Complete Writings of the Lutheran Mystical Spiritualist Valentine Weigel* (1964–   ).

PREFACE

During the night of August 2, 1759 in Freudenberg, West Germany, a nineteen-year-old youth left his father's home and country since he had been forbidden to read Boehme's *The Way to Christ*. He fled to Amsterdam "because Boehme's book was printed there," but, finding no work, he went to sea. His immersion in Boehme's works gave him support and consolation on his many adventurous voyages and protected him from the temptations and vulgarity of ship life. After long years of inner growth and basic theological studies this man, Johann Christian Stahlschmidt, served from 1775 to 1779 as Reformed pastor in many congregations in Pennsylvania. In 1826 at Saarn near Mülheim on the Ruhr, the eighty-six-year-old Stahlschmidt died, a close friend of the hymn-writer Gerhard Tersteegen.

It is astonishing how great an influence Boehme's *The Way to Christ* had on the faith and life of the young

Stahlschmidt. It was to this book, he wrote, that he owed not only his spiritual awakening, but also the powerful impulse to a completely new spiritual consciousness. In time he received strength and consolation from the volume. In his experience Stahlschmidt did not stand alone. Numerous men in the sixteenth and seventeenth century, by themselves or in small groups, found in the thought of the quiet Görlitz shoemaker and in his writings a depth of piety which they often missed in the orthodox proclamation of the church of that day. Johann Heinrich Jung-Stilling, whose life's work led him from tailor to village school master, physician, university professor and writer, once set forth the striking idea that the religious spirituality of extensive lay circles in seventeenth- and eighteenth-century German Protestantism was in its foundations "mystical Boehmism and occasionally Paracelsian."

Historically, Boehme's significance lies in the fact that his profound thought is bound to a living piety in which mystical and Reformation influences are united in an harmonious whole. This was discovered not only by the Pietist conventicles of the seventeenth and eighteenth centuries, but also by the idealist philosophers and Romantic poets of the nineteenth century. Not only simple laymen but the cultured and learned also were actively drawn and stirred by the personal piety and the wealth of thought of the Protestant mystic from Görlitz.

Thus, for example, the painter Philipp Otto Runge was introduced to Boehme by the poet Ludwig Tieck. In his letters, Runge continuously returned to the thoughts of Boehme. "We discover," he once wrote, "that an unrelenting strength, a dreadful eternity and a sweet, eternal and infinite love arise forcibly against one another in vehement strife, as hard and soft, rock and water; everywhere we see these two, in the smallest as in the greatest, in the whole as in the particular. These two are the being of the world, are grounded in the world and come from God; God alone is above them." With Boehme, Runge sees in the basic colours blue, red and yellow,

the "whole symbol of the Trinity" which painting charac-
teristically brings to view and re-presents in art.

Contemporary man, as well, so easily given to
thoughtlessness and superficiality, can learn from Jacob
Boehme's profound spirituality. Our age, which suffers in a
purely external, material mode of thought, is at the same time
filled with a deep longing for authentic interiority. The
modern orientation to mystical reflection on the self arises in
no way from an introverted egoism. The man of the present
longs from the depths of his being to gain inner unification in
face of manifold distraction and to find the central and essential in face of the peripheral and extraneous. In the widely
practiced preference to place meditation before action, this
tendency of our time is clear.

To those who wish to gain self-discovery and self-
actualization through reflection on the self, Boehme can offer
significant spiritual aid. As his book *The Way to Christ* indicates, Christian piety begins with repentance, that is, with
self-understanding in which man comes to know the unfathomable self-seeking at the base of his being. Only by
repentant, humble self-understanding does man come to himself and to God.

Boehme's marvelous prayer book presents further a true
spiritual treasure which leads out from true repentance. What
Boehme writes on the true inner prayer of the heart belongs to
the most beautiful and refined thoughts on prayer in the history of religion. The examples of prayers which breathe in
their totality his ardent, longing, spirit of prayer can direct
modern man, for whom prayer is so difficult, on the path of
his own life of prayer. From Boehme one can learn the deci-
sive step from meditative religiosity to spiritual worship.

Today one often speaks of the virtue of equanimity, that
concept of "aequanimitas" which Western thought owes to
the philosophy of Stoicism. Jacob Boehme, however, unites
to this concept another spiritual tradition, namely Christian
mysticism. For the medieval mystics, the concept of "resigna-

tion" (*Gelassenheit*) is not in any way understood as the ability of man to remain passionless under all circumstances. Rather, for them and for Boehme, the expression "resignation" retains its full mystical meaning. "Resignation" means, in the Christian sense, to leave one's own will and to leave oneself to God's will alone. The Lutheran theologian Heinrich Bornkamm correctly pointed out that Jacob Boehme is to be described as a voluntaristic mystic. Man's bearing to God stands, according to Boehme, in the relationship of two wills which must be brought into agreement. According to the teaching of the mystic, the will of man is thus to be conformed—"of the same form" (*gleichförmig*)—with the will of God. The primary consideration of the mystic and Boehme is thus not for a philosophic concept of God which defines God's being, but for a genuine spiritual relationship by which man looks to God as the spiritual power which determines his will and changes his life.

Jacob Boehme turns himself to those who are "in earnest regarding holiness." For him religion is simply concerned with the salvation of man. In his teaching on the new birth, Boehme speaks of the new man who is born of God and has experienced salvation. Only the new-born man is able to direct the lost world back to God as the source of salvation. The Pietists and the revival movement of the nineteenth century eagerly took up Boehme's doctrine of the new birth, yet Boehme's thoughts were of value not only for past historical movements. His teaching on the new man comprises the keystone of his religious thought and sensitivity and commends the same importance for all times. Some years before Boehme, Johann Arndt in his four books on *True Christianity* had shown that the Bible describes holiness, not learning, as the ideal desired by God for man. Boehme's doctrine of the reborn new man reminds Christians, in an age in which Christendom is broken externally by doctrinal antagonisms and confessional divisions, of the true destiny desired by God for man.

PREFACE

All unrest in the world is caused by the inner anxiety of man. Boehme agrees with Augustine that only the man who has found peace of heart in God is able to bring the world to peace. In the soul of man himself lies the basis of his feeling of misfortune. Deep in his interior dwell melancholy and dread. In his doctrine of the humours Boehme indicates how strongly man is ruled by the basic experience of melancholy. Without the consolation of the Holy Scriptures man would be lost. The example of Stahlschmidt indicates in how astounding a manner Boehme's *The Way to Christ* can work as a book of consolation.

Only he who has found in religion, to quote Schleiermacher, "the sense and taste of the infinite" will bring proper understanding to Boehme's profound dialogue "on the supersensual Life" and his explications "on divine contemplation." And yet the reader may perhaps begin with the dialogue between the master and student in which Boehme's agreement with the traditions of Christian mysticism is most clearly expressed. Moreover, here Boehme's language achieves a marvelous simpleness, born as it is out of the silent simplicity of the great mystic. Immersion in the ideal of unaffected and simple piety could help man today to conquer the horrid reductionism and frightful simplification which makes the thought and language of contemporary man appear so insipid and primitive.

In spite of the narrowness of his environment, Jacob Boehme was a man of universal spirit. His thought extended itself far and contained an original theology of nature. Yet, however greatly his profound ideas influenced the history of Western philosophy, his greatest significance lies in the area of spirituality. He was truly "a man of God" (2 Timothy 3:17).

Professor Doctor Winfried Zeller
Marburg on the Lahn

FOREWORD

The Way to Christ is a collection of nine treatises on the spiritual life by the Görlitz shoemaker and visionary Jacob Boehme (1575–1624). Following the circulation of his first book in manuscript form in 1612, Boehme was attacked by the orthodox churchmen of his city and was forbidden to write. He remained silent for seven years but then once again, at the urging of friends, took up the pen to formulate more fully his complex vision of the nature of good and evil and their one source in the divine abyss.

The treatises in *The Way to Christ* were written during the last four years of his life and were collected and published under that title by his followers a number of times over the next century. The book was intended to serve as a meditational guide and as an aid to edification and consolation. Together, the treatises epitomise the breath and depth of Boehme's thought in its final form.

FOREWORD

Published as directives to a wayfarer, travelling from his sinful state to an ecstatic visionary experience with divine wisdom (the Virgin Sophia), *The Way to Christ* begins with a discussion of the need for repentance and provides examples of daily prayer literature. It then treats the nature of true resignation and the new birth by which the soul is betrothed to the divine Sophia. The remaining sections introduce the reader into the mystery of this new life, the modes of its development and the joy of its maturity.

INTRODUCTION

Jacob Boehme's *The Way to Christ* provides the best introduction to his thought and spirituality. A collection of nine separate treatises, its parts were written late in his career and reflect his final theological position, a position established not aside from his earlier work but on it. The work is a cross section of both his theological and literary styles. It includes highly speculative pieces, practical devotional guides and edificatory material for thought and action.

The Way to Christ immediately introduces the reader not only to Boehme, but to the Boehmist tradition, a tradition from which its inaugurator cannot always be easily extricated.[1] Following Boehme's death in 1624, his disciples Abraham von Franckenberg (1593-1652) and Johann Theodor von Tschech (1595-1649) carried his works and ideas throughout Europe with missionary zeal. Among others, the Silesian poets Quirinus Kuhlmann (1651-1689), who was burned at the stake for his sectarianism in Moscow, and Johann Scheffler (1624-1677), better known as Angelus Silesius—the "Silesian Angel" who converted from Lutheranism to Catholicism, transformed Boehme's thought and symbols into poetry. By 1661 Boehme's complete works were translated into English by John Sparrow (1615-1665) and shortly after the Philadelphian Society was established in London by the Boehmist visionaries John Pordage (1607-1681) and Jane Leade (1623-1704). Boehme was known to men of the stature of Benjamin Whichcote (1609-1683) and evidence of his influence can be traced in the works of the 17th-century writers John Milton (1608-1674) and Isaac Newton (1642-1727) among others. In the Lowlands his thought was taken up by the Quietists Pierre Poiret (1646-1719) and Antoinette Bourignon (1616-1680).

The Way to Christ exists, in title and form, because of this Boehmist tradition. On New Year's Day 1624 Boehme's friends printed, seemingly without his knowledge, three of his treatises: *On True Repentance*, *On True Resignation*, and *On the Supersensual Life*. The work was reprinted in 1628 to include *On the New Birth* and other smaller pieces. In this form it was translated by Sparrow into English in 1648. With other slight additions Sparrow included *The Conversation Between an Enlightened and Unenlightened Soul*. Johann Georg Gichtel (1638-1710), the most important of Boehme's editors, interpreters and popularizers in the late 17th century, printed *The Way to Christ* with its present contents for the first time in 1682. Gichtel knew of all earlier printings of the work and of individual publications of the separate treatises in Dutch and German, and was concerned to establish an order of the treatises that would best serve the uninitiated reader. His order, with one slight variation (Gichtel's third treatise was reprinted as the second because it treated the same theme as the first), was maintained by later editors.[2]

The treatises as they were printed were to mark stages on the way to Christ. After proper repentance (treated in the first two treatises; the second treatise was generally printed as an addendum to the first), the reader is to pray properly (the third treatise), resign himself fully to God (the fourth treatise), experience the dimensions of the new birth that results from such resignation (the fifth treatise), and grow in divine contemplation (the sixth and seventh treatises). The eighth treatise is a dialogue summation of the earlier works; the ninth provides practical advice for souls who walk on the path of the new birth. As the reader proceeds, the language becomes ever more technical, the structure more contorted and the ideas more difficult to grasp. The reader is progressively introduced into the Great Mystery (*Mysterium Magnum*). Reading is not a simple activity of the mouth; it is an incorporation of the principles seen by the reader. The reader is called upon to understand, to know intellectually and emotionally, the depth of the subject treated. The Great Mystery to which he is introduced is the Mystery of the divine and is thus infinitely understandable. Boehme is aware that all reading involves a shaping of consciousness and therefore he warns his reader at the very beginning not to continue if he is not in earnest. The person who finishes a book is not the same person who began it. If he understands its content even in part, he takes upon himself a great burden. He must accept and follow, accept and not follow, or reject the contents. Whichever he does, he re-forms his orientation in an unchangeable way. The reader is not the same man he was before he began to read Boehme's words; he is one who has heard the words and has gained insight from them, or one who, having seen the words, considers them of no consequence and sets them aside. His consciousness thereafter will be different because of this encounter.

When the encounter is with the idea of being and nonbeing, of Nothing and Something, of all, then by the very ultimate nature of the encounter, one's consciousness is ultimately shaped to blessedness or damnation. Because of this, Boehme taught, it is better to avoid the encounter if one is not in earnest, for, if one is not "wholly and completely" so, one will too lightly set aside the seriousness of the questions and suffer damnation. The increasing difficulty in Boehme's vocabulary and treatment is, therefore, as Boehme's followers would have seen it, providential since it restricts readership. Only the most earnest, the most serious readers will continue on the path outlined in the spiritual guide *The Way to Christ*.

Boehme had experienced concurrent growth in earnestness and insight in his own life, and, out of love for neighbour and God, he wished to describe the path he had taken. The idea at times suggested that Boehme was a recluse, a solitary visionary who sat quietly at his bench and humbly repaired shoes, must be set aside. His spirituality developed in a remarkably active life. He was born in 1575 into a pious Lutheran farming family of substantial means.[3] His father held offices in the local church in Boehme's native village of Alt Seidenberg near Görlitz. A child of weak constitution, Boehme was apprenticed to a shoemaker following an elementary education in the local school.

Almost nothing is known of Boehme's first twenty-four years. His disciple and first biographer, Abraham von Franckenberg, tells of visions that came to Boehme (the discovery of wealth in a hidden cave; a prophecy regarding his future greatness by a stranger) during this period, but the accounts are hagiographical and are paralleled by other legends in the area. In its indications of Boehme's deep piety as a young man, the von Franckenberg biography is valuable, but it does not suggest anything of what must have been a busy, difficult and at times frustrating and debilitating life as a young tradesman. In 1599, Boehme became a citizen in Görlitz and entered into business there as a shoemaker. In May of that year he married a local butcher's daughter, Catharina Kuntzschmann, and shortly thereafter purchased a home. Between 1600 and 1611 his wife bore four sons. Throughout his life he was an active business and family man involved in problems relating to the transference of goods, controversy among the guilds, the sale of property and private and public litigation. Later in his life he would leave shoemaking and take up the linen trade. With other citizens in Görlitz, he would face the personal and economic difficulties brought on by the Thirty Years' War.

For a man of Boehme's religious interests, Görlitz was an exciting location. In the city were followers of the Silesian nobleman, the spiritualist Caspar Schwenckfeld von Ossig (1489-1551)[4] and other groups who took interest in the work of the alchemist Theophrastus Bombastus von Hohenheim, Paracelsus (1493-1541), and the nature mystic Valentine

Weigel (1533-1588).[5] The Paracelsians and the Weigelians in particular would have had an interest in Renaissance Neoplatonism and the Jewish mystical tradition, the Cabbala. The influence of all these groups can be noted in Boehme's work from a very early period, and as his career developed, he made greater use of their language, symbols and thought structures, many of which were reshaped and incorporated into his own system.[6]

The spark that ignited this environment for Boehme was provided with the arrival of Martin Moller (d. 1606) who came to the city as a Lutheran pastor in 1600. Moller had read much medieval mystical literature and was of that sector within Lutheranism that by the turn of the 17th century was consolidating its opposition to what has been labelled Protestant Orthodoxy or Scholasticism.[7] In the religious controversy of the mid 16th century, the debating theologians, Lutheran and Calvinist, developed a precise theological methodology and vocabulary particularly influenced by the Spanish-Jesuit scholasticism of the 16th century, and its formulations quickly took control in university and church. Protestant Orthodoxy insisted on the acceptance of closely worded doctrinal statements of faith. To its enemies it was seen as a dry, intolerant defense of a single denomination's position, and as lacking any concern with issues relevant to religious life or the practice of Christian virtue and devotion.[8] From its beginnings Lutheran Orthodoxy was opposed by men who were primarily interested in the practice of piety: personal renewal, individual growth in holiness and religious experience.[9] This practically oriented opposition found a spokesman in Boehme's contemporary, the Lutheran pastor and author Johann Arndt (1555-1621), who in his *True Christianity* and numerous devotional works established the direction of the movement.[10]

As part of this movement Moller immediately organized

his "Conventicle of God's Real Servants" and Boehme, awakened in the revival, joined. Later in 1600, Boehme experienced his first great revelation. Exactly what comprised the revelation is not known, but von Franckenberg's explanation of the experience as resulting from the reflection to him of his soul in a pewter dish is suggestive in that the image of an eye reflecting back upon itself from its mirrored likeness is one that Boehme used at a number of points in his later writing. In this instantaneous and overwhelming experience, Boehme saw an answer regarding that question which gave him greatest concern, the troubling question of theodicy. Boehme's initial insight developed over the next twelve years, during which his prophetic role became clear to him.[11] Awakened he saw many about him sleeping. He began to write, and in 1612 finished his *Aurora* or *Day-Dawning* which, he hoped, would open the moral, intellectual and spiritual eyes of all. What Boehme intended to do with the work is uncertain. It may have been meant for only a small group of associates, but one of them, without Boehme's knowledge, made copies and circulated them. Early in 1613 one of these copies fell into the hands of Martin Moller's successor, the chief pastor Gregory Richter, who in addition to his concern for the defense of Lutheran Orthodoxy had personal reasons for attacking Boehme. He had Boehme's book confiscated and on July 30, 1613, its author was banned from further writing.

Boehme ceased writing for a "sabbath of years," as he described it, but the period merely afforded an opportunity for him to increase his learning and further his speculation. In January 1619, after another illumination that once more incited his prophetic spirit, he broke his silence with his *De tribus principiis, or On the Three Principles of Divine Being*. His fame had not waned during these years and it may be that a large part of his decision resulted from the prompting of friends. Alchemical images shaped the form of his arguments in his works of the next year and a half and they remained strong for some time thereafter.

In 1670 he wrote *On the Threefold Life of Man, Fourty Questions on the Soul, On the Incarnation of Jesus Christ*, the *Six Theosophical Points* and the *Six Mystical Points*. The following year was primarily devoted to apologetic writing. With the completion of *De Signatura rerum, or Concerning the Birth and Designation of All Being* in 1622, Boehme's probing of the nature of the universe with alchemical tools came to an end and from then to the end of his life he reformulated the main patterns of his thoughts within the more common themes and images of traditional Christianity. During this period he wrote *On Election to Grace, On Christ's Testaments*, the commentary on Genesis entitled *Mysterium Magnum*, his largest work, and the *Clavis* or *Key* to his chief doctrines. It was during these years, as well, that he wrote the treatises contained in *The Way of Christ*, the first and second in 1623, the third, eighth and ninth in 1624. Treatises four to six were written in 1622. Only the seventh treatise was written much earlier, in 1620.

The last years of his life were marked with conflict. As early as 1618, the year in which his *Theosophical Letters* begin, mention is made of Boehme's converts; his disciples were meeting regularly in Görlitz in 1623. Their enthusiasm had its effect and, as rumours of the circle grew, Richter became newly enraged. The authorities did not know of the works written since 1619 and supposed that to that date Boehme had maintained silence. The publication of *The Way to Christ* on New Years Day 1624 immediately brought forth angry broadsides and sermons by Richter against which Boehme attempted defense. In March he was told by the municipal council to seek his fortunes elsewhere and went for a short time to Dresden. Late in 1624, ill and working on the *Theosophical Questions*, he returned to his home in Görlitz. Richter was dead by this time and his replacement was called to Boehme's home to minister to the dying prophet. His confession was accepted by the pastor as orthodox and after receiving the Supper he died several days later on November 17.

* * *

The thought that influenced so many, Boehme insisted, was from his own experience, and not that of any other mind.[12] Thus he wrote, "I do not wish to set down anything strange which I did not myself experience so that I do not find myself as a liar before God."[13] Yet the reason Boehme "set down" his works was not his own. "I do not write of my own accord but by the witness of the Spirit which no one can withstand. It stands in its own strength and does not depend on our desire or will."[14] "I have always written as the Spirit dictated and left no place for reason."[15] By such statements however Boehme did not wish to deny that he had used many sources or that he had learned much from them. Reason was not to be rejected as he noted several times in his *Way to Christ* and elsewhere;[16] it was to be directed to its proper end.[17] Boehme believed that his writing had come from the Spirit. It was intended to direct his fellow-believers back to the Spirit as he had been directed.[18] "If you grasp the Spirit of the Creator, you will need no more admonishment, but you will rejoice and be happy in this light, and your soul will laugh and triumph with it."[19]

The path on which Boehme wished to lead an earnest reader was a path of experience, a path that led from self-knowledge to conversion and patience in persecution, expressed properly in love for God and neighbour. It was a path on which a visitation of the "eternal light" might be granted. Such a visitation came to Boehme at a number of points in his own career. In it his "spirit saw immediately through all and in all creatures, knew God in plant and grass, who He was and what His will was."[20] Under such an impulse his will was immediately driven to describe God's being.

The being of God that Boehme experienced and wished to describe was primarily a burning love, the light of which illuminated God's image to which man had been created. Once illuminated, Boehme believed, a man knows his proper direction. He must then leave all false images of the world, his total "I," all creatures he possesses. He must detach himself from the things of the world and with firm resolution and continual prayer seek the grace of God. In this search the image corrupted in the fall would come alive and he would experience mystical union or, as Boehme often described it, the marriage of the Virgin Sophia with the soul.

Sophia or wisdom is one of the most difficult concepts in Boehme's system to grasp. No tongue nor person can describe Her, Boehme insists.[21] His continual attempts to portray Her, to create proper images in which She may be best understood, adds to the difficulty. "In [wisdom] is revealed what God is in His depth. Wisdom is God's revelation and the Holy Spirit's corporeality; the body of the Holy Trinity."[22] "She holds the *Mysterium Magnum* out of which the Spirit reveals the wonders of eternity. The Spirit gives Her essence, since She is His food for His hunger. She is a being of wonder without number or end and has no beginning. The Spirit began Her in desire from eternity and remains into eternity. She is a body of the Number Three so that the Spirit stands in an image without which He would not be known."[23]

Boehme speaks of Sophia always by analogy (*im Gleichniss*).[24] As the revelation of God, Sophia is related to all three persons of the Trinity. "As the soul is in the body and reveals itself in the flesh's essence . . . God's wisdom is the outspoken being by which the power and Spirit of God . . . reveals itself in form. She bears . . . but she is not the divine principle. [She is] the mother in which the Father works. And therefore I call Her a Virgin because She is the chastity and purity of God and brings no desire behind Herself . . . but Her inclination goes before Her with the revelation of the Divinity."[25] Above all, "She is the dwelling place of the Spirit of God . . . She is a mirror of the divinity, for each mirror is silent, and bears no likeness except the likeness it receives. Thus the Virgin wisdom is a mirror of divinity in which the Spirit of God beholds itself . . . and in Her the Spirit of God saw all the forms of creatures . . . At the same time she is like the eye that sees."[26] She is the seeing as Holy Spirit, the mirror as Son and the eye as Father. In Her Adam reflected the Trinity in Paradise, but he fell asleep. He slept as one and woke as two. He slept to eternal being and woke to the elemental existence in which he came to know evil and good.

The way to Christ is the way back to Paradise and union with the Virgin Sophia. Despite the alchemical images in much of Boehme's work, his first treatises in *The Way to Christ* are best understood in the context of Lutheran theology rather than aside from it. Luther himself was opposed to speculative mysticism yet his thought provided a source for the many Lutheran mystics in the 17th century. Warning against speculative mysticism early in his career, for example, Luther wrote, "Many labor and dream many things regarding mystical theology. They are ignorant, knowing not of what they speak or what they affirm."[27] One must not suppose, however, that these negative attitudes were applied by Luther to all mystical writing. Mystical theology was, he believed, a legitimate topic for theological study,[28] and as a young man he praised the life of contemplation.[29] Mysticism he understood with Bernard of Clairvaux as "the experience of God,"[30] but for Luther this was the immediate experience of every believer and not the experience of chosen souls who had reached the highest rung on a ladder stretched toward the divine. For Luther, mystical union defined not the end of the search for Christian perfection, but rather the beginning, the incorporation of every believer into the body of Christ.[31] The terminology of mystical theology was applied to this initial union; it was democratized as it were.[32] For later Lutherans, the goal of the Christian life tended to be defined in terms of holiness, of each individual's resignation and obedience to God's will as expressed in Scripture or directly by the Spirit. The language of mystical theology was for them reduced to the needs of moral theology, although among certain theologians including Boehme, a possibility for mystical experience in an ever-present faith union was left open.[33]

It was not Luther's initial concern to set aside mystical literature; rather he wished to point out the theological and spiritual dangers involved in speculation on mystical union. His aim was first to clarify the role of faith in the life of a Christian, a role he continuously discussed in terms borrowed from late medieval mystical writings.

> Moreover faith is that light above our every achievement. Nothing other than the light of faith can lift us to it because it itself is most high. It pours forth over us; by it we are raised up. From this it is able to be described as closed and incomprehensible to us although it comprehends us.[34]

This selection strikes the keynote of Luther's theology. Every possibility of gaining access to the divine on one's own merit is closed. God works all in man. He strips the soul, effecting faith in it, and in the stripping man experiences the wrath of God, God's "No." Yet, in this turmoil, faith grasps God's "Yes" to man. It clings to the experiential knowledge of the promise that although a sinner, man is justified—*simul justus et peccator*. Before death man can never hope to rise above this paradoxical situation. He can know God's love only through the torment of the cross. Any other attempt on man's part to comprehend the glory of the divine is in reality the flaunting of man's own supposed abilities, an act of idolatry.

Elsewhere Luther treats the same theme with texts from the Song of Songs, so popular among medieval mystics, and in explicitly mystical vocabulary,[35] although he reshaped that vocabulary to suit his particular needs. This reshaping is best seen in his use of the word *exstasis* (ecstasy). Luther was influenced in his use of this term by Augustine, in whose work it has both positive and negative connotations; *exstasis* can describe the panic in the fear of death or the experience of revelation, much in the same way as Luther's word "faith" does.[36] Luther, then, had little difficulty in associating *exstasis*, so popular among medieval mystics, with *fides* (faith), thereby changing the denotation ascribed to *exstasis* by those mystics who applied the term to the experience of mystical union at the end of an ascent to God. His meaning is particularly clear in his commentary on Psalm 115:

> *Exstasis* is in the first place the sense of faith which literally exceeds the sense in which the unfaithful remain. In the second place it is a rapture of the mind into the clear cognition of faith and this is properly *exstasis*. In the third place it is alienation or trembling of the mind in persecution. In the fourth, it is the transfiguration *(excessus)* which martyrs achieve just as the transfiguration of Christ, Moses and Elijah as discussed in Luke 9.[37]

Here the word *excessus*, similarly popular among medieval mystics, is drawn into his treatment of faith, and shortly after in the same commentary he draws parallels between *excessus* and *fides* in explicitly mystical terminology: "That is *excessus* when a man is elevated above himself . . . and illuminated sees that he is nothing. He looks down, as it were, from above into himself, into his own shadows and darkness. Nevertheless he is looking down from his position on a mountain."[38]

Leaving aside those references to union between God and

man in Luther's works that are textually questionable,[39] a number of related terms and images remain that describe a union of the believer with Christ in faith[40] so close that the two become as it were *(quasi)*[41] one thing. As he had made use of the mystical terms *exstasis* and *excessus* to describe the experience of faith, so too Luther used other medieval images related to mystical union. In his treatise *On the Freedom of a Christian Man*, for example, referring to Ephesians 5:31-33 he wrote, "The third incomprehensible gift of faith is this, that the soul is joined with Christ just as a bride with a bridegroom and by this sacrament . . . Christ and the soul are made of one flesh."[42] That union, like the mystical, is real, but in it no confusion of persons occurs. Nor does such an image endanger the doctrine of forensic justification. "*Faith* makes it that Christ becomes us; *his love* makes it that we become him."[43] (italics mine).

It is Christ's love alone that brings about holy actions in the believer. In it we love the neighbour.[44] The love of God does not lie dormant; it is effective. It gives the Son, and having done so, draws the believer back to his source in love.[45]

In describing the reality of this union then, Luther found some of the vocabulary of late medieval mysticism such as *exstasis* and *excessus* useful, but he always took care to distinguish his meaning from that of his medieval predecessors. Nevertheless, there was one aspect of his teaching that allowed later Lutherans to reemphasize earlier mystical notions on the imitation of Christ, the ascetical ascent and the mystical union.[46] As already noted, the union of a believer in faith with Christ is, for Luther, affected and made effective by God's love. Faith receives that love and acts in accordance with it. It is manifested in reciprocal love for God and neighbour, and only in it is there a possibility for a human, experimental, loving knowledge of God.[47] For Luther, however, it must always be emphasized, the love that is experienced for God is man's psychological love; it is the action of a thankful soul, not the result of an infusion of grace.

There is much in Boehme's initial treatises in *The Way to Christ* that reminds one of Luther.[48] Fallen man, called on to consider earnestly the depths to which and heights from which he has fallen, is to be ever mindful of the grace available to him in the person and work of Christ. Man is to recall the covenant made for him in his baptism.[49] In it "he promised his Saviour faith" (*Way to Christ* I, 3) and received a cloak of righteousness that he has since soiled. His meditation is to remind him of that covenant, to bring him to true repentance for his disloyalty, and to lead him to accept once again the promise of redemption in Christ, a promise of both in Law and Gospel (II, 10).[50] Christ's Spirit, not man's mind, leads him in his repentance. No work of man's is necessary; "he need only seize Christ's words and wrap himself in Christ's suffering and death" (I, 10).

Like Luther, Boehme emphasizes that such faith appears as foolishness to the world.[51] In it, one obtains the noble Sophia's love. In his use of Sophia imagery in *The Way to Christ*, Boehme is doing much the same as Luther did with images and concepts taken from late medieval mystics. Sophia is united with the soul at the beginning of the believer's life of faith. In that initial union one experiences Her presence. It is faith in this union that imitates the whole life of Christ, his incarnation, suffering, death, resurrection, ascension and glorification (I, 30). It is faith that hungers and can only be fed by Christ's body and blood. All conquering is done only by Christ's merits; the kiss of Sophia is received in Christ. Sophia reveals Herself "in the precious name of Jesus" (I, 30). Boehme does not suggest that the attainment of the Virgin's love takes one out of his world. The pearl he has received will be attacked by evil on all sides. The way of Christ must continue to be followed; the joy and light of such life penetrates to the dark recesses of the soul. Like Luther, as well,

Boehme makes a division between the inner and outer aspects of the sacraments. The Spirit speaks internally in the external preached word; it washes internally in the external waters of baptism and feeds the soul in the bread and wine. There is an external physical church in which the true believers worship. Luther had already made these distinctions and Boehme continues them although in Boehme emphasis is always placed on the internal spiritual to the neglect of the external aspects, whereas in Luther the two are much more closely related. Nevertheless, Boehme is not opposed to Luther on this point. He is only lifting up an aspect that he felt was badly neglected in his day.

Boehme's works differ from Luther's in two other major ways. Firstly, Boehme is much more open to describing man's own activity and at times his language comes very close to that of Semi-Pelagianism. Secondly, Boehme emphasized the unitive mystical experience possible for the believer in language Luther would not have used. Moreover, in Boehme's work the various aspects of the application of saving grace to the believer, chief among which is the mystical union, tend to be formed into a progressive order, whereas Luther had included them within the single concept of faith. In this Boehme has much in common with his contemporary Johann Arndt.

Arndt opens his major work, *True Christianity*,[52] with a description of man created in the image of God, the Holy Trinity. Lost in the fall, the man who is redeemed in Christ lives toward full renewal of the image in the world to come. Without such renewal man remains lost, yet of himself, fallen as he is, he has no power to correct his situation. He must in faith experience a new birth, be justified and sanctified to the image of God, that is, according to the person of Jesus Christ.

The gift of faith as the basis of the new birth brings with it repentance, true sorrow for all past sins, and an unwillingness to commit them further. But faith brings much more. In it and with repentance comes the mystical union of the be-

liever with Christ and all Christ's attendant merits. Out of the
mystical union, the newborn creature directs his steps in imitation of the life of Christ, dying to his own wishes in daily
amendments and acting in love. All these activities lead to the
full renewal of the divine image. Arndt insists, with Luther,
that God has freely intended the mystical union from the
beginning; that it is announced to the individual believer
through God's word, externally in Scripture and internally in
the heart; that it is totally a gift of grace; and that it is primarily union with Christ in his body, the Church. Like Luther, as
well, he interprets it in close relationship with purification
and repentance, describes it in nuptial and sacramental images, and sees it as the root of continuing love toward God and
full renovation of life, finally completed in glory.

With the exception of his use of the term Sophia,
Boehme's concept of mystical union in *The Way to Christ* is
much the same as Arndt's. The difference between Boehme
and Luther must not be overlooked, however. Over half a
century separates them and their attitudes are consequently
different. The agonizing terror experienced by Luther is presented in balanced phrases in Boehme's discussion of repentance. Boehme insists on the need for divine election and
proffered grace, but tends to take it for granted. Whereas
Luther is concerned with faith first and shifts the meanings
inherent in mystical terms such as *exstasis* to bring them completely under the rule of his doctrine on justification, for
Boehme faith and union are broken apart and become separate
stages in an ordered movement leading from birth to rebirth
and a new life thereafter. The theological density in Luther's
use of the word faith is diffused by Boehme, and Arndt, into a
path to Christ that, as later Lutherans would describe it, was
an order of salvation *(ordo salutis)* from election, through vocation, illumination, conversion, regeneration, justification,
mystical union, renovation and preservation to glorification.

In Luther's work the love described as growing out of

faith toward God is closely tied to faith throughout the believer's life, as are all other stages later included in the order of salvation. Boehme, as noted, tends to let this centrality of faith fade; at the same time he emphasizes the importance of love for Sophia and by so doing, in a theological setting initiated and concluded by a concern with the restoration of the image of God in fallen man, he changes the tone of Luther's position.

In Boehme's work also the possibility for a perfected experience of the faith-union with Sophia is continually expressed in words that might well have sounded to Luther like those of the speculative mystics he so vehemently attacked. Boehme is no longer describing a union solely of the type discussed by Luther. Rather, the believer is directed to explore the nature of his faith-union with Sophia. He is admonished to cast aside all love for the creaturely and to learn progressively to love, in fullness, the God who has united Himself with the believer. Spiritual joy, he believes, will crown the fulfillment of this unitive experience, the mystical marriage, the gift of the pearl.

For Boehme, Sophia is already with the soul at the first stage on the path to mystical marriage. She is both beginning and end. She is present at the beginning calling the believer in Christ to Her and away from his falsehood. As he proceeds on his path of resignation, his insights into the nature of the divinity increase. These insights center on the contradiction inherent in reality, in its very root, its ground, or as Boehme preferred to call it, its "un-ground," its abyss. All of Boehme's work was done to explain this contradiction. It arose out of a desire "to grasp the possibility, indeed the necessity of evil in the highest Good."[53] The fourth to eighth treatises of *The Way to Christ* are difficult to understand outside of the context of Boehme's treatment of this question.

In his attempt to deal with the contradiction of reality, the "Yes" and "No," the wrath and the love of God, Boehme began with nothing, the Nothing, unknown even to itself. The Nothing is subject and object and thus in its very nothingness "it is a search for Something."[54] The Nothing reaches to Something and discovers itself in it. It is an eye that sees itself in its own reflection looking back. Thus "in the being of all being, there is strife and opposition."[55] Any revelation is possible only in division. The subject is conscious of an object, an object that has meaning only as standing over against the subject.

In Boehme's work this dualism in unity that makes possible revelation is directed outward as trinity. The Nothing is a single unified will willing something. The will turns in upon itself and within the will the Son is begotten, the discovery on the part of the Nothing of the Something within itself, which is itself, the ground of the abyss. The unfathomable will proceeds simultaneously from the Son and comes to an eternal contemplation of itself. The procession is the Holy Spirit; the contemplation is the wisdom of God. The movement of the Nothing to Something is completed in this contemplation in which are all created beings, and which has an inclination or desire to reveal the individual characteristics of its being. This contemplation or wisdom, this image of the Trinity, is the center of the divine but is understood by Boehme in special relationship to the Son although the Spirit is seen as its form. The image in which and to which man was created was this image of the Trinity, this virginal wisdom of the Nothing. In this image too the angels were created.

The Word of John I:1 is spoken in the wisdom of God. All three persons bear a relationship to this Word but the Son again has special affiliation. He is the knowledge and essential cause of the speaking. The speaking is the Spirit. The Word was with God then in two ways. Firstly, it was *in* God as an unformed power, as Son and Spirit; secondly, it was *by* God as a formed power, that is, as wisdom, and as such was the basis of all created being. God conceived the various possibilities of being in His Word and created them by it.

God's conception of these possibilities took place in a moment. The moment is, as it were, the ignition of fire that shines forth as light in God. The will of the Nothing looks out in search of Something as light (love) and having achieved self-revelation in the Son, draws it back to itself in desire as fire (wrath). Yet, the two exist in union. They are a coincidence of opposites. God rests, as Boehme puts it, in love-play. In the moment the Nothing knows itself, and in the knowledge eternal nature has its being.

Fire and light are two of the principles (*principia*) discussed by Boehme. They reflect themselves in a third. There is a fire of eternal nature, a light of divine power, and the being of the observable world, eternal and temporal nature. It was necessary for the Nothing's complete manifestation of itself that creatures be formed that would out of their own freedom reflect the majesty of the divine back to its source. For this reason eternal nature was created from eternity.

This third principle is manifested in seven properties, qualities or, in the term generally used in *The Way to Christ*, characteristics. God created through His Word. He who was from the beginning in the Trinity understood in his wisdom individual beings. The seven characteristics progressively reveal the Word. The first is harshness, God's conception of Himself. It is followed by attraction, followed by dread, the result of the first two. The fourth is the ignition of fire, the basis of sensitive and intellectual life. From the fire the fifth characteristic or love-light is emitted, which dissipates the individualism of the first four characteristics. The sixth is the divine power of speech; the seventh is the speech itself. Each of the seven characteristics is present in all being and images the motion from all eternity. They are moreover divisible into three, the first three representing the first principle; the fifth and sixth, the second principle and the seventh the third. The fourth is the center of this nature, on which the whole turns.

As free, the beings in the third principle can turn toward either of the other two. If they maintain the balance, all is well. Lucifer however refused to accept the role of the principle of light and love within himself and turned to the fire in an endeavour to control its might. In his attempt to gain power enough to establish his position as lord of all things, Lucifer broke the unity and turned himself toward the fire principle that, without the tempering principle of light (love), was experienced by him as wrath. He sought to be the fire that emanated light, and discovered it as fire. He fell as a result into the kingdom of his own fantasy, into a darkness in which the only light available was that which he himself formed, and in which he and those who followed him lived. Locked out of his former position, he found himself fantasied into matter, which had been prepared for him.

Temporal nature came into existence at the desire of eternal nature and by God's fiat at the moment of Lucifer's fall. At God's Word light came forth into the creation and God divided the light from the darkness that living unto itself could no longer comprehend the light, the quintessence in which creation stood. The highest point of creation, original man—Adam—was created according to the image of God. The most perfect work of Sophia, he reflected Her most completely in his spirit. In him there was no strife; there was harmony. Containing all three principles, Adam was fire and light. Male and female (androgynous), he could bear children from his own being. "If Adam would have remained in such innocence he would have remained . . . in the two principles and ruled over all. He would not have known the angry kingdom nor would it have been revealed to him."[56] In his two-fold fall, however, in his sleep and disobedience, he broke the harmony in which he lived. Rather than experience the seven characteristics in balance, he chose to know them separately. Thus "the image of God was destroyed . . . and the light of the being of the holy elements in which he knew God went

20

out. The balance died and awoke the four elements and improper knowledge that made him ill and finally brought death to him."[57]

Like God, man was both fire and light. Man's soul began in the fiery inception of eternal nature and was to stream back to its source as light, as love, or, in Boehme's other image, as the spiritual water of new life that would temper the fiery source. Without such water the soul would be consumed, damned in its own fiery root. Adam chose that fiery origin, but God was merciful. Because God would not allow man to remain fallen, He provided a way for him to become holy once again. The light of reason (philosophy) and of revelation (prophecy) were provided to guide him. The light-love was finally and fully revealed in the person of Christ who flowed with His light, love and water in all the principles in which man was created, and reestablished the balance. In the new androgynous Adam, Christ, man lives again in harmony and in unity with the Virgin Sophia. In Him, he gains his most precious pearl; a conqueror's crown waits for him at his journey's end.

As Boehme's two favourite images describe it, the prodigal son returns (Luke 15:11 ff.), but work still remains to be done in the vineyard (Matthew 20:1-16). With a resigned will the journey back is undertaken and with a resigned will the work in the vineyard is completed. The arrival home is an experience of divine contemplation and the conclusion of the work ushers in contemplation of the divine. For Boehme, as for Luther, faith is a present reality of God with man *and* a future hope.

* * *

Every reader of Boehme's works is immediately faced with the problem of language. There are numerous technical terms that require definition. The images and structures shift within his thought: They take on new meanings, are defined differently at various points and are applied in contexts and to structures other than those in which they are first used. In *The Way to Christ* in particular there is a difficulty in fixing the points of the way in time. In one sense a progression can be noted from regeneration to divine contemplation, yet the union with Sophia, the end of the progression, is already described as achieved at the earliest points. It occurs, as later Lutheran scholastics described the mystical union, in an instant, in a mathematical point, which is stretched out in time for men to see.[58]

In the very topic Boehme chooses to discuss he has pushed language beyond its limits. He is one who, as the 15th-century mystic Nicolas of Cusa may have said, has gone beyond the axiom of contradiction.[59] For Boehme, A is both B and non-B, and he must develop a language to describe his experience, an experience for which there is no human language. The problem is increased for Boehme because of his doctrine of the inner relationship of all things. There is a Trinity in the One, a revelation of the Trinity of Father, Son and Holy Spirit in each of the three principles, and a trinity of these principles in man. Seven characteristics may be categorized as trinity, trinity as seven categories. Macrocosm and microcosm blend in their parallels.

But there is an even greater problem, that of the relationship between being and word.[60] All things are created in and by the Word and are reflected in man's word. All things have *Kraft*, here consistently translated "power," which is paralleled by the *Kraft* above all, the Word of God. Because of the close relationship between macrocosm and microcosm, man's words are therefore to be carefully spoken. A man speaks and has creative power in his word. Speaker, word and power are one and yet three. They reflect the Trinity. Empty words are destructive. In their existence they create either in the Word or aside from it. If they are spoken outside of the Word, they make idols; in their power to create they blaspheme. Only the prophet, the man directly inspired by God, is free of this danger. Danger remains for the reader who misuses the words spoken by the prophet and for this reason, late in life, Boehme wrote a *Clavis* or *Key* to the chief points and words that he used. Yet Boehme does not fully overcome the reader's difficulties in his *Clavis* and he is aware of this fact.[61]

In *The Way to Christ* many of the words are intended in their simplest sense. Thus *centrum* refers in most cases to the center or root of a being, *matrix* to the source of a being or beings, *locus* to the place established for a specific being, *contrarium* to the opposition between things, *Separator*, to the power of opposition and *principium* simply to the principle, most often used in the sense of the three principles. A number of words may be read with their obvious Latin meanings: *corpus*, body; *hierarcha*, ruler; *nutrimentum*, nourishment; *polus*, the end of an axis; *materia*, matter; *cloaca*, sewer. *Complexio* is most often used to describe a personality temperament but to avoid confusion with Boehme's *tempermentum* it has been rendered by the now slightly archaic English word "humour." *Limbus* (changed in some manuscripts to *limus*, earth), when applied to man, refers to that aspect of man by which Christ dwells in him. Other words, too, have specific meaning for Boehme: *Tempermentum* is the proper balance of a being; *turba magna*, the imbalance of anger aroused in Lucifer's and Adam's fall; *Verbo fiat* is the Word in which creation occurred; Paradise is "the being of essence in the first being."[62] In this sense it is *ens*, although *Ens* can also refer to the quintessence, the *Ens* of fire and light, out of which the four elements are born. *Ens* is the element desired by the *tinctur*. *Tinctur* is the power by which things are changed, it is the Word in act, it is the life of wisdom. Externally *tinctur* is the power by which the base metals are turned into gold. The *spiritus mundi* is the power working in the four elements; *Signatur* is the external manifestation of a thing.

Each of the seven *Eigenschaften* (here translated *characteristics* to best define both its aspects of being: understood as the specific characteristic of a thing and as a characteristic of a greater entity)[63] is associated with one of the planets, Saturn with the first, Mercury with the second, Mars with the third, the sun with the fourth, Venus with the fifth, Jupiter with the sixth, and the moon with the seventh. Vulcan is associated with the second characteristic and together with the first and third is seen as the cause of the fourth. At times, Venus is related to the second light principle. The elements of salt, mercury and sulphur are also associated with the first three characteristics. Sulphur as the source begets mercury, the divider, from which two salt arises. All three reflect the trinity in man.

Imagination is that aspect of man by which he orients his consciousness. In itself it is neutral,[64] able to turn to either fire or light principles. It develops the *impression*, a *sensus*. Where *imagination* leaves off, *magia* begins. *Magia* is that which pierces through the *imagination* toward the *Mysterium Magnum*. This search and discovery of *magia* is "the best theology. In it faith is founded and discovered."[65] It is to be trusted in that its search is that which was present in the eternal beginning and which discovered itself therein: "The Nothing is a search toward Something. Yet there is Nothing that gives Something; rather, the search is itself the gift of that which is also a Nothing except for a desiring search alone. This is the eternal foundation of Magia, which makes [things] in itself where no thing is. It makes Something out of Nothing,"[66] and it does this aside from the activity of will.

"The will has nothing, nor is there anything that gives something to it. The will has no place where it can discover itself or rest."[67] On man's part, therefore, only when the will has been totally resigned can the creation of the Word in nothingness take place and the marriage with the divine Sophia be fully consummated.

INTRODUCTION

A Note on the Text*

The present translation of *The Way to Christ* was made from the 1730 Leyden edition done by Johann Wilhelm Ueberfeld. This edition made extensive use of earlier editions and manuscripts of the work. When significant alternate readings occurred, Ueberfeld noted them in his edition in parentheses. These alternate readings have been retained in this translation. The most significant alternate readings from Boehme's own manuscripts of separate treatises have been included in notes.

In my translation I am indebted to the earlier translation of *The Way to Christ* by John Joseph Stoudt (New York, 1947). Although Stoudt's work is marred by many inaccuracies and omissions (including all of the ninth treatise), and is at times too loosely translated, it does regularly provide valuable insights into Boehme's meaning.

Unlike Stoudt's, this translation is an attempt to remain as close to Boehme's original as possible. Boehme's word *Kraft* has been translated "power" consistently. For his word *Ernst* and its derivatives I have used "earnest" rather than the more common English rendering "serious." With some reservation I have retained the English "lust" for Boehme's *Lust* where the term refers to the earthly passions of fallen man. In many cases *Sinn* has been rendered "thought" rather than "sense" to avoid confusion for English readers who might tie "sense" too closely to "the five senses" and to best capture Boehme's intention. All Latinate words have been kept as in the original. Only in the case of *complexion*, meaning "humour," and *constellation*, which occur with great frequency in the ninth treatise, have I not italicized them. In most cases the *Du* (You) at the

*I am particularly indebted to my colleagues Miss Nancy Saunders and Mr. Fred A. Grater for their help in completing the final draft of this translation.

25

beginnings of addresses to God has been omitted because the inclusion of the word is clumsy in English. I have not retained the editors' punctuation in all cases and have often omitted coordinating words for readability. Square brackets indicate insertions of material not in the original.

THE FIRST TREATISE
ON TRUE REPENTANCE
(1622)

How a man must arouse himself in his will and mind, and what his consideration and earnest resolution are to be when he wishes to powerfully repent, and with what kind of a mind he is to come before God when he wishes to request and receive from Him forgiveness of sins.

Together with short formulas for prayer; how a man's soul is to awake itself in the grace of God, and to grasp and hold the same.

Preface of the Author to
the God-loving Reader

Saint Paul says: Whatever you do, do in the name of the Lord and thank God and the Father in Christ Jesus [Colossians 3:17].

God-loving reader, if you wish to use this little book correctly, and are in earnest, you will truly know its value. However, I wish to warn you if you are not in earnest, leave untouched the precious Names of God (in which the highest holiness is named, made known and mightily desired), so that they do not ignite the wrath of God in your soul, for one is not to misuse God's holy Names. This little book belongs only to those who wish eagerly to repent, and who have a desire to begin. They will experience both the words that are in it and the source that gave rise to them. With this receive the eternal goodness and mercy of God.

1. When a man wishes to proceed to repentance, and turn himself to God with his prayers, he is to examine his mind before any prayer, [considering] how it is completely and wholly turned from God; how it has become faithless to God; how it is ordered only in the temporal, fragile, earthly life and directs no correct love to God or to its neighbour; and

27

how it thus lusts and seethes against God's law and seeks only itself in temporal, perishable, fleshly lust.

2. Secondly, he is to consider how all this is an enmity against God that Satan, by his deceit, awoke in our first parents, for which abomination we must die and perish in our bodies.

3. Thirdly, he is to consider the three abominable chains by which our souls are bound fast to the time of this earthly life. The first is God's stern wrath, the abyss and dark world that is the *centrum* and creaturely life of the soul. The second chain is the devil's desire against the soul by which he continually sifts the soul, tempts [it] and constantly wishes to drag it away from God's truth into vanity, as into pride, covetousness, envy and wrath, and to kindle and continually increase these same evil characteristics by his desire in the soul. Through this the soul's will is turned from God and enters into self. The third and most abominable chain by which the poor soul is bound is the corrupted, and completely vain, earthly, mortal flesh and blood, full of evil desires and inclinations. Here a man is to consider how, with body and soul, he lies captive in the slime of sin, in God's wrath, in the jaws of hell's abyss; how God's wrath burns in him, in soul and body; and how he is a stinking swineherd who has wasted and used up his father's inheritance, God's love and mercy, in earthly pleasure with the devil's fatted pigs; and [how he] has not perceived the precious covenant and reconciliation of the innocent suffering and death of Jesus Christ, which God, out of pure grace, placed in our humanity, reconciling us in Him; also how he has so completely forgotten the covenant of holy baptism (in which he promised his Saviour faith and loyalty), and that, [living] so completely in sin, he has defiled and darkened the righteousness (which God gave him by grace in Christ), so that he now stands in God's presence with the beautiful cloak of the innocence of Christ that he has soiled, as a dirty, tattered and ragged swineherd who has continually

eaten the husks of vanity with the devil's pigs, and is not worthy to be called a son of the father and a member of Christ.

4. Fourthly, he is to consider earnestly that angry death waits for him every hour and moment, and wishes to seize him in this swineherd's cloak, in his sins and abominations, and cast him into the hellish abyss as a perjurer and faith-breaker, to be held in the dark death chamber for God's judgement.

5. Fifthly, he is to consider the earnest and stern judgement of God when he, with his abominations, will be set alive before the judgement; and that before the eyes of Christ and before all holy angels and men, all those whom he has wronged by word or work and caused to do evil so that they sinned by his instigation will come before him and curse him; and how he will stand there in great shame and scorn, as well as in great fright and eternal despair; and how this will make him eternally regret that for so short a time of pleasure he lost such great eternal happiness, and that he did not better perceive that he might be among the community of the saints, and enjoy eternal light and divine power.

6. Sixthly, he is to consider how the godless man loses his noble image (how that God made him to His image) and becomes a formless spectre, like a hellish worm or abominable beast since he is then an enemy of God, against heaven and all holy angels and men; and how his community is eternally in horrid darkness among devils and hellish worms.

7. In the seventh place, he is to consider earnestly the eternal punishment and pain of the damned, how in eternal horror they suffer pain in their self-created abominations and do not see the land of the saints in eternity nor receive any revival, as is to be seen with the rich man [Luke 16:22]. A man is to consider this earnestly, and think how God created him in such a beautiful and majestic image, in His likeness, in which He Himself wished to dwell; and that He created him

29

to His praise, to His own eternal joy and majesty; that he might dwell with the holy angels, with God's children, in great joy, power and majesty, in eternal light, in the song and sound of the harmony of the angelic and divine kingdom of joy; that he ought eternally to have enjoyment with the children of God without fear of any end, where no evil thought can disturb him, neither suffering nor grief, neither heat nor cold, where night is unknown, where neither day nor time are any longer, but eternal bliss, where soul and body tremble in joy and rejoice in infinite wonder and power, in beauty of colour, in the adornment of the infinite birth, in the wisdom of God on the new crystalline earth that is as transparent glass. And [he is to consider] how he thus wantonly forfeits this for so brief and vile a time, which, in this vanity, in the evil life of the lustful flesh, is full of sorrow, fear, and restlessness, of vain misery; and [how] the godless fare as the pious; how one must die even as the other [does], but [how] the saints' death is an entrance into eternal rest, and the death of the godless man is an entrance into eternal restlessness.

8. Eighthly, he is to consider the course of this world, how everything is a plaything by which he spends his time in restlessness; that it happens to the rich and powerful as to the poor; that we all live and move among the four elements; and that the poor man's bite tastes as good in his weariness as the rich man's in his cares; that we all live in one breath, and that the rich man has nothing for his advantage but a connoisseur's palate and a lustful eye. Otherwise everything is for the one as it is the other. Because of this lustful eye man has lost so great a blessedness and leads himself because of this into such great eternal restlessness.

9. In such consideration a man will feel in his heart and mind—especially if he continually pictures his end—that he will have a deep longing to gain God's mercy and [he] will begin to feel sorry for his past sins, and that he has spent his days so evilly and neither perceived nor considered how he

stands here in this world, in a field, as a plant [bearing] fruit either in the love of God or in wrath. He will first begin to realize that he has not yet begun to work in Christ's vineyard, and that he is a dry branch on the vine of Christ. In many [a man] whom Christ's spirit stirs to such consideration there mounts up great sorrow and heartache, complaint against oneself, over these days of evil that he has so spent and lost through vanity without effect in Christ's vineyard.

10. He whom Christ's spirit leads to sorrow will have his heart opened so that he can know his sin and be sorry for it. It will be easy to advise him. He need only take the promises of Christ that God does not wish the death of the poor sinner (Ezekiel 33:11) but calls all to come to Him (Matthew 11:28), and that there is great joy in heaven over one sinner who repents (Luke 15:7). Let him only seize Christ's words and wrap himself in Christ's suffering and death.

11. But I wish to speak to those who feel in themselves a desire for repentance but cannot in any way come to knowledge nor to correct true sorrow for past sins, since the flesh always says to the soul, "Now listen, tomorrow is good enough," and then, when tomorrow comes, the flesh says again, "Tomorrow." Since the poor soul groans and stands in weakness, and receives neither true sorrow for past sins nor any comfort, I say to it: "I shall describe a way in which I myself have gone, which he is to do, and what happened to me." If he desires to follow it, he will experience what is hereafter described.

Way of Repentance

12. When through the aforementioned consideration, a man finds within himself a hunger, so that he would eagerly repent, but finds in himself no proper sorrow for his past sins, and yet a hunger for sorrow (as the poor, captured soul ever groans, fears itself and acknowledges itself as guilty of sins

before God's judgement), he can do no better than to gather sense, mind and all reason together into one and in that hour commence his first consideration; when he feels a desire to repent he is to make a powerful resolution, that in this hour, in this minute, he will enter into repentance, and leave his godless way, give no attention to any worldly power and honour and, if it must be, leave all for true repentance and esteem nothing.

13. And [he] is to make such a firm and stern resolution for himself that he will never again leave [repentance], even if the whole world considers him a fool; and that he will wish to lead his mind obediently away from the beauties and pleasures of this world into the sufferings and death of Christ, under His cross, and order his whole hope to the coming life and enter into Christ's vineyard, in righteousness and truth to do God's will, and begin and complete all his work in this world in Christ's spirit and will. For the sake of Christ's word and promise by which He promised us heavenly reward, he should eagerly suffer and bear all misfortune and suffering, so that he may be counted among the community of Christ's children, and so that he may be incorporated and united into His humanity by the blood of the lamb of Jesus Christ.

14. He is strongly to consider, and completely wrap his soul [in the idea] that he has made the resolution to gain the love of God in Christ Jesus, and that according to His true promise God will give him the noble pledge of the Holy Spirit as a beginning so that in himself he might be reborn in Christ's humanity, according to the heavenly divine being, and that the spirit of Christ might renew his mind in His love and power, and strengthen his weak faith so that in his soul's desire that continually hungers and thirsts, he might receive the body and blood of Jesus Christ as meat and drink (John 6:55) and in the soul's thirst drink from the sweet fountain, Jesus Christ, the water of eternal life according to Christ's promise and truly firm pledge (John 4:10).

15. He is to consider fully the great love of God, that God does not wish the death of the sinner, but that he be converted and live (Ezekiel 33:11). And he is also to [consider] how Christ, in a friendly manner, calls poor sinners to Himself, since He desires to revive them (Matthew 11:28); and that God sent His son into the world to seek and to make holy that which was lost, the poor, repentant, converted sinner; and how, for the sake of the poor sinner, He gave His life unto death, and for him died in our humanity, taken on [for us].

16. He is to consider strongly also that God in Christ Jesus will more readily hear [him] and receive him into grace than he himself wants to come to Him; and that in the love of Christ, in the very precious Name JESUS, God can desire no evil, that there is no glimpse of wrath in this Name, but that He is the highest and deepest love and faithfulness, the great sweetness of the Godhead in the great Name JEHOVAH that He revealed to our dead and corrupted humanity in its heavenly part, which disappeared through sin in Paradise; that [God] therefore was moved in His heart so that He would pour His sweet love into us so that the Father's wrath, which was enflamed in us, might be put out and changed into love. All of this occurred for the sake of the poor sinner so that he might again gain the open gate of grace.

17. In such a consideration he should firmly imagine that at this hour and moment he stands in the presence of the Holy Trinity, and that God is truly present in him and outside of him, as the Holy Scripture says, Am I not He who fills all things? (Jeremiah 23:23). (Again: The word is near you, even in your mouth and in your heart [Romans 10:8].) Again: We will come to you, and make our home in you (John 14:23). Again: I am with you always, until the end of the world (Matthew 28:20). Again: The kingdom of God is within you (Luke 17:21).

18. Thus, he is to know and believe for certain that he stands, with his soul, before the face of Jesus Christ, before

the holy Godhead, and that his soul has turned from God's face; and that he now, this hour, wishes to turn his soul's eyes and desire to God, and, with the poor, prodigal and returning son [desires to] come to the Father. With downcast eyes of soul and spirit, in fear and deepest humility, he is to begin to confess his sin and unworthiness as follows.

A Short Form of Confession before the Eyes of God

Each one may change and enlarge this form of confession according to his situation, as the Holy Spirit teaches. I desire to set down only a short guide.

19. O great, unsearchable, holy God, Lord of all being, who in Christ Jesus, out of pure love for us, revealed your holy being in our humanity, I, a poor, unworthy, sinful man, come before your revealed face, in the humanity of Jesus Christ, even though I am unworthy to raise my eyes to You, and [I] implore You, and confess to You that I have been faithless and disloyal to Your great love and grace that You have given us. I have forsaken the covenant that You, out of pure grace, made with me in baptism, in which You took me as a child and heir of eternal life. [I] have led my desire into the vanity of this world, and defiled my soul thereby, and made it completely bestial and earthly, so that, because of the mire of the sin, my soul does not know itself, and sees itself wholly as a strange child before Your sight, unworthy to desire Your grace. I lie as deep as my soul's lips in the mire of sin and in the vanity of my corrupted flesh, and have only a small spark of breath in me that seeks Your grace. In vanity I have thus become dead to myself so that, in this vanity, I dare not raise my eyes to You.

O God in Christ Jesus, who for the sake of poor sinners became man so that You could help them, to You I cry; I still have a spark of refuge for You in my soul. I have not regarded Your purchased inheritance that through Your bitter death You purchased for us, and I have shared the inheritance of vanity in Your Father's wrath, in the curse of the earth, and am trapped by sin and half dead to Your kingdom. I lie in weakness before your power, and angry death waits for me. The devil has poisoned me so that I do not recognize my Saviour. I have become a wild shoot in Your tree and have devoured my inheritance from You with the devil's pigs. What shall I say before You, I who am not worthy of Your grace? I lie in the sleep of death that has trapped me, and I am bound fast with three strong chains. O help me, You Breaker of death. I can and am able to do nothing. I have become dead to myself and have no power before You, and dare not lift my eyes to you because of my great shame. I am a defiled swineherd and have spent my inheritance with the false adulterous whore of vanity, wasting it in the lusts of the flesh. In my own lust I have sought myself and not You. Now I have become a fool in myself and am naked and bare; my shame stands before my eyes; I cannot hide it. Your judgement waits for me. What am I to say to You, You who are the judge of the world? I have nothing more that I can bring to You. Here I stand before You naked and bare, and fall down before Your face, and complain to You of my misery, and cry for Your great mercy. Although I am not worthy, take me into Your death and let me die Your death in my death. Strike down my assumed "I" and destroy by Your death my "I," so that I no longer live, since in myself I only sin. Kill the evil beast full of false cunning and self-desire, and redeem the poor soul from its heavy bondage.

O merciful God, it is because of Your love and patience that I am not already lying in hell. I give myself up with my whole will, thought and mind to Your grace, and ask for Your mercy. By Your death I call out of the small spark of my life surrounded by death and hell, which open their jaws to me, and seek to swallow me up in death. You have promised You will not put out the glimmering wick. I have no other road by which to come to You than [by] Your suffering and death, because You have made our death life by means of Your humanity and have broken the chains of death. Therefore I sink my soul's desire into Your death, into the broken gates of Your death.

O great Fountain of the love of God, let me die to my vanity and sin in the death of my Redeemer Jesus Christ.

O Breath of the great love of God, revive my weak breath in me so that it may begin to hunger and thirst after You. O Jesus, sweet power, in Your fountains of grace give my soul to drink the sweet water of eternal life so that it may wake from death and thirst after You. O how it has become completely exhausted in Your power. O merciful God, convert me; I cannot. O Conqueror of death, help me to strive since the enemy holds me with his three chains and will not let my soul's desire come before You. Come, and take my soul's desire into You. Be my pull to the Father, and redeem me from the devil's bonds. Do not look upon my deformity, that I stand naked before You, and have lost my cloak. Clothe my breath that lives in me and desires Your grace and let me once again see Your salvation.

O deepest Love of all, take my soul's desire into You, and, by Your death, lead it into You out of death's bonds through Your death into Your resurrection. Revive me in Your power so that my desire and will begin to grow anew. O Conqueror of death and God's wrath, conquer my "I" in me. Break its will, and crush my soul so that it is in fear before You, continually falling on the ground before You, and make it ashamed of its own will before Your judgement so that it may become an instrument obedient to You. Bend it in death's bonds; remove its power so that it wills nothing without You.

O God, Holy Spirit, my Saviour in Christ, teach me what I ought to do so that I might turn to You. Redirect my will in me to You. Draw me, in Christ, to the Father, and help me so that from now on I might leave sin and vanity and nevermore enter into them. Awake true sorrow for past sins in me. Keep me in Your bonds, and do not let me loose from You so that the devil may not lead me again into the death of deaths. Enlighten my spirit so that I may see the divine way, and continually walk in it. Take me from myself and give me completely to Yourself alone. Do not let me begin, will, think nor do anything without You. O how long, Lord, will I not be worthy of what I desire of You? Let my soul's desire dwell merely in the doorways of Your outer room. Make it a servant to Your servants. Preserve it from the horrible pit in which there is no solace or refreshment.

O God in Christ Jesus, I am blind to myself. I do not know myself because of vanity. In my blindness You are hidden from me, You who are yet close by me. Yet Your anger that my own desire has ignited has made me dark. Take the breath of my soul's desire to Yourself. Test it, Lord, and shatter it, so that my soul may reach Your beam of sweet grace.

I lie before You as a dead man whose life, like a small spark, hovers at his lips. Ignite it, Lord. Direct my soul's breath to You. Lord, I wait on Your promise, for You have said, As I truly live, I have no desire in the death of the sinner, but that he turn and live [Ezekiel 33:11]. I sink myself into the death of my Saviour Jesus Christ, and wait on You, Your word is truth and life. Amen.

20. In this, or a similar manner, as each one feels in his conscience what sins he led his soul into, may he confess. Although [I say], if his resolution is truly earnest, he needs no formula, for the spirit of God who is soon in the will of the mind will make [one] for Himself, for it is He Himself who in

true earnest desire works repentance and represents the soul before God through the death of Christ.

21. But I do not wish to hide from the dear reader, who stands in Christian resolution, how it usually goes with those who have such a firm resolution. Indeed, [it is] different with one than with another, according to how earnest and great his resolution is. For the spirit of God is not bound and it customarily uses many methods as He knows each [person] individually. It is just the same as when one who has been in battle can give an account of it and how it went with him [even though each account will be different].

22. If it so happens that such a heart comes thus before God with serious resolution and enters into repentance, it might go with it as with the Canaanite woman [Mark 7:24-30]. If God does not listen, the heart remains without comfort. [A man's] sins and unworthiness still present themselves before his eyes as if he were worthless. His mind is as if dumb. The soul groans in the depths. The heart receives nothing, neither can it pour out its confession before God almost as if the heart and soul were locked up. The soul is eager, but the flesh holds it in captivity. The devil covers everything completely over and shows it again the road of vanity, and tickles it with fleshly lust, and says in the mind, "Wait. First do this and that. Gather some money for yourself so that you do not need the world. Then live a pious life in penance. There is time enough."

23. O how many hundreds [of people] have perished in such a beginning and have returned once again into vanity. They are like little twigs broken off by the wind or parched by the heat.

24. Listen, dear soul. If you wish to be a conqueror of death and hell in your Saviour Christ, and wish that your young shoot might be and grow as a tree in the kingdom of Christ, you must stand firm in your first earnest resolution, even if it costs you your first parental inheritance, as well as

your body and soul. Either [be] an angel in God or a devil in hell. If you want to be crowned, you must strive. You must gain victory in Christ, and not lie under the devil. Your resolution must remain firm. You must not prefer temporal honours and wealth to it.

25. If the spirit of the flesh says, "Wait, it is not yet fitting," the soul must say "It is now my time and hour to return again to my fatherland out of which my father Adam led me. No creature shall hold me, and you, evil earthly body, you who have swallowed my pearl that God gave my father Adam in Paradise, will be extinguished in Christ's death, the will of your pleasure in vanity will be broken, and I will [enter] again the rose garden of my Redeemer Jesus Christ. As an evil dog you will be bound in the chain of my just resolution and therefore you will be as a fool before all men. Thus you will be obedient to my soul's first resolution. No one will free you from this chain except temporal death. In this may God and His power help me. Amen."

A Short Suggestion

How the poor soul shall come before God again, and how it is to strive for the noble, knightly crown; what kind of armour it must wear if it would strive against God's wrath, also against the devil, the world and sin, against flesh and blood, against the stars and elements, and against all enemies.

26. Dear soul, for this [undertaking] earnestness is required. There must not simply be a repetition of such words. An earnest, resolute will must pursue this or it will not be attained, for if the soul wishes to obtain Christ's conqueror's crown from the noble Virgin Sophia, [it] must court Her with great love-desire. It must pray for it to Her in Her holiest of Names and must come before Her in highly chaste humility, not as a lustful bull or wanton Venus. As long as it is such, it ought not to desire such [things], nor will it receive them.

And although something may be received during this time, it is only a ray compared to such [things].

27. But a chaste mind may well attain to it, so that the soul in its noble image, which died in Adam, might be alive. [This is to be] understood in the heavenly corporeality, according to the inner ground, so that She sets a victory-crown on [it] which, if done, is again taken away from the soul and as a crown laid aside, as one crowns a king and afterwards the crown is secured. Thus it also happens to the soul since it is still surrounded with the house of sin, so that if it should fall again, its crown would not be dirtied. To the children who have known and experienced this it is said clearly enough. A godless (pig-man) is not worthy to know more about this.

The Way

28. For this [undertaking] a sober mind is needed that comes before God in earnest resolution and in deepest humility, with repentance for its sins, since it has an inner resolution that it will no longer walk in the old footsteps of vanity. And even if the whole world should consider it a fool because of this and if it should lose honour, and temporal life as well, still it must persist in it.

29. If a man wishes to obtain the noble Virgin Sophia, Her honour and love, he must make such a vow to Her in his resolution and mind. For Christ says this: He who does not forsake wife, children, brothers, sisters, money, goods and all that he has, indeed even his earthly life, and follow me, is not worthy of me (Matthew 10:37-39). This Christ understands as [referring] to the soul's mind, so that if there were anything that would keep the mind from it, no matter how beautiful or majestic it might seem in this world, the mind ought not to look to it, but rather wish to give it up than to lose the noble love of Sophia in the growth of the flower of Christ, in His tender humanity in us, according to the heavenly corporeal-

ity. For this is the flower of Sharon, the rose in the valley, of which Solomon [Song of Solomon 2:1] sings and calls his dear beloved, his chaste betrothed, whom he loved as have all the saints before and after him. Those who have obtained Her have called Her their pearl. How this is to be prayed for, follows in this brief guide. The work, however, is commended to the Holy Spirit in each heart when it seeks Her. This Spirit Himself forms the prayer.

Prayer

30. I, a poor, unworthy man, come again to You O great, holy God, and lift my eyes to You although I am unworthy to do so. Yet Your great mercy and Your precious promise in Your word have made me brave enough that I now lift the eyes of my soul's desire to You, for my soul has now grasped the word of Your promise in itself, and with this comes before You. Even though it is yet a strange child before You, one disobedient to You, now it desires to be obedient. Therefore my soul wraps itself now with its desires in the Word that became man, that became flesh and blood, that broke sin and death in my humanity, that transformed wrath into love in my soul, that took the power from death and the victory from hell in soul and body, and that made an open gate to the clear presence of Your power for my soul. I have directed my soul's hunger and desire into this most holy Word O great, most holy God, and I come now before You and cry in my hunger through the Word that was made flesh and blood. O living Source, because Your Word has become the life in our flesh, I grasp it, in my soul's desire, as my own life and I press it to You in my soul's desire by Your Word in Christ's flesh (by His holy conception in Mary the Virgin and by His whole incarnation, by His holy birth, by His baptism in the Jordan, by His temptation in the wilderness when He in [His] humanity overcame the kingdom of the devil and this

world, by His mighty miracles that He did on earth, by the mockery and scorn [directed at Him], by His innocent suffering and death, by the pouring out of His blood when God's wrath was drowned both in soul and flesh, by His rest in the grave when He awoke our father Adam from his sleep into which he fell in Paradise, by His love that pierced through wrath and overcame and destroyed hell in the soul, and by His resurrection from the dead, by His ascension and the sending of the Holy Spirit into our souls and spirits, and by all His words and promises that You, God, Father, will give the Holy Spirit to those who pray to You in the name of and through the Word that has become man).

O life of my flesh and soul, in Christ my brother, I cry to You in my soul's hunger and pray to You with all my powers, although they are weak. Give me what You have granted and promised me in my Saviour Jesus Christ: His flesh for food and His blood for drink, to nourish my poor hungry soul so that it may become strong in Your Word that became man, and revive itself so that it may desire and hunger for You.

O deep Love in the sweetest Name JESUS, come in my soul's desire. This is why You came into human nature and revealed Yourself according to Your great sweetness, and call to Yourself those of us who hunger and thirst for You. You have promised to revive us. Now I open my soul's lips to You, O holiest sweet Truth. And although I am unworthy to desire this from Your holiness, I come to You nevertheless through Your bitter suffering and death since You have covered my impurity with Your blood, sanctified it in Your humanity, and made an open gate for me by Your death into the sweet love of Your blood. Through Your holy five wounds, out of which You poured Your blood, do I lead my soul's desire into Your love. O Jesus Christ, Son of God and man, take into Yourself Your purchased inheritance, which Your Father gave You. I call through Your holy blood and death within me. Open Yourself in me so that my soul's spirit may reach You within itself. Reach into me with Your thirst to [quench] my thirst. Bring Your thirst, which You had upon the cross for us men, into my thirst and quench with Your blood my thirst so that my death in me that holds me imprisoned may be drowned in Your blood, and so that my corrupted image (which in my father Adam was corrupted in the sin of the heavenly kingdom) may be made alive in Your powerful blood. Reclothe my soul with it as with a new body that dwells in heaven, in which Your divine power and Word that became man might dwell within it which is the temple of Your Holy Spirit that dwells in us. As You promised us: We will come to you and make our dwelling with You [John 14:23].

O great Love of Jesus Christ, I can do nothing but sink my desire into You. Your Word that became man is truth [John 17:17]. Since You called me to come, I now come; let it happen to me according to Your Word and will. Amen.

Warning to the Reader

31. Dear reader, with good intentions I do not wish to hide from you what has been earnestly shown to me. If you are still in the vanity of the flesh, and if you are not in earnest resolution on the way to new birth intending to become another man, leave the above words in the prayer unsaid or they will be the judgement of God in you. You are not to misuse the Name of God. Be rightly warned. These [words] belong to the thirsty soul, but if it is in earnest it will experience what they are.

Guide

How the soul ought to meet its dear lover when He knocks in the centrum *in the locked room of the soul.*

32. Dear soul, you must always be in earnest, without relenting. You will obtain the love of a kiss from the noble Sophia in the holy Name JESUS for She stands immediately

before the soul's door and knocks and warns the sinner of [his] godless ways. If he desires Her love She is willing and kisses him with a beam of Her sweet love, by which the heart receives joy. But She does not immediately enter the marriage bed with the soul, that is, She does not immediately awaken the corrupted heavenly image that was lost in Paradise in it [the soul]. This is dangerous for man; since Adam and Lucifer fell, this may occur again, because man is still firmly bound in vanity.

33. There must be a true covenant in your pledge. If She is to crown you, you must be first tested. She takes Her ray of love beams from you again and sees if you will remain true. She allows you to cry and does not answer with a glimpse of Her love. If She is to crown you, you must first have been judged: You must taste the sour beer that you have poured into yourself by your abominations. You must first come to the gates of hell and show your victory in and for Her love in power in the face of the devil's attacks so that She will again look at you.

34. Christ was tempted in the wilderness. If you wish to clothe yourself in Him, you must follow His whole way from His incarnation to His ascension. Even though you cannot nor dare not do this as He did, you must nevertheless enter His way completely, and ever die to the soul's vanity, for in this way the Virgin Sophia weds Herself to the soul only by this characteristic that sprouts in the soul through Christ's death as a new growth that is [rooted] in heaven. The earthly body at this time does not grasp this because it must first die to vanity. But that heavenly image which was corrupted in Adam, the true woman's seed in which God became man and brought His living seed of heavenly being into it [human nature], grasps the noble pearl in the [same] way in which it came to Mary in the fulfillment of the covenant.

35. Therefore watch what you do. When you give your word, keep it. She wishes to crown you more than you want

[to be crowned]. But you must stand firm when the tempter comes to you with the world's pleasure, beauty and glory. The mind must cast these out and say, "I shall be a servant in the vineyard of Christ, not a lord. I am God's servant for all that I have and [I] ought to use it as His word teaches me. My heart grows foolish in the dust and continually ought to be humble."

36. In whatever position you are, humility must be at the top or you will not reach marriage with Her, although true humility is first born in marriage to Her, but the free will of your soul must stand as a knight, for if the devil cannot conquer the soul with vanity, so that it will not bite [at his lure], then he comes along with unworthiness and with all the sins in the book. Then perseverance counts.

37. Christ's merits must be placed first for the creature cannot otherwise conquer the devil. Here it goes badly with many as even their external reason thinks that the person is senseless and possessed by the devil. Thus fiercely the devil defends himself in many because he has a great robber's castle in them, but if he weakens he must leave it. Here the fight begins, for heaven and hell strive with each other.

38. If the soul remains firm here and conquers the devil in all his attacks, and pays no attention to temporal things for the love of the noble Sophia, the precious conqueror's crown will be given to it as a sign of victory. Then the Virgin [Sophia] will come to the soul. She has revealed Herself in the precious Name JESUS as Christ the serpent-treader, as the anointed of God. She kisses [the soul] completely inwardly with her sweet love and presses love into its desire as a sign of victory. Here Adam according to his heavenly part is resurrected from the dead in Christ. Of this I cannot write; there is no pen in the world with which to do it for this is the marriage of the lamb when the noble pearl is sown with great triumph, although it is first but small, like a mustard seed, as Christ says [Matthew 17:20].

39. When this marriage has taken place, the soul should see that it has promised the Virgin [Sophia] that the pearl tree will grow and increase. Then the devil will come quickly with his stormy weather with godless men who will scoff, mock and shout out that it is madness. Then the man must enter Christ's way under the cross. Here for the first time it will be shown by demonstration that he who allows himself to be called a Christian must allow himself to be called a fool and a godless person; indeed his very best friends, who had earlier praised his fleshly lust, now become his enemies and, although they do not know why, they hate him. Therefore Christ covers His bride under the cross so that it may not be known in the world and the devil also does this so that these children of the world are hidden so that more such branches may not grow in the garden that he thinks he owns. This I write for the information of the Christian-minded reader, so that if similar things happen to him he knows what to do.

A Very Earnest Prayer

in temptation against God's wrath in the conscience; also against flesh and blood, when the tempter comes to the soul and contends with it.

40. O deepest Love of God in Christ, do not abandon me in this need. I am indeed guilty of sins that now rise up in my conscience. If You abandon me I must sink. You have promised me in Your word: Even though a mother forgets her child, which is painful, yet You will not forget me [Isaiah 49:15]. You have shown me [the wound] in Your hands, Your hands pierced through with sharp nails, and You have shown me Your pierced side out of which ran blood and water. I, poor man, held in Your wrath, can and may not do anything now. Before You I sink myself into Your wounds and death.

O great Mercy of God, deliver me from the devil's

bonds. I have refuge in nothing other than in Your holy wounds and death. I sink into You in the anguish of my conscience. Treat me as You will. In You will I now live or die as You will. Let me only die and perish in Your death; bury me in Your death so that hell's anxiety will not disturb me. How can I excuse myself before You, who test my heart and inward parts, and set my sins before my eyes? I am guilty indeed of them and give myself to Your judgement; judge me Yourself through the death of my Redeemer Jesus Christ.

I cry to You, O true Judge, through the anguish of my Redeemer Jesus Christ, who sweated His bloody sweat in my stead on the Mount of Olives, who let Himself be beaten for me before Pilate and who allowed a crown of thorns to be pressed on His head in mockery so that blood flowed from Him.

O righteous God, You have set Him in my place. He was guiltless, and I was the guilty one for whom He suffered. Why ought I then to despair in Your anger? Wipe out Your wrath in me through His anguish, suffering and death; I give myself into His anguish, suffering and death; in His anguish and suffering I shall be silent before You. Do with me what You will, only let me not depart from His anguish. You have granted me His anguish, and drowned Your anger in Him. Even though I have not accepted it, but have turned from Him and become faithless, You have given me this precious pledge in my own flesh and soul in that He has taken my flesh and soul into His heavenly [being] and with His heavenly blood has reconciled the wrath in my flesh and soul in Himself. Take me, now, into His reconciliation and place His anguish, suffering and death in Your anger that is enflamed in me, and break Your judgement in me in the blood of His love.

O great Love in the blood and death of Jesus Christ, break the self-made robber's castle of the devil that he has built in me, since he stands against my following the way of Your grace. Drive him out of me so that he might not seek me, for before You no living being can stand if You take away Your supporting hand from us.

O come, You Breaker of the wrath of God. Break his power. Help my poor soul to strive against him and overcome him. Lead me to Your victory and keep me in You. Break his seat in the enkindled vanity of soul and flesh. Kill the desire in my vanity in flesh and blood that the devil, by his false desires, has now ignited with hellish anxiety and doubt. Extinguish them with Your waters of eternal life, and lead my anguish out through Your death. I sink into You fully and completely, and even if body and soul should fail in this hour and perish in Your anger, I would not forsake You. Even though my heart clearly says no, my soul's desire will hold fast to Your truth, and no devil nor death shall take it from me since the blood of Jesus Christ, the Son of God, cleanses us from all our sins [I John 1:7]. I grasp this, and God's wrath may now do with my sin what it wills and the devil may fume in his own self-made robber's castle as much as he wants over my soul. Neither devil, death nor hell will tear me from Your wounds. You stinking devil, you must at last be shamed within me, and you must abandon your robber's castle, for I shall sink it into the love of Jesus Christ, and you may live in it as best you can. Amen.

Instruction in Temptation

41. Gracious reader, it is no joke. He who has not undergone [temptation] and sees it as a joke is inexperienced. Even though he be spared it until the end, which is obviously dangerous, he must still go through this judgement. O blessed is he who goes through it in an earlier time, in his youth, before the devil has firmly built his robber's castle [in the soul]. He can hereafter be a worker in Christ's vineyard and sow his seed in Christ's garden; he will reap the fruit in his

time. This judgement lasts for a long time, years and years for many a person, if he does not earnestly put on Christ's armour when the judgement of temptation first admonishes him to repentance. He who comes to it of his own earnest resolution, and thinks to leave the godless way, to him it will not be difficult nor last long. Even though he must stand fast against the conquering victory of the devil, he will be strongly supported and will gain the best so that hereafter, when dawn breaks in the soul, he will greatly praise God that the enemy has been conquered.

A Short Formula of Prayer

[to be used] when the noble Sophia kisses the soul with Her love and offers love to it.

42. O holiest and deepest Love of God in Christ Jesus, give me Your pearl, press it into my soul. Take my soul into Your arms.

O sweetest Love, I am unclean before You. Break my impurity by Your death. Lead my soul's hunger and thirst through Your death into Your resurrection, into Your triumph. Strike down my "I" in Your death. Take it captive and lead my hunger into Your hunger.

O highest Love, You have appeared in me. Remain in me. Embrace me in Yourself. Keep me in You so that I cannot bend from You. Fill my hunger with Your love. Feed my soul with heavenly being and give it as drink the blood of my Redeemer Jesus Christ. Let it drink from Your fountain.

O mighty Love, awaken in me my corrupted image that died in my father Adam in the heavenly kingdom through Your word in the woman's seed in Mary. Awake and move it, Lord.

O Life and Power of the Godhead, You have promised

us: We will come to you and make our dwelling in you [John 14:23]. O sweet Love, I lead my desire into the word of Your promise. You have promised indeed that Your father will give the Holy Spirit to them who ask for it. Therefore I lead my soul's hunger into Your promise, and take Your word in my hunger. Increase my hunger for You in me, O You sweet Love; in Your power, strengthen me. Make me alive in You so that my spirit may taste Your sweetness. Believe through Your power in me for without You I can do nothing.

O sweet Love, I pray to You through that love with which You overcame God's wrath and changed it into love and into the divine kingdom. Change also the wrath in my soul through this great love so that I may be obedient to You, and that my soul might love You eternally in it. Change my will into Your's; lead Your obedience into my obedience so that I shall be obedient unto You.

O great Love of Jesus Christ, I cry to You. Lead my soul's hunger into Your wounds from which You poured Your holy blood and extinguished the wrath in the soul. Into Your wounded side, out of which blood and water ran, I lead my hunger, and throw myself completely into it. Be mine and revive me in Your suffering, and do not let me leave You.

O my noble Vine, give sap to Your branch, so that I might sprout and grow with Your power and sap in Your essence. Beget true power in me through Your power.

O sweet Love, You are my light; illuminate my poor soul in its dark prison, in flesh and blood. Lead it continually on the right path. Break the devil's will and lead my body through the course of this world, through death's chamber, into Your death and peace so that on the Last Day it will be resurrected out of Your death into You and live with You eternally. Teach me what I ought to do in You. Be my will, knowledge and activity and do not let me do anything without You. I give myself fully and completely to You. Amen.

A Prayer for Divine Action,
Protection and Guidance

How the mind in the life tree ought to act with and in God for Christ.

43. In You, O living Source, I lift up my soul's desire, and call with my desire into You through the life of my Saviour Jesus Christ.

O You Life and Power of God, awaken Yourself in my soul's hunger. Ignite my soul's hunger with Your love-desire through the thirst of Jesus Christ that he had for us men on the cross, and draw out my weak power through mighty powers into Your Spirit. Be with Your power the working and willing in me. Bloom in me through the power of Jesus Christ so that I may bring forth praise as the proper fruits in Your kingdom and never allow my heart and desire to turn eternally from You.

But since, in this troubled valley, in this external earthly flesh and blood, I swim in vanity and my soul and noble image, [made] according to Your image, is surrounded on all sides by enemies as with the devil's desire against me, with the false desires of vanity in flesh and blood, as well as with the opposition of those godless men who do not know Your name; [since] I swim with my external life among the stars and in elements where my enemies within and without [lie in] wait for me, [including even] temporal death that is the destroyer of this vain life; therefore I fly to You, O holy Power of God, because You have revealed Yourself with love in grace in our humanity through the holy Name JESUS, and have given Him as a companion to us. Therefore I do pray to You, let His holy angels, who serve Him, wait on our souls, and place themselves about us and protect us from the fiery arrows of the evil one's desires, which he shoots daily at us by the curse of God's wrath that has been awakened in our earthly flesh. Let Your power hold back the opposition in the beams of the star in which the evil one with his desire enters to poison us in soul and flesh, and to lead us into false desire as well as into sickness and misery. With the holy Name JESUS keep away these beams of wrath from our souls and spirits so that they do not disturb us and let Your holy and good angel be by us so that he drive off these poisonous beams from our bodies.

O great Love and sweet Power, JESUS, Fountain-source of divine sweetness, I call to You with my soul's desire from the eternally great Name JEHOVAH. My soul calls in that spirit from which it was breathed into the body, which formed it to the image of God and in its thirst it desires in itself the sweet fountain-source JESUS [who is] from JEHOVAH, as refreshment in its fire-breath of God, which is its own self, so that its fire-breath may rise up through the fountain-source JESUS [who is] from JEHOVAH, the sweet love JESUS and the holy CHRIST, and may reveal in my corrupted image the heavenly, spiritual corporeality, and become man, so that the poor soul might again receive its dear bride into its arms and might rejoice with her forever.

O Emmanuel, you Marriage of God and man, into Your arms, into Your desire toward us and in us I give myself. I desire You. Wipe out Your Father's wrath with Your love and strengthen my weak image in me so that it may overcome and tame the vanity in flesh and blood, and serve You in holiness and righteousness.

O great, holiest, Name and Power of God JEHOVAH who has moved Yourself in our corrupted heavenly humanity by Your sweetest power JESUS in the promised fulfillment of the covenant made with our father Adam in the woman's seed of the Virgin Mary, You have led Your living being in Yourself, Your holy power, in the Virgin Wisdom of God, into our corrupted humanity, and have given us life, victory and a new birth. I pray to You with all my powers, bring me forth in

Your sweet power JESUS to a new and holy life. [In this way] I might be revealed in You and You in me, and Your kingdom in me so that my soul's will and walk might be in heaven.

O great, incomprehensible God, who fills all, be my heaven in which my new birth in Christ Jesus might live. Let my spirit be the stringed instrument, music and joy of the Holy Spirit. Play on me in Your reborn image and lead my harmony into Your divine kingdom of joy, into the great praise of God, into the wonders of Your glory and majesty, into the community of the holy angelic harmony, and establish in me the holy city Zion in which we, as the children of Christ, shall all live in one city that is Christ in us. I sink myself fully and completely into You. Do in me what You will. Amen.

A Prayer in and against Temptation under the Cross of Christ

in the time when all enemies storm against us, and when we in the spirit of Christ are persecuted, hated, slandered and reproached as evildoers.

44. I, poor man full of anguish and sorrow, wander again on my pilgrim's path into my lost fatherland, and go through the thorns and thistles of this world again to You, O God my Father. On all sides I am torn by thorns, plagued and despised by enemies. They mock my soul and despise it as an evildoer who has become faithless to them. They despise my way to You and consider it foolish. They think I am senseless because I travel on this thorny way and do not take their hypocritical road with them.

O Lord Jesus Christ, I fly to You under Your cross. Ah dear Emmanuel, take me, and lead me to You through Your own pilgrim's path that You travelled in this world, through

Your incarnation and Your wretchedness, through Your [experience of] scorn and mockery, and through Your anguish, suffering and death. Conform me to Your image. Send Your good angel with me who will show me the way through this horrid, thorny, waste of the world. Stand by me in my wretchedness. Comfort me with the comfort [with] which the angel in the garden comforted You when You prayed to the Father and sweated Your bloody sweat. Uphold me in my anguish and persecution, under the scorn of the devil and those false men who do not know You and who will not go on Your way. O great love of God, they do not know Your way and do this out of blindness, by the devil's deception. Have mercy on them and lead them from blindness to light so that they will learn to know themselves, how they lie captured in the devil's mire and slime in a dark valley firmly bound with three chains. O great God, have mercy on Adam and on his children. Redeem them in Christ, the new Adam.

I cry to You, O Christ, man and God, [I] who must wander on the pilgrim's path in this dark valley on all sides mocked, in anguish and held to be a false and godless man. Lord it is Your judgement on me that my sins and inherited vanity may be set up in this pilgrim's way and carried as a sign of the curse in which Your wrath might be lessened, and thus thereby it might take the eternal scorn from me. It is Your love-token, and You lead me by it into the mockery, anguish, suffering and death of my Saviour Jesus Christ so that in my Saviour I might thus die to vanity and in His spirit, through the mockery, scorn and death [which came to Him] my new life might sprout forth.

I pray to You O Christ, patient Lamb of God, by all the anguish and mockery [toward You], by Your suffering and death, by the contempt of the cross beam when You were scorned in my place, give me patience in my way of the cross and lead me to You like a patient lamb into Your conquest. Let me live with and in You and convert my persecutors who, altogether unknowingly, with their scorn, offer up my vanity and inherited sins before Your wrath. They do not know what they are doing. They think that they are doing evil to me, but they do me good. They do before You what I ought to do. I ought to uncover and acknowledge my shame daily before You and sink myself with it into the death of Your son so that it might die in His death. But, since I am too weary, feeble and weak, You use them in Your anger so that they might uncover my shame before Your wrath, which Your anger grasps and which sinks them into the death of my Saviour.

O merciful God, my vain flesh cannot know how You intend good for me in that You allow my enemies to take my offensiveness from me and offer it to You. My earthly mind thinks that You thus plague me because of my sins and then I am in every way afraid, but Your spirit in my inner, new man tells me that this happens to me because of love, that You intend it as good for me when You let my enemies persecute me, so that it serves me the best, that they do the work in my stead and uncover my sins before You in Your wrath so that it might swallow them and so that they might not follow me into my fatherland. Because they are yet strong and fat they can do it better than I since I am weak and weary in the will of vanity. You know this, O righteous God.

I pray in You, therefore, O righteous God, since You use them as my servants to do the best for me, although my earthly reason does not really know [that] You wish to bring them also to a knowledge of my way, and to send them also such servants, and to lead them sooner to the light as You have led me, so that they might know You and thank You.

O merciful God in Christ Jesus, I pray to You in my knowledge from out of the depths of the love for us poor men that You have revealed in me, according to [our] hidden human nature, call all those to You who are in You. Move Yourself once more in us in these last troubles, in which Your wrath has been enflamed in us. Withstand Your wrath in us so that it may not swallow us in body and soul.

O Dawn of the day of God, break forth completely. When You have come forth reveal Your holy city Zion, the new Jerusalem, in us.

O great God, I still slumber and do not see the depth of Your power and might. Awaken me completely in You so that I might be alive in You. Break down the tree of Your wrath in us, and let Your love sprout up within us.

O Lord, I lie before Your face and pray to You: Do not punish us in Your wrath [Psalm 6:2]. Are we not Your own purchased possession? Forgive all of us our sins and redeem us from the evil of Your anger and the devil's envy and lead us under Your cross in patience into our paradise. Amen.

A Little Prayer, or Conversation

in the internal ground of man, between the poor wounded soul and the noble Virgin Sophia, as between the spirit of Christ in the new birth and the soul; how much joy there is in the heaven of the new, regenerated man; how graciously the noble Sophia presents Herself to Her bridegroom the soul when the soul enters repentance, and how the soul acts when the Virgin Sophia is revealed to it.

The gates of the paradisaical rose garden no one but the children of Christ who have experienced this may understand.

45. When Christ the cornerstone moves in the corrupted image of man in his deep conversion and repentance, the Virgin Sophia appears in the movement of Christ's spirit in the corrupted image in Her Virginal clothing before the soul. Before Her the soul is frightened in its impurity so that all its sins are first awakened and before Her they are horrified and trembling. Then judgement comes over the sins of the soul so that it turns back in its unworthiness ashamed of its beautiful lover; it turns into itself and rejects itself as altogether un-

worthy to receive such a treasure. We who have tasted this heavenly treasure understand this but no one else does. But the noble Sophia draws Herself near to the soul's being and kisses it in a friendly manner and tinctures the dark fire of the soul with Her love beams and penetrates the soul with Her loving kiss. Then the soul leaps in its body for great joy in the power of this virginal love. It triumphs and praises the great God, by virtue of the noble Sophia.

I will now present a short introduction as to what happens when the bride takes the bridegroom to the heart. [It is presented] to the reader who may not yet have arrived at this place for his consideration if he desires to travel after us and to tread the paths where one plays with Sophia.

If this happens, as is described above, the soul rejoices in its body and says:

Soul:

46. O great God, now may my praise, thanks, strength, glory and honour be to You in Your power and sweetness, because You have redeemed me from the instigator of anguish. O beautiful Love, my heart grasps You. Where have You been so long? I thought I was in hell, in God's anger. O gracious Love, remain with me. Be my joy and revival. Lead me in the right paths. I give myself unto Your love. Ah, before You I am dark. Make me light. O noble Love, give me but Your sweet pearl. Lay it in me.

O great God in Christ Jesus, now do I honour and praise You in Your truth, and in Your great might and majesty because You have forgiven me my sins and have filled me with Your power. I rejoice with You in my life. I praise You in Your castle, which no one can open but Your spirit in Your mercy. My bones rejoice in Your power; my heart plays in Your love. Eternal thanks be to You because You have redeemed me from hell and made death in me to be life. Now I discover Your promised truth, O sweet Love. Let me not bend from You again. Give unto me Your crown of pearls and stay with me. Be my possession so that I may eternally rejoice in You.

Then the Virgin Sophia Speaks to the Soul:

47. My noble bridegroom, my strength and might, be always welcome to me. How have you forgotten me so long that I, in great sorrow, had to stand before your door and knock? Did I not always cry to you, [and] call on you? But you turned your face from me; your ears had left my land. You could not see my light for you walked in the dark valley [Psalm 23:4]. I was near to you and continually cried to you, but your sins held you captive in death, so that you did not know me. I came in deep humility to you, and called to you, but you were rich in the might of God's wrath and you could not see my humility. You had taken the devil as a lover, and he had defiled you and built up his robber's castle of vanity within you, and turned you completely from my love and faith, toward his hypocritical false kingdom in which you have done much sin and evil, and broken off your will from my love; you have broken my marriage, and have had a strange love affair, and lost me, your God-given bride, [and caused me] to stand, a crushed being, without the strength of your fire's might. Without your fire's might I have not been able to be happy, for you are my husband; by you my own brightness is revealed. You are able to reveal my hidden miracles in your fire-life, and lead them into majesty. Apart from me you are a dark house in which is only anguish and pain and an enemy's torment.

O noble bridegroom, keep your face before me and give me your fire-beams. Lead your desire into me, and ignite me. By my meekness, I shall then change your fire-beams into a white-light, and direct my love through your fire-beams into your fire's essence and I shall kiss you eternally.

O my bridegroom, how good it is for me in your marriage. Kiss me, then, with your desire in your strength and might. Then will I show you all my beauty and bring you joy in your fire-life and sweet love and bright light. All holy angels rejoice with us now that they see us married once more. Now, my dear beloved, remain faithful to me. Do not again turn your face from me. Work your miracles in my love, for which God awakened you.

The Soul Speaks Further to Its Noble Sophia As to Itself in Its Own Regenerate Love-play:

48. Ah, my noble Pearl and Flame of my light opened in my anguished fire-life, how You changed me into Your joy. O beautiful Love, I broke my faith with You in my father Adam, and, by the fire's might I have changed myself into the pleasure and vanity of the external world. I took a foreign lover and I would have had to walk in a dark valley in a foreign love if You had not remained in great faith and come into the house of my misery through Your penetration and destruction of the wrath of God, hell and dark death, and had [not] brought Your meekness and love to my fire-life again.

O sweet Love, You have brought the waters of eternal life from out of God's fountain, and revived me in my great thirst. In You I see God's mercy that earlier my foreign love had hidden. In You I can be joyful. You changed my fire-anguish into great joy. Ah gracious Love, give me Your pearl so that I may remain in such joy forever.

Thereupon the Noble Sophia Replies to the Soul Again and Says:

49. My dear lover and great treasure, your beginning gives me the greatest joy. Through the deep gates of God, through God's wrath, through hell and death I have broken into the house of your misery, and I have given you my love

out of grace, and released you from the chains and bonds by which you were bound fast. I have kept my faith with you, but you beg me now for a serious thing, which I do not eagerly wish to risk with you. You want to own my pearl as your possession. My dear bridegroom, think how you previously lost it in Adam! Because of this you still stand in great danger, and wander in two dangerous kingdoms: In your fire-source you wander in that land where God calls Himself a strong, jealous God and a consuming fire; in the other kingdom you wander in the external world in lust, in the vain and corrupted flesh and blood, where the world's pleasures with the assaults of the devil rush over you every hour. In your great joy you might bring earthiness again into my beauty and darken my pearl for me. Moreover, you might also become proud like Lucifer when he had the pearl as his possession, and you might turn away from God's harmony. Then I would be robbed eternally of my lover.

I shall keep my pearl to myself and shall dwell in your corrupted humanity now again made alive in me in the heaven within you and preserve my pearl for Paradise, until you lay aside your earthiness. Then I will give it to you as a possession. But I will eagerly give you my presence and the sweet beams of the pearl, during the time of this earthly life. I shall dwell with the pearl in the inner choir, and be your faithful, dear bride. I do not marry your earthly flesh for I am a Queen of heaven and my kingdom is not of this world [John 18:36]. Yet I shall not cast aside your outward life, but I shall often visit it with my love-beam for your external humanity shall return. But I do not wish the vain beast of vanity. God in his intention did not create it so uncouth and earthly, but your desire grasped this bestial grossness in Adam through lust out of all the essence of awakened vanity, [and of] earthly characteristics, in which heat and cold, pain, enmity and destruction stand.

Now my dear beloved bridegroom, give yourself to me in

my will. I shall not abandon you in this earthly life in your danger. Even if God's wrath should soon come over you so that you are afraid and think that I have left you, I shall be with you and defend you because you do not know what your office is. You must work and beget in this time. You are a root of this tree from which branches are born, which must all be born in anguish. I press through your branches into the sap and bear fruit on your boughs, and you do not know it. The Highest One has ordered me to dwell with and in you.

Therefore, cover yourself in patience, and guard yourself from the pleasures of the flesh. Break their will and desire. Keep them in the reins like an evil horse, and I shall often visit you in your fiery essence, and give you my love-kiss, and crown you with a crown from Paradise as a sign of my love, with which you will have joy. But my pearl I will not give you at this time as your own. You must remain in resignation and hear what the Lord plays in your harmony. Moreover, you must give Him the sound and essence of your tone by my power, for now you are a messenger of His mouth, to make known His fame and honour. For this reason, I have bound myself to you again and crowned you with my warrior's victory crown that I obtained in the battle against the devil and death. But the pearl-crown with which I have crowned you I have now laid aside for you. You will not wear it anymore until you are pure before me.

The Soul Speaks Further to the Noble Sophia:

50. My beautiful and sweet Spouse, what ought I to say before You? Only let me be committed to You for I cannot protect myself. If You do not wish to give me the pearl now, then let Your will be done. Give me however Your love-beams and lead me through this pilgrim's path. Awake and bring forth within me whatever You will do through me. I had wasted Your sweet love, and not kept my faith with You

by which I fell into eternal punishment. Yet since You came to me out of love in my hellish anguish, and redeemed me from pain and took me again as a bridegroom, I shall now break my will for Your love and be obedient to You and wait for Your love. I now have enough, since I know that You are with me in all my need, and You do not abandon me. O gracious Love, I turn my fiery face to You. O beautiful crown, take me immediately into You and lead me out of my restlessness. I wish to be with You eternally and nevermore depart from You.

The Noble Sophia Answers the Soul Comfortingly, and says:

51. My noble bridegroom, be comforted. I have engaged myself to you in my highest love, and in my faith [have I] bound myself to you. I shall be with you in all the days to the end of the world. I shall come to you and make my dwelling in you in your internal choir. You will drink from my fountain, for I am now yours and you are mine, and the enemy shall no longer separate us. Work in your fiery characteristic [and] I shall give my love-beams in your activities. We wish to build Christ's vineyard. You give the essence of fire; I shall give the essence of light and growth. You be fire; I shall be water. We shall bring about in this world what God has foreordained for us [to do]; we shall serve Him in His temple which we ourselves are. Amen.

To the Reader

52. Dear reader, do not treat this an uncertain story. This is the true ground and contains the whole Holy Scripture for in this book is the life of Jesus Christ clearly depicted, even as it is known by the author himself, for this was his way. He gives you the best that he has. May God give the increase. There is known to be a heavy judgement on the one who scorns this. Let him be warned.

A Little Morning Prayer

when one arises, to dedicate himself to God, before he allows anything else into him.

53. May God, Father, Son and Holy Spirit have rule, O one true God! I thank You through Jesus Christ (Your dear Son), our Lord and Saviour, for Your defense and protection, and all blessings, and I now dedicate myself with body and soul, and with all that You have set me to do in my calling under your defense and protection. Be the beginning of my sensing, seeking, endeavouring and of all acting. Work in me so that I might begin everything to the praise of Your name and might perfect in it Your love for the service of [my] neighbour; send Your good angel with me so that he shall turn away the poisonous beams of the devil and the corrupted nature from me. Protect me from all evil men's desires. Be good to all my enemies in my presence [Psalm 23:5], and lead my mind into Your vineyard so that I may labour and work in it in my office and calling as Your obedient servant (or maid). Bless me and all that I use and do with the blessing of Your love and mercy. Keep Your grace in the love in Jesus Christ in and over me, and give me a cheerful mind to perform Your wonders. May Your Holy Spirit govern me from my beginnings until my final day and be my will, work and completion. Amen.

An Evening Prayer

54. I lift my heart to You, O God, Fountain-source of eternal life, and thank You through Jesus Christ, Your dear Son, our Lord and Saviour, that You have this day protected me from all accidents and stood by me in my calling and position. I dedicate my calling and position and the work of my hands to Your providence and cry with my soul to You. Work in my soul so that neither the evil enemy and no other influence and desire might come into and cleave to my soul.

Let my mind only play in Your temple in You and let Your good angel remain with me so that I may rest with certainty in Your power. Amen.

(Note: See more in the treatise *On Holy Prayer*.)

THE SECOND TREATISE
ON
TRUE REPENTANCE[1]
(written February 9, 1623)[2]

*A short guide on the key to the understanding of divine mystery,
how a man may reach divine contemplation within himself.*

Whichever man desires to attain to divine contemplation
within himself and speak with God in Christ must follow this
way and then he will achieve it.

1. He ought to gather up all his sense and reason, with
all his imagination, into one thought, and conceive within it a
strong imagination in himself to consider himself, what kind
of person he is. Scripture calls him an image of God (Genesis
1:27), the temple of the Holy Spirit (I Corinthians 6:19) who
dwells in him, and [it] also calls him a member of Christ and
offers him Christ's flesh and blood as food and drink.

2. He ought to examine himself in his life [to see] if he is
worthy of this great grace and capable of this high title of
Christ. He should begin to consider his whole life, what he
has done, and how he used his whole time, whether he discovers himself in Christ, whether he stands in God's will, or
toward what he is inclined, or whether he discovers any will
in himself that looks intentionally toward God and would
eagerly be holy.

3. And if he now discovers such a deeply hidden will
within himself, which would gladly turn to God's grace if
only he could, let him know that this will is the Word of God
that was incorporated and spoken into him in Paradise after sin
[and] that God JEHOVAH, as the Father, still draws him to
Christ, for in our own characteristic we have no more will for
obedience.

4. But the same pull of the Father, as that grace that was
incorporated and spoken, draws all men from their false activ-

ities, even the most godless (when they are not completely like a thistle but willing to remain quiet under the pull [of grace] for a moment).

5. Therefore, no man has cause to doubt[3] God's grace, if he then discovers in himself a[4] desire to be converted.

6. Let him not put this off for a moment, as it is written: Today when you hear the Lord's voice, do not harden your ears and hearts [Hebrews 3:7-8].

7. The desire for future conversion at some time is God's voice in man, which the devil, by his imported[5] images, covers and holds back so that it is put off from one day and year to the next, until the soul at last becomes a thistle and can no longer reach grace.

8. Let such a man merely do this thing in a (sensual)[6] consideration and look at the whole course of his life, and hold it up against the Ten Commandments of God and against the love of the Gospel that asks him to love his neighbour as he loves himself, so that he be a child of grace only in Christ's love. Let him see how far he has wandered from this, and what his daily practise and desire is. Then the same pull of the Father in God's righteousness will be led into him, and point out the images built up in his heart that he loves[7] instead of God, that he held and still holds[8] as his best treasure.

9. These images will be: (1) pride, love of self, and a wish to be honoured by others. Moreover it will be an image of might and authority in his pride. In honour he wishes to step up above all others. (2) Moreover, it will be an image of a pig, as covetousness, which wants to have everything [for itself] alone. Even if he had the world and heaven, he would also want to rule hell. He would desire more than he needs for his temporal life and have within himself no faith in God but would be a filthy pig that desires to draw everything to itself. (3) Moreover, it will be an image of envy in him, which strikes out at other hearts and is not willing to accept them if they

have more temporal possessions and honour than he has. (4) Moreover, it will be wrath, which envy lifts up in itself as a poison and, for almost no reason, strikes out, attacks, raves and wishes to justify itself. (5) Moreover, it will also be a heap, yes many hundreds of earthly beasts in him that he loves. For he loves everything that is in the world, and has placed it in Christ's stead and honours it more than God. Let him look only at his words, how his mouth secretly slanders other men and brings forth evil among his friends, often speaking evil without any certain cause and rejoicing in the misfortune of his neighbour and hoping misfortune comes to him. These are all the hooves and horns of the devil and the image of the serpent that he carries within him.

10. Then let him hold these[9] up against God's word in law and Gospel, and he will see that he is more beast and devil than true man. He will clearly show how these imagined and inherited images[10] hold him back and lead him away from God's kingdom so that often when he eagerly wishes to repent and convert himself and turn himself to God, these devil's hooves hold him back and lead him away from it, and the poor soul imagines that these spectres are divine. It places its lust in them again, it remains firmly in God's wrath and finally steps into the abyss when the grace and the pull of the Father are extinguished.

11. To such [a man] we tell our own way so that, as soon as he is aware of these beasts, immediately, in the same hour and minute, he will understand and lead his will accordingly into his soul so that he will wish to leave the bestial will and through true repentance turn to God. Even though he neither will nor can do this in his own powers, he should take Christ's promises to himself, for Christ said: Seek, and you shall find; knock, and it will be opened unto you [Luke 11:9]. No son asks bread of the Father and He offers him a stone; or an egg, and He offers him a scorpion. If you who are wicked know

how to give good gifts to your children, how much more will my heavenly Father give the Holy Spirit to those that ask Him for it (Luke 11:13).

12. Let him take this promise into his heart. It is poison and death to the devil and to all inherited and fabricated beasts. Let him come immediately before God in his prayer at this same hour thinking on these promised words. Let him consider all these abominable beasts, of which he himself is one. Let him think that in himself he is nothing other than a filthy swineherd who has wasted his father's possessions and his birthright with the pigs of the world and with evil beasts; that he now stands before God's face as nothing other than a miserable, naked, ragged swineherd who has prostituted and adulterated his father's inheritance with the world's bestial images; and [that he] has no right any longer to God's grace, and is unworthy of it; much less can he be called a Christian or a child of God. Let him despair of all those good works that he has ever done for they arise only from hypocritical appearance of godliness by which the man-devil wishes to be called an angel. For without faith it is impossible to please God, the Scripture says [Hebrews 11:6].

13. But let him not despair of God's grace, only of his own self and of his own abilities and possibilities. Let him bend his soul with all his powers before God, even if his heart clearly says: "No," or "Wait. This is not a good day," or, "Your sins are too great; it is not possible for you to come to God's mercy." Then he will also become anxious, so that he cannot pray to God nor receive comfort or power in his heart, so that it seems to him as if his soul is completely blind and dead to God. But he ought to stand firm and hold God's promise as a certain, unfailing truth, and sigh with dejected heart for God's grace and, in his great unworthiness, give himself to Him.

14. And, though he sees himself as too unworthy, as if he is a stranger, to whom the inheritance of Christ no longer

belongs and [as if] he has lost his right, he should consider seriously that Christ says: He came to seek and make holy that which is lost [Luke 19:10], as the poor sinner, dead and blind to God. This promise he is to accept and [he is to] make such a strong resolution in himself that he will not forsake the promised grace of God in Christ, even if his body and soul should suddenly be cut asunder. Even if he should not gain consolation of forgiveness in his heart all the days of his life, God's promise will be more firm than all the comfort that may come to him.

15. Let him resolve and firmly commit his will to his resolution that he never again will wish to enter the old bestial images and evil, and even if all his pigs and beasts mourn for their herdsman. Even if he should be a fool to the world because of this, let him wish nevertheless to remain firm in his resolution and in God's promise of grace. However, if he is a child of death, let his wish be in Christ's death in Christ's promise, and die and live in Him as He wills. Let him but direct his resolution to God in continual prayer and sighing, and let him give all the beginnings and productions of his work into His hands, remaining quiet before the imagination of covetousness, envy and pride. Let him give up only these three beasts and the others will soon begin to be weak and sick, and to approach death. Christ will soon be in His promised words that He places in him and with which He wraps him, a form of life. He will begin to work in him. His prayers will be more powerful (and ever stronger) in the spirit of grace.

16. Just as a seed works in the mother's womb, and grows under many natural movements and external accidents until the child receives life in the mother's body, so it happens in this matter. The more a man moves himself from the images, the more he enters into God until Christ becomes alive in embodied grace,[11] which occurs in great earnestness of resolution. Immediately the marriage with the Virgin

Sophia[12] begins when the two lovers receive each other in joy, and press into each other with completely inner desire, in the sweetest love of God. Then in a short time the marriage of the lamb is prepared when the Virgin Sophia (as the worthy humanity of Christ) is wedded with the soul. And what happens then, and what kind of joy then arises, Christ indicates [by referring to] the great joy over the repentant sinner that is held before God's eyes and all angels in heaven for the man than for more than ninety-nine righteous who need no repentance (Luke 15:7).

17. We have neither pen nor words to write or to tell what the sweet grace of God in Christ's humanity is, and what happens to those who are worthy to come to the marriage of the lamb, which we in our own way have experienced, and which we know, so that we have a true ground for our writings. We have shared this gladly with our brothers in the love of Christ. If it is possible for them to believe our precious childlike counsel, they will experience in themselves that from which this simple hand understands and knows such great secrets.

18. Since we already have written a detailed tract *On True Repentance* and *On New Birth* we shall leave off here with only a mere guide, and direct the reader himself to it, as well as to the large work on Genesis [*Mysterium Magnum*]. There the ground of all that which he may ask will be found in enough detail. And, in a Christian manner, we admonish him to follow us in this way. Thus he will come to divine contemplation in himself, and hear what the Lord says to him in Christ. And with this we commend him to the love of Christ.

THE THIRD TREATISE
ON
HOLY PRAYER
WITH AN ORDER FOR EACH DAY
OF THE WEEK[1]
(1624)

How a man is continually to examine the office, position and way of life in which God has placed him; and how he is to commit the beginning, middle, and end of all his activities to God and continually do all his works with God even as the branch of a tree bears its twigs by the power of the root and from these bears its fruit; and how in all his beginnings he is to fetch the power for his works from God's fountain and thank his Creator for all blessings.

Together with a heartfelt consideration of the suffering, death and resurrection of Jesus Christ; how a man is continually to lead his soul's hunger and desire through Christ's death into His resurrection in God and press forward to the new birth so that he might pray in spirit and in truth and present himself before God. Written at the request and desires of his[2] dear and good friends for the daily practice of true Christianity in their heart- and[3] house-churches.

Foreword of the Author to the God-loving[4] Reader on the true ground of a proper art of prayer; what prayer is and why God calls us to pray.[5]

1. Dear Christian reader: Correct prayer is not simply a custom in which one need only say the words of the prayer. No, such mouthing of words without careful consideration and divine desire is an outward thing, an external formation of words.

2. The mouth forms the words of its prayer only with the external power of the stars and the elements, and makes only a form of willing in which there is no proper, actual power. Nothing pleases God in a thing except what He Himself works and does.

3. In His prophets˙ God testifies against such external mouth-prayers without power, when He says: With their lips do they draw near to me, but their heart is far from me (Isaiah 29:13). Again, Christ says: Not all who say to me, Lord, Lord, shall enter into the kingdom of heaven; but those who do the will of my Father in heaven (Matthew 7:21). And further in another place He says: Apart from me you are not able to do anything (John 15:5). He is the living source and the throne of grace by and through whom we are able to press before and into God in prayer.

4. If we wish to pray properly we must look in the first place at ourselves and consider well whether our heart has formed itself in another creature, and whether such a desire as we wish to receive from God is proper; whether our desires that we direct to God in prayer are opposed to the advantage and to the love of neighbour; whether in them [our prayers] we seek temporal things to take advantage of our neighbour and to draw to ourselves what is his; whether we desire universal love and simplicity in them; or whether with such prayer we seek only our own advantage.

5. We are to consider well in the second place whether we also desire and love something more in our prayer than the mercy of God; whether we desire only those things from the divine hand and cooperation that we desire from temporal things; or whether we sigh to gain them by our art, cunning and intelligence and only ask God for His permission to do so; whether we rely on ourselves; whether we wish to succeed with God's cooperation so that hereafter we can say, "God has given this to me in His fatherly providence; I am only His hand and instrument"; or whether we wish to say: "I have done this by my own art and understanding."

6. Thirdly we are to consider what we wish to do with that which we ask and desire from God; whether we seek in it the world's honour and glory alone for temporal pleasure; or whether we wish to turn[6] what God gives us with His bless-

ing through our prayer to God's honour and the love of neighbour and [thus] return it to Him; and whether we believe ourselves [to be] the only ones,[7] those workers and servants in His vineyard of whom God will demand an account of His gifts,[8] as to how they have been [faithful servants] in their tasks.

7. We are fourthly to consider that in this world we have nothing of our own, and that we ourselves are not our own, but that we are only workers and foreign guests in this world for a short time; that we are only managers for our God over His creation and creatures; that what we work and produce we do not only for ourselves but for God and our neighbour; and that all together we are one in Christ our salvation, who is Himself[9] in all of us; and that because of this we are to have a common love between ourselves and seek to desire to deeply love as God has loved us in Christ our Saviour; and that we are to heartily and willingly wish to share the gifts that God gives us through our prayer, be they heavenly or earthly, to our fellow-members loving and upholding them; and to keep ourselves as the tree does its branches, or the earth does giving itself willingly to all its fruits, loving and bearing all of them.

8. We are fifthly to consider that of our own power we are not able to pray correctly before God, as Christ says: Without me you can do nothing (John 15:5). And Saint Paul says: We do not know what we pray for [or] how it is fitting before God, but the Holy Spirit[10] presents Himself for us before God with sighs too deep for words (Romans 8:26).

9. For this reason, if we wish to pray to God our heavenly Father, we are to call upon Him in the name of His dear Son, Jesus Christ, for the illumination of the Holy Spirit, so that He might forgive us our sins for the sake of His bitter passion and death, and give us what is good and holy for us. We are to place everything that is earthly in His knowledge and will, and not only come before God with naked breath and words if we want to pray correctly and be heard, but [we

are to come] in proper earnest repentance and turn from our false way of life.[11]

10. And we [are to] wish to leave all pride, falsehood, wrath, envy and stubbornness and to give our whole heart and soul to God, the Holy Spirit, so that He might be our work of repentance and power in prayer; that He might grasp our will and desire in Himself, and lead them into God, and that we might put to death our false vanity and desire, which are inherited by us, in the death of Christ, and be born and rise up in the spirit of Christ with a new will, mind and obedience to God; and [that] hereafter we might walk [live] before God in our new will and birth in such a power of righteousness and purity, as His children, which He dearly bought[12] through the blood and death of His dear Son, and be born again in His Spirit.

11. You are to consider well what prayer is and why God calls us to pray. It is not [such a] matter as when a man comes before a worldly king, or lord, to whom he has attached himself, and prays for grace and often thinks quite differently in his heart. No, it is rather a going out of himself, so that a man gives himself to God with all his powers, with everything that he is, and that he possesses. Yes, in correct prayer he gives himself as a possession to God. He comes again with the prodigal son to the Father, into his first fatherland and inheritance out of which Adam, our first father, led him. He has no longer a natural right to the heavenly possessions; he lost them with Adam's departure, and wasted [them] in vanity with the devil's adultery.

12. With the prodigal son he must thus come once more to God in great humility and faith, in true hope in God's offered grace in His Son Jesus Christ, and see himself as unworthy of heavenly possessions by natural rights and fall down before God, his heavenly Father, and pray for the mercy offered in His Son Jesus Christ, so that He might still accept him as a day-labourer and worker in His vineyard, and

again give him heavenly meat and drink for his weakened, hungering and thirsting soul, so that he no longer need eat the devil's pig's husks of vanity, lies and falsehoods, and thus die in unbelief, without heavenly power. He must offer his hungering and thirsting soul's mouth toward God's grace and mercy, in his prayer, with deep sighs for expectation of grace, and give Himself wholly and completely to God's grace.

13. Then he will immediately hear in his soul that God will come to him in His grace, and give him in his soul the grace that He offered in Jesus Christ, so that the poor, hungering soul will receive in power and essence what it begs and desires from God, that is, the flesh and blood of Jesus Christ, its Saviour, which out of grace is offered to all hungering, repenting souls.

14. He will discover properly within himself how the old father of the prodigal son comes toward the poor, changed repentant soul and falls around the neck of its essence of life with His love, and with His love embraces and kisses it, grasping it in His arms, and speaking to it with power: "This is my dear son: This is my dear soul that I lost. It was dead and has come alive again. Now slaughter the lamb, Jesus Christ; [the soul] is to sit down at the table with me in my power and eat with me from the food I ordered, of the proper nourishment of my Son Jesus Christ, and it is to rejoice with me eternally." Then the signet ring, as the precious testament of the covenant of God in the blood of Jesus Christ, will be placed again [upon the son], and, through such a covenant and sealing, it will be received again as a child of God.

15. Therefore I say this to the Christian reader: that praying is not only a mouth-work, as when a man comes before a lord and requests temporal things, or release from debt. God calls us to pray not only for external, available grace but also for childlike, active grace in which the Holy Spirit in the service of Christ asks and prays in us so that He might make grace powerful in us and by such action blot out

sin in us, drowning it in Christ's death, destroying hell and opening in us the gates of eternal life (Christ's payment) through God's wrath and taking the devil's power from him and dressing us with Christ, so that in the spirit and merit of Christ we cry out to the Father of all mercies, and say, "Abba, dear Father" [Romans 8:15].

16. Saint Paul says: For we have not received the spirit of bondage so that we again must have to fear ourselves, but a childlike spirit so that with joyful hearts we may ask of the Father with all confidence that He will give it to us (Romans 8:15; Ephesians 3:12; Galatians 4:6).

17. For the sake of giving and receiving God calls us to ask and pray, as Christ says: My Father will give the Holy Spirit to those who ask Him for it. Again: Ask, and it will be given you, seek and you will find, knock and it will be opened unto you (Luke 11:9-13).

18. Every prayer that does not find and receive is cold and indifferent, and is held in the hindrance of temporal, earthly things; that is, the soul does not draw near to God purely, it does not want to yield itself wholly and completely to God, but it still hangs on to earthly love that holds it captive so that it may not reach the city of God.

19. If a man wants to pray correctly, he must turn from all creatures and come before God pure in will and mind. He must be resolute and in earnest like the publican in the temple, and the prodigal son,[13] who thus came to God. And if reason in flesh and blood speaks a pure "No, you will not be heard; your sins are too great," or "Now is not the time; wait; do this or that first so that hereafter you will have leisure and time," or it says: "Why are you praying? Can you not come before God; do you not receive power in yourself?" do not be mistaken; the power is in the internal ground, in the desire of the will and works with God. Remain silent and wait for the Lord. It will finally press through so that you will feel it in your heart and thank God.

20. He who wishes to pray correctly and by prayer to reach God's power and spirit should forgive all his enemies and put them in his prayers, and ask God to convert them, and to reconcile them to Him in His love so that not a serpent might remain in his heart to hold him back and tear the power of prayer from the soul, as Christ says: The devil tears the word from their hearts, lest they should believe and be holy (Luke 8:12). Again: When you bring your gift to the altar, and there consider that your brother has something against you, leave [it] and reconcile yourself to your brother; then come and offer your gift (Matthew 5:23-24). Again, in the Lord's prayer: Forgive us our debts as we forgive our debtors (Matthew 6:12), so that the evil enemy may not tempt us by built-up hatred, and hinder us and lead us to doubt.

21. God aids a pure, empty, and naked soul in prayer. Even if it is surrounded by vanity, its will is to come before God in purity so that He may begin to work in its will and afterwards might daily put to death the vanity of the flesh. So certainly is the will with desire to be directed so to God, that it might say with Jacob when he wrestled the whole night with God: Lord I will not let You go, until You bless me (Genesis 32:26).

22. Even though the heart struggles and doubts, and all kinds of hindrances befall it, yet the will ought to remain firm and fix its mind on grace and not wish to leave it. Even though the devil flourishes before it the lusts of the flesh by which the soul is frightened and thinks that it is rejected by God, yet the will should hang on to grace as a child to its mother's breast, and continually strive against the devil and his desire in the flesh and blood until it is finally victorious and conquers the devil by the spirit of Christ. Afterwards he will see and discover great wonders in himself, so that he will know that there is such a great joy in heaven over the converted soul as [there is] over the ninety-nine righteous persons who do not need such repentance (Luke 15:7).

23. Therefore, he who wants to pray correctly is firmly to consider that he will come to divine grace and favour, and that he will receive what he asks for. Therefore, his prayer is also to be so directed that it does not run against God's order. Rather, [he] is to think that in his prayer he will work with God as the wood on the tree works with the tree's power. So he is also to wish to work with God's power, or else his prayer will only be a work in the shell of the true tree of life, for he works with it only externally in the elements and not internally and with God.

24. However, he who properly prays, who works internally with God, but bears good fruit externally, [is] like the tree [that] brings forth its power and with its power lets itself be seen in its fruit. So also the true divine power in man lets itself be seen externally with good works and virtues. Otherwise there is no faith there, unless the works follow. Thus prayer is merely hypocrisy and makes only an external form and does not reach the place of God.

25. I do not wish to hide this from my good friends, both male and female, in Christian love. [I wish to note this] out of my little treasure chest as a Christian reminder of how man is to be prepared for prayer. And although I know well that they stand beside me in such work and are fit for and partake of the gifts of the Holy Spirit, in this and the following prayers I wanted to revive myself somewhat with them and point to and share the grace of God with them by my power and gifts (just as one lamp ignites the other, one gift of God [ignites] the other) so that we may revive ourselves in the One Love that is Christ in all of us and that I might thus enjoy your divine gifts and knowledge so that we might grow together, increase and bear much good fruit to the praise of God.

26. I hope to have written the following prayers for each day (so that a man may take his special hours as opportunity arises) only for the encouragement and awakening of the good gifts that are first in all of you. I do not begin with the com-

plete ground and beginning of Christian doctrine, but [I write] only for [your] practice and awakening. I commend all of you to the working love of Jesus Christ and myself to your brotherly and Christian favours.

Direction

How one for such order and practise is to maintain himself for proper prayer.

27. Dear Christian reader, proper prayer is also proper earnestness and must be [done] in earnest or it is useless before God. If we wish to pray properly, we are to think of nothing except that we stand before God's bright face, before the Holy Trinity and the choirs of His holy angels and that God tests our soul, spirit and heart in our prayers and looks on our will in a most inward manner [to see] whether it is completely directed toward Him, whether it has given itself completely to Him.

28. If this is so, He stirs the will with the power of His Holy Spirit[14] and smashes it so that it is properly desirous and hungry for grace, that it begins earnestly to press out of itself and to press into God's mercy.

29. The will is far too weak in its own powers, but when the divine power stirs it, it is awakened so that it becomes fiery and properly desirous. In this desire God Himself works. Then a man speaks properly with God and God actually speaks with the soul of man.

30. Such speaking or working is nothing other than that the poor soul eats of God's mercy (which he has again turned to us in the death of Christ) and revives itself with the balsam of divine love in Christ in which it is strong against the temptations of the devil.

31. Divine hearing is the power of grace that He has again brought into humanity in the Name of Jesus and has

again disclosed an open door for us to His hearing by which we are able actually to hear God speaking[15] in us even as He speaks His mercy through the same open gates of grace, and in itself the soul speaks again with God through these same open gates. In such conversation [we are] nourished as well as enlightened and renewed by God's speech.

32. It [the soul] eats of the expression of God who became man, that is of the flesh and blood of Christ in the form and manner that a plant eats the sun's power in itself, by which it is tinctured, and becomes fragrant and good, so that it grows and blooms. In the same way the soul [grows] under the divine sun, under which it becomes light and powerful.

33. This is now the value and fruit of correct prayer, which an external mouth or a will turned from God cannot reach but only the [will] turned [and] wholly given to God.

34. If this is to occur the will must turn from all creatures and from all earthly things, and stand pure before God so that works of the creatures, those things that it wishes to ask from God in temporal things, follow it only in the flesh and stand behind the pure will, so that the pure will might bring the needs of the body before God, and the flesh itself does not work with its lust, or it would direct earthly lust into the divine work in the soul.

35. Thus, there always belongs to proper prayer, if we want to receive something from God, correct repentance and inner humility. Correct prayer is a taking of that which the soul desires, concerning which Christ says: Until now the kingdom of heaven suffers violence, and those who do violence tear at it by force (Matthew 11:12).

36. Because of this, I wish to set down a short formula and[16] preparation of confession, of how a man is first to prepare himself beforehand if he wants to bring his short prayers and requests before God. He may be heard just as well in a short prayer, in which his heart stands correctly before God, as [he is] with many words. Many words are not needed, but

only a believing, repentant soul that gives itself up with all earnestness into the mercy of God and God's comfort. One single sigh suffices with God if the will stands pure before God and if it has cast the earthly cloak, false lust, away from self. [This is intended] to bring the reader to remembrance and to encourage him.[17]

37. It is not necessary to use only this form of confession, but the Holy Spirit makes a form for Himself in the heart when the will turns in true earnestness to God.

38. I wish to set down this confession [of sins] only as an introduction for one who does not yet know how a person who prays correctly shall act, so that his soul may be guided. And I commend the work of confession together with prayer in each soul that is in earnest to the Holy Spirit. He will make confession and prayer for Himself. If one comes with proper earnestness to the gates through which God the Lord speaks in man, then he will discover this.

A Confession and Proper Act of Repentance before God's Face

39. O deepest, great unsearchable holy God, after the terrible fall of our first parents out of pure grace and mercy, You revealed Yourself with Your great love and mercy in our humanity in Your Son Jesus Christ, and again made for us poor men a gate of grace open to Your presence in Him, and wiped out sin and death in His blood; and now as a merciful God, You call us to such grace. We poor sinners must only be converted and come to You and You will give us new life (Matthew 11:28).

I, poor, unworthy, sinful man, come to You invited by Your word and confess to You that I am not worthy of such grace that You offer us. I stick fast in the mire of vanity and I am overburdened with vain fleshly lust and my own will. My sins have caught and darkened me so that I neither taste nor see Your grace in me. I have neither proper trust nor faith in You and I have wholly given myself to the vanity of the world and the flesh and am captured by it. I have dirtied with fleshly lust my beautiful garment with which You clothed me in baptism, and I lie caught in the devil's net, in Your anger. Hell opens its jaws before me and my conscience nags at me. Your judgement stands always before me and the bonds of death wait for me. I lie in the mire of sin and vanity so that I can neither know nor regret my sins. They have hidden me from Your face and have [left] only a small spark of living breath in me that, through Your pull, desires Your grace. I come before You now with the prodigal son and the publican in the temple, and cry for Your mercy, and ask You in my weak power, through the bitter suffering and death of my Redeemer Jesus Christ, which You have set forth as the throne of grace and You offer us His[18] grace through His payment. You wish to take me again as a child and heir in Your Son, and wish to awaken in my heart proper earnest repentance and contrition and suffering for my past sins so that I might leave the godless ways and wholly and completely turn my heart to You.

O great God, strengthen my weak faith in me. Smash my heart so that it knows and regrets its many sins. Stir my poor soul with Your power so that it knows that it is turned from You.

O Breath of the great mercy of God, draw me to You through my Redeemer Jesus Christ's death and resurrection and wipe out my sins in His blood and death, and make my poor soul alive in His blood and wash it pure from its sins so that it with its desire may press to You, O holy God, and fetch power from Your fountain of grace. Awake a proper hunger and thirst for true repentance and sorrow in me for past[19] sins so that I might hate and oppose them and turn to You.

O great depth of mercy, I, poor man,[20] am far from You

and cannot reach You with my weak power. Turn to me and take up my desires in You, and ignite them Lord so that I might taste Your grace.

Forgive me my transgression and sin, and heal my weakness. Smash my heart and soul so that I might know myself and humble myself before You. Be my beginning to conversion and lead me on the right path so that I might walk with You. Give me Your Holy Spirit in my soul and spirit and sanctify me in Your grace as Your dear Son Jesus Christ has promised me: My Father will give the Holy Spirit to those who ask for it (Luke 11:13). Again: Knock and it will be opened (Matthew 7:7; Luke 11:9). Now do I, poor sinner, invited by Your word, come and take Your promise in my soul and heart, and do not leave You until You bless me, as [you did] Jacob. And even though my sins are many, You are the almighty[21] God and the eternal Truth that[22] cannot lie, and You have promised in the prophet Isaiah: If we turn and repent, our sins[23] will be as snow-white as wool (Isaiah 1:18). I trust in Your promise and give myself wholly and completely to You, and from the heart ask You to take me in grace and lead me to Your children who walk on the way of the living; let me go with them, and walk in Your law. Grant me a true, humble and obedient heart that might always fear Your wrath and no longer sin.[24]

O You Fountain-source of all grace, what shall I say before You? What shall I pretend [or with what] comfort my evil will and desire? I desire no consolation from You in all my earthly, evil will, but I ask You out of my power, which is still within me by Your grace,[25] to kill my earthly, evil will, let it no longer live before You. It desires only hypocrisy and its own love, and it is never righteous before You. It gives You good words and agrees to truth, and yet it is a continual liar before You. Only grant me Your will so that I will nothing without You. With Your will tread down my evil will to the ground, and allow me to will and act in Your power.

O Lord, what in my vanity shall I ask from You? I ask nothing from You but the death of my Saviour Jesus Christ, that You kill me in His death and in His resurrection make me alive so that I no longer walk after my spirit's will in me, but in Him, that I may be His temple and dwelling, so that He may lead and direct me, so that I can neither will nor do anything without Him. Bind me with Him, so that I may be a good branch on His vine and in His power bring forth good fruit. I sink wholly and completely into Your promise. Let it happen with me according to Your word and will. Amen.

A Thanksgiving and Prayer when Man, after Such an Act of Repentance, Discovers the Divine Power in Himself

40. O God, Fountain-source of love and mercy, I praise and glorify You in Your truth, and thank You in my heart that You offer to me Your face once more and look on me, unworthy and wretched [as I am], with the eyes of Your mercy, and give me again a beam of comfort so that my soul can hope on You.

O superabundant[26] Love, Jesus Christ, You who have broken death and have changed God's wrath into love, to You do I give myself wholly and completely. My soul praises and extols You. It rejoices in Your power and love, that You are so good. My spirit plays in Your power and rejoices in Your truth. All Your acts are proper and true. You rule over sin and shatter death's power. You hold hell's might captive and show us the way of life. No one is like You, Lord, who releases captives from the dungeon of death and revives the wretched. You give them drink in their thirst, and give them the water of eternal life. You direct their feet on the right path and herd them with Your staff [Psalm 23:4]. The dry places of the heart and soul You water with Your rain, and give them the water of Your mercy. In the midst of death, You make them alive, and set them up before You so that they live. You make them think of the mercy and the covenant that You have made with us through Your blood and death, and You forgive us our sins. You give Your power into us so that we may know You. You give us the food of eternal life by which we are revived and always hunger and thirst after You. Now does my soul know this; therefore it praises You and rejoices in Your great might and majesty.

O Fountain-source of divine sweetness, take my soul into You and fill my spirit with Your love, and bind me in Your bond so that I may nevermore turn from You. (Strengthen my weak faith and give me sure hope and confidence.²⁷) Purify my heart and soul, and give me chastity in conscience so that I might be ashamed of my sins before Your face and turn from them. Put to death all my evil lusts in me so that I may cling to You with pure desire and walk in Your will. Keep me in Your power and knowledge, and give me a humble heart toward You and to my neighbour so that I may always know and love You. Help me also that I love my neighbour as myself, through Jesus Christ our Lord. Amen.

A Prayer to the Fiery Burning Love of God, in Order to Properly Love It²⁸

41. O holy God, You who dwell in light to which no one can come but only the love of Your Son Jesus Christ, by it You loved us poor human men before the world's foundation [was laid], and redeemed us through this love from Your anger and from the power of death and hell. You declare to us now such love through Your Son Jesus Christ in Your fire-flaming spirit, so that if we should pray to You for it, You will give it to us.

I, poor unworthy man, acknowledge myself unworthy [of such love]. However, since You have revealed it in our humanity that You took on, [You have] called poor, lost sinners by it, and came therefore in flesh so that You might search them out in sins and misery and thereby release [them] from sin and make [them] holy, as Your word teaches.

Therefore, I come, O Father rich in love, invited by Your word, and take Your word and truth into my heart and soul and grasp it to myself as Your gift. And I pray, O fiery flaming Love of God given to us poor thirsty souls in the covenant of Jesus Christ, ignite my soul with this love so that it might receive a new life and will and be redeemed from the prison of Your wrath and from the jaws of death.

O fiery Love of God, You have broken death in our humanity, and destroyed hell, and performed our soul's victory in Christ through death. On holy Pentecost Day You moved in the mouths and hearts of the apostles in fiery flame and ignited all Your saints and did Your miracles through them; You who love and keep the whole world and all Your creatures, to You I come and give myself wholly into You.

O You great Fountain-source of God, arise in my spirit in my interiority, and ignite within me the fire of Your love so that my spirit[29] burns in Your love and I might praise and know You in it.

O great Holiness, through the merit of my Saviour Jesus Christ, through His blood and death, I press into You myself and give myself to Your flames. Through His resurrection and ascension I lead my will in You, and give it wholly and completely to You. Do with it as You will. Redeem it from false lust and break its power so that it sees only You.

O holy Power of God, You move in and over heaven and earth, and are near to all things. Pour out Yourself also into me so that I may be born again in You and sprout forth within me and bring forth good fruits, like a branch on the vine of my Saviour Jesus Christ, to His eternal praise and majesty.

O Gate of God's holiness, illuminate Your temple in my spirit so that I might walk in Your light, and praise You all the time, and serve You in holiness and righteousness as pleases

You, You who are One God, Father, Son and Holy Spirit, highly praised in all eternity. Amen.

Now follow the prayers for all days of the week; for morning, noon, and evening; how a man is to be in constant practise and action.

Christ said to His disciples: Watch and pray so that you do not fall into temptation (Matthew 26:41).

And Saint Peter: Your adversary, the devil, goes about as a roaring lion, and seeks whom he may devour, [that is] the one who stands against him steadfastly in the faith, in prayer and in the hope that your hearts may be preserved from the darts of the evil one (I Peter 5:8-9).

Prayers[30] for Monday
A Short Prayer and a God-directed Sigh when One Wakes Early before One Arises

42. My eyes look to the Living One who made heaven and earth and rejoice in His goodness, that He is so gracious and has held His hand over me during this dark night and by Your holy angels has protected me from all harm and suffering. To You, O living Source, I press. Bless me with Your holy cross, upon which You underwent death and brought us again to life, through the blood of our Lord Jesus Christ, in the name of the Father, and the Son and the Holy Spirit. Amen.

Prayer and Thanksgiving when One Rises

43. I thank You, O God my heavenly Father, through Jesus Christ, Your dear Son, our Lord and Saviour, for all the good things; for Your gracious protection and defense, that You held Your hand over me, and protected me this night from the devil's cunning and deception and from all evil. Now I place into Your hands my body and soul (and all that which

You gave me and in which You set me as Your servant), as well as all my senses, thoughts and desires. Rule over me this day, and all time, with Your Holy Spirit and lead me on the right path. Give me Your Word in my heart, and teach me Your truth, that this day and at all time I neither speak, think nor do anything but what is proper and true. Protect me from lies and from all evil men who live in lies and deception so that I do not follow them; but lead Your truth into my heart and guide [it] on the right path. Clothe my heart and soul with the cloak of salvation and with the coat of righteousness and purity. Wash my heart with the blood of the little lamb, Jesus Christ. Let my eyes look on Your path so that I walk on it. Give me Your holy angel to guide and lead me and to protect me from the devil's suggestions and false net, so that I do not allow myself to lust after unrighteousness. Give me pure and chaste eyes so that no false lust be wakened in me. Protect me from wrath and cursing that I do not misuse Your Name, but walk as it pleases You, through Jesus Christ, Your dear Son, our Lord and Saviour. Amen.

A Prayer when a Man Dresses and Washes Himself

44. O eternal God, with these clothes I remember the cloak of innocence of our first parents, how they had no need of clothes like these; these earthly clothes had their beginning in sin.

O merciful God, You brought us again the beautiful cloak of Paradise in Your Son Jesus Christ; put it on my soul, since the earthly body is not worthy of it, until I am once again resurrected from the dust of the earth when You will completely reclothe me again with the clothes of Your power and majesty. This do I believe and hope according to Your

Word. And as I wash myself now with external water, thus, O dear God, wash my heart and soul with the blood of the lamb, Jesus Christ, so that I might be pure before You, and please You well as Your bride. Take me in Your arms like Your own dear bride with whom You are given and promised in faith and in love.

Clothe me with the cloak of Your innocence in which You in our cloak have taken to Yourself the scorn of all men. O Lord Jesus Christ, You have put off from Yourself in Your suffering and death our earthly clothes. The soldiers took them from You and offered You up, naked and bare, to Your eternal Father. Thereby You have purchased for us the pure and holy cloak of innocence that our first father Adam had before the fall, when he knew that he was naked.

O dear Lord Christ, clothe my poor soul again in it. Did You not come into our humanity so as to help us, and to give us the cloak of Your power? Take my mind in Your cloak so that it may step before God in such a cloak, and pray to Him.

O Lord Jesus Christ, without the cloak of Your power and satisfaction I cannot come before God. My prayer cannot reach the place of the Godhead in any way, unless You clothe[31] my mind and desire with the victory of Your resurrection. In it alone I can come with my mind to Your holy Father. Therefore, I now give my mind and will to You as a possession. Clothe it, Lord Jesus, with Your power as I now clothe the body with earthly clothes. Wash away all impurities from my mind as I now wash my face with water. Wash my mind inwardly with the power of Your grace, so that it will be awake to look on You and have an opposition to all falsehood and to impurity of lies, untruth, pride, covetousness, envy, wrath and all that is contrary to God.

O God, Holy Spirit, let me enter and walk in Your power. May Your holy angel whom You have given me lead me, through Jesus Christ, our Lord. Amen.

A Prayer when a Man Desires
To Go to His Work and to the Calling
in Which God Has Placed Everyone

45. Almighty, eternal God and dear Father, Creator of heaven and earth, You have created all things to Your praise, and man to Your image, and have set him as lord and ruler of Your works, and placed everything under his hand.

I, poor, miserable, sinful man, remember the grievous fall of our first parents, by which Your curse came upon this work and over the earth. I remember how our first parents were driven out of Paradise into this curse, in which we must all swim in trouble, sorrow and necessity, and [must] trouble and hurt ourselves to keep and refresh our lives, until once again we finally enter the dusty essence from which we were taken. There we are to await Your true promise that You will awaken us from the dust of the earth in the last days and again form us in the beautiful paradisaical image. I remember this now as I take up the work and calling in which You, by nature, have placed me. I pray for Your great mercy, which You, after the grievous fall, have turned again toward us in the grace of Jesus Christ. Bless me in my calling and position, and turn me from Your curse and wrath through Jesus Christ's love, so that the evil spirit does not search me out and grasp me in my calling and position and lead [me] into falsehood, and so that I do not offend or deceive my neighbour nor do wrong, by word or work, nor desire what I should not.

Give me, O dear Lord, a wise heart and mind so that I, with good conscience, without false desire and also without pride, greed, envy and wrath, might do my work, and carry out my responsibilities according to Your will, and let me accept what You give me in Your grace, and, with the work of my hands in my office and responsibility, in which You have set me, let me seek to serve not only myself but also my neighbour and the poor, the miserable and those without ability. Moreover may the weak and feeble who do not have understanding of Your miraculous works, or the ability to do them, have help from You.

Help, O dear God, that I properly know myself, that in my office and responsibility, in my work, I am Your servant only, and that all that I do comes from Your hand, that in this world I have nothing of my own but am only a pilgrim and house-guest on earth, and that You, O God the Father, work to bring about and direct all with Your son, Jesus Christ, in the power of the Holy Spirit, and all that is Yours alone, and not mine.

Give me to recognize correctly that all men come from One, and therefore all are my members, brothers and sisters, as a tree with its branches; that I am to love all of them as You, O dear God, loved and still love us with the one love in Christ Jesus from the foundation of the world, and have reconciled to Your wrath (Your Son) all in an eternal love. So, O dear God, awaken this one love in me, and ignite my soul and mind with it so that with You and in You, in Your love, I might love all my fellow-members. I am prepared and willing to serve them, so that Your name might be made holy in all of us, and Your kingdom might come into us, and Your will be done to us, so that all of us might eat and drink Your blessing in one love. Take the evil and grievous guilt as Your curse and wrath from us so that the devil's envy and greed does not rise up in us and lead us into vengeance and evil so that we must love ourselves deeply and forgive one another's failings and weaknesses[32] as You daily[33] forgive us in Your love in Jesus Christ.

O Lord, keep Satan's deceitful graspings [from us] so that he might not tempt us and raise up our evil inclinations in us, by which we fall into false lust. Release us, O dear God, from all such evil by the blood and death of our Lord Jesus Christ.

Grant me a joyous mind to do Your wonders and help so that without Your power I can neither work, will nor do anything. Lead my life by Your miracles and creatures into the eternal, heavenly activity, into the hidden spiritual world. Let me receive power and knowledge in Your miracles so that my inward ground might grow and flourish in Your power into Your miracles, for the revelation of the new Jerusalem where You, O true God, will work, will and be all in all in us. Give me [the ability] to know this continually so that I might have a memorial in my mind, and not sin or break off my will from You and bear a false image that only lusts after pride, covetousness and its own honour, and will be damned with the evil spirits. Give me, rather, a spirit and will to be with You, and to work with You in the power of my Saviour Jesus Christ and the Holy Spirit. Amen.

A Prayer for Monday Noon, or when One Is Moved to Such Meditation, To Consider His Position

46. O God, eternal Father, I thank You and praise You that You have placed me in this position and given me goods and nourishment (or given me to pious people whom I am to serve with[34] my gifts), and have granted me reason and understanding and created me a rational man, so that I acknowledge to You that I am not a dead, foolish, ignorant man, who knows nothing of You and who does not thank You for such goodness. But You have created me in the light of the world so that I live in and work with Your lights, and You show me all Your wonders in Your light. For this I thank You, that You have created me to Your image, and placed Your wonders under my hands so that I may know them and rejoice in the works of Your creation.

I pray to You, eternal God, give me understanding and wisdom that I might not misuse Your creation but use it only for my needs, for the good of my neighbour, myself (and my family). Give me gratitude for all Your gifts, so that my reason does not say: "This is mine. I have purchased it. I will possess it alone. I am noble with it, majestic and beautiful; it belongs to me because of this honour and glory." All this comes from the devil and the grievous fall of Adam.

O dear Lord Christ, help me that I might always consider Your humility, lowliness, and temporal poverty, and do not let my mind lift itself above the simple, poor and needy, so that my soul is not broken away from them, so that in their misery they do not weep over me and my way to You is not hindered. Help my heart to lie in the dust for the simple, and always acknowledge that I am not more than they, that my position is Yours, and that I am only Your servant in it.

O great, holy God, I pray to You: Open my own interiority to me so that I properly know what I am. Unlock that within me which was locked shut[35] in Adam. Let me see and discover in my interiority of mind the beautiful morning-star in the holy Name JESUS, which offers itself out of grace to us poor men, and dwells in us and wishes to work powerfully in us.

Break down the hard posts of the selfishness of my own will so that His will might shine forth through me and I might discover in my mind the beams[36] of His love-fire.

Ignite the fiery life of the soul's ground with the beams of Your light so that I might carry You. Pour Your love and meekness into my fiery life so that the fiery brightness does not completely consume and destroy me because of my continuing impurity.

O great holy God, I now come near to You in my mind, as into Your poured-out power that You have formed into an image of Your likeness according to Your work, and I give myself again to You as Your possession. Work Your wonders in my mind, as in Your counter-image, as You will, and keep my mind within Your power as Your instrument so that it may neither will nor do anything without You, but that it may work and do everything with You. Lead my inclinations with Your might so that I with You may rule over sin, death, devil, hell and [the] world.

Since in the beginning in my father, Adam, You made me ruler of all creatures, and after the terrible fall You brought me into [that position] again in Jesus Christ, so that in Jesus Christ I am to rule with Him, and in Him, and He with me and through me over all His enemies until all have been laid as a footstool before His feet and mine, I therefore give You, my Lord Jesus, my whole mind and soul, and all that I am. Rule in me over all my enemies that are in me and outside of me. Lay them before You as Your footstool and lead my mind as God's image into God's power so that as an instrument of the Holy Spirit it might will and work and perform the good so that Your high Name, God, might be revealed in it and again come to community with Your holy angels, to which You in the beginning ordained it.

O great God, it is indeed a beam of Your power, majesty and knowledge, a playmate of divine wisdom and glory, a servant of the majesty and unity of God, a knower of Your revelation, and a figure of the great Name of God that made all the world and all things! In His essence, before it became creature, all the forms of Your will stood. These forms, O great God, You brought into creaturely being, and set the noble mind to rule over them because with Your holy Name and in Your power You wished Yourself to rule by [Your] mind.

O God, the mind turned from You in Adam, and entered into the possessiveness of its own will, and made itself dark, dry, prickly, antagonistic, hungry and greedy, and became a hellish source and abomination before You, like to all evil spirits. O great God, You turned it again to Yourself and regenerated it with Your[37] holiest Name, JESUS. Therefore do I willingly give it to You in Your sweet, offered grace, and hereby deny my own will and natural rights and give them to

You, Lord Jesus, as Your possession, so that I am no longer myself, but that You are [my life, Galatians 2:20], according to You and Your eternal Father's good acts, so that God is all in all [I Corinthians 12:6] a true triune being, Father, Son, Holy Spirit, in heaven and on earth, working and ruling all in all. Amen.

Another Prayer for Monday Noon To Contemplate the Day's Quality and Characteristic, and To Rise Up into the Correct Noon of the Internal Moon's Heavenly Being

For the Elevation of the Mind

47. O God, You brilliant, eternally shining Light, You have given the external world the light of the breath of Your might through the beams of Your light, and rule with the sun and moon in all Your works of this world's being. You bring forth all temporal life by these lights. All that has breath, that works and lives in these lights, praises You in Your power. All stars take light and appearance from Your outpoured brightness. You adorn the earth with fair plants and flowers through this light and make joyful all that lives and grows. You point out to us men Your majesty in it so that we might know Your kingdom that is hidden inwardly, and see thereby how You have made Your eternal Word visible and active,[38] so that we may contemplate by it Your inner, spiritual kingdom where You dwell in a hidden way and fill Your creatures, and You Yourself do all in all.

The heavens as well as earth tell of Your honour, power and great might [Psalm 19:7]; the elements are counter-strokes of Your wisdom, since Your Spirit plays with the counter-stroke before You, and all things praise You and rejoice and frolic in Your power. And You, O great God, have made my mind over all this as knower and playmate of Your wisdom, so that I might praise You in it, and help You to bring about and increase Your miracles. You have had good pleasure in this, in that you subjected such strength to me to work in all things and to make all things my own.

O great God in Christ Jesus, where is my might and majesty now? It is blind. Guide me again into my place in your creation so that I see again in Your light and know Your wonders. Illuminate again the light of my external sun and moon so that I might learn from its external being to know Your inward power.

Ah super-illuminated Light of the great hiddenness, give me the beams of Your hidden holiness so that I might see in my light the light of Your gleam.

O Fire and Light of the great interiority, take pity on my misery, and help me out of this dark house in which I am trapped. Give me again a true knowledge of Your being to which You initially formed the mind in nature and ordered it to the will of Your figures and creation. Direct me again in Christ my Saviour into my once-possessed majesty.

And even if, in this time, the body is not worthy of it, since it has become a stinking *cadaver*, shine through my noble mind as Your image, and let it dwell in Christ my Saviour in heaven, in the community of Your holy angels.

Place it within that noon of Your wonders to which You have formed it, and O Lord Jesus Christ, rule through it over all things, as in Your inheritance. Help me to be humble, and not to take to myself this which You do, but help me to look toward You and praise You [with] my desires, and continually live in Your harmony, and neither begin nor do anything without You.

O Lord, holiest Light, let my mind dwell in Your forecourts so that it may rejoice in the brightness that flows forth from You, and [let] it never again bend away from You.

Direct it back again into the community of the holy angels to which You have ordained it.

O holy Name Emmanuel, it is Yours. Do with it as You will. Amen.

Prayer for Monday toward Evening To Remind Oneself of the Difficulty of the Work of Our Hands in the Curse of God's Wrath

For the Elevation of the Mind

48. Ah God, how wretched, full of grief, sorrow and care, full of anguish and trouble is our time. If we think we stand upright, and wish to rejoice in the work of our hands, You overshadow us with Your anger and [bring us to] anguish. We walk and are anxious and there is nothing that pursues us but the wrath in our corruption. We distort our days like a gossip; as a speech that is forgotten, our days pass, and we are ever in restlessness; inconstant is our way of life; we lean on our arm and we hang on the work of our hands, and do not completely trust You. Therefore You allow us to travel in our anxiety and misery. We always[39] consider that You, O God, work and do all, for no breath can come without You, and no blade of grass may crown the earth without You. We see all this and still we build on our own nothingness, on the works of our hands, and we do not really trust You any longer. We gather it and do not enjoy it. A stranger makes himself suffer it in vanity, and there is no end to the miseries that we bring forth.

O God, think on our hardships and misery, and turn Your wrath and curse from us. Let us walk again toward Your goal so that we may come again into our inheritance, and rejoice in Your wonders. Look on the anxieties of our mind and the allurement of our will, and think that we live locked up in the being of dust. Lord, release us and lead us home again. We are in a foreign land, with a foreign mother, who harshly beats us in Your anger, and who lets us starve and run in vain hunger for Your sweet food. With the prodigal son we must eat the husks of vanity. Our cloak is old and full of shame, and we stand in great scorn before Your holiness.[40] The driver of Your wrath leads us captive: If we think we have grasped You, You hide Your face before us and let us suffer.

All this makes our self-will, so that we turn ourselves from You into vanity and desire only perishable being. We swim with our lust in it like a fish in water, and always say to our soul that it has no need, although we stand on hell's abyss and angry death waits for us every hour. All of us travel[41] toward the night, and walk toward our grave, as a messenger walks along his way.

O Lord Jesus, stay with us and in us, and teach us to consider that our external life, on which we trust so much, walks toward evening and its end, and that it is soon over for us. Teach us to travel the right way. Be with us on our pilgrim's path, and lead us home to You. When the time of our night draws near, and death opens up its jaws toward our flesh and external life, and swallows us up within itself and grinds us as dust, then take us into Your power, and allow us to be sweet bread in the essence of the outflowing Word of Your mouth.

Help, my dear God, that I continually think on this, that with my outer life always (each hour) I go toward evening and toward the dusty existence; that I come always closely to the night of earth; that the way of my flesh is only a walk to the grave when the worms shall destroy me.

Ah, Lord! I must give myself as food to that which nauseates me here. I must fall into its throat. Where does the lust for earthly things that I pursue in the world remain? If everything becomes a mockery for me, why do I so lift myself up in temporal lust toward that from which I cannot release myself? Why does my soul torment itself and be anxious for its enemy, which leads it to the dark night?

O God, teach me to know that I may turn my heart from the hardships of the work of this world to You, and not consider death for my life, so that I might live in continual repentance, and move my mind to You and work with You, so that my flesh, properly created in Adam, might be brought out of dust and into mind again.

Redeem me from the gross husks of the earthly flesh in which the devil has brought his poison, which is of no value for Your kingdom (John 6:63); and bring forth the heavenly spiritual body in me again in which there is immortality and in which no evil inclinations or false lust can arise; and let me rest in Christ Jesus in You until the lordly reappearance and revelation of Your majesty. Amen.

A Prayer when One Stops His Work in the Evening and Wishes To Go to Sleep

49. I thank You, O God, Father of all good, through Jesus Christ, Your dear Son, our Lord and Saviour, for all goodness and that You have graciously protected me from all evil and shame this day. I now place my work to Your protection, and flee with my mind to You and wholly and completely give myself to Your holy work. Work in me this night, and at all times, with Your power of grace, and break in me the vain desire of false activity, since Your curse and anger, as well as the devil's injected lust, desire to work within my flesh, and inspire my whole mind into the lust of vanity. Destroy this, O dear God, with Your power and ignite in me the fire of Your pure love, and wipe out the false love of impurity.

Withstand all the evil influences of the constellations and the ignited elements, and let me rest in Your power so that my mind will not be led into false desire and inclination.

O great, holy God, I sink wholly and completely into Your grace and mercy. Let Your good angel be with me so that he may hold back the fiery beams of the evil one, so that I may rest secure in Your power, through Jesus Christ our Lord. Amen.

A Little Prayer when One Undresses and Lies Down To Sleep

50. O merciful God, take off from me the false cloak of the serpent that my father Adam and my mother Eve, by their false lust, put on me. In it my poor soul is clothed with Your wrath and stands before Your holy angels in shame. Make bare my mind and soul so that my mind might be free of such clothing and stand purely before Your face. Clothe it with Your power, and with the cloak of the humanity of Jesus Christ, so that it may again walk before You with the holy angels.

O dear Lord, Jesus Christ, to You I give my soul and mind completely naked and bare. Take from me the unclean cloak in which I stand in great shame before God's holiness.

Clothe me with Your conquest, and place me before Your Father again as a newborn child, which You have washed in Your blood, and whose evil will You have destroyed in Your death and [whom You have] regenerated in Your resurrection. Ignite Your light in this new birth so that I might walk in the light, and remain a branch of You. Amen.

A Thanksgiving of the Repentant Soul for the Bitter Suffering and Death of Jesus Christ[42]

51. O deepest Love of God in Christ Jesus, I give You praise and thanks that You have redeemed me from the fiery source of pain, and have given Yourself with Your own love

and grace into my fiery source, and changed me into a love-fire and a divine light. You have laid Your power and might into my being, into my body and soul, and have made me Your own possession. Indeed You have bought me for Yourself as Your possession with Your grace through the treasure of Your precious blood. For this I eternally thank You; and I ask You, You outpoured Love in the holiest Name JESUS, lead me back again (when I have here died to the temporal life) into my first fatherland (in which my father Adam dwelt in his innocence) into Paradise, and bury my body and soul in the divine rest. Moreover, let it be that I may live daily in repentance, and in the leaving of my earthly will, and remain steadfast in it for my whole life, and bring forth many good fruits in such a position, until You again lead me to rest, into my proper fatherland, into the proper land of promise in which there flows the milk and honey of divine power. Amen.

Prayers[43] for Tuesday

Of God's righteousness and strict commandments and laws; what God demands of us, and how this may be fulfilled, [explained] through the 10 Commandments and [Articles of] faith, and presented in the form of confession and prayer.

A Mirror Earnestly To Be Considered
The First Commandment

God spoke to Israel on Mount Sinai: I am the Lord Your God. You shall have no other gods besides me (Exodus 20:2-3; Deuteronomy 5:6-7). Again: You shall love the Lord your God with all your heart, and with all your soul, and with all your mind (Deuteronomy 6:5; Matthew 22:37).

Prayer[44]

52. O great Holy God, You have made man out of the *limus* of the earth, in which Paradise sprouts forth, as in Your

holy power, [to be] a majestic, powerful and beautiful body, without changeability or destructibility, a likeness of the elements. Out of Your power You have breathed into him the inner soul and the external, elemental life by the power of Your inner, divine activity and knowledge as the great Name GOD; and You gave him his own will that he might be an image of Your miracles, might and majesty, and might rule over all Your creatures in this world. You also gave him the external life of all activity with the interior life of the soul by which You rule the world.

You set him as a ruler above Your wondrous works, and gave him no commandment nor law except that he was not to lead himself into his own lust and will, but that he was to work and will alone in Your power (in the will that You gave him) and not direct himself into his own possessiveness, to test good and evil so that the anger of the fire and the might of darkness might not be aroused in him to destroy the noble image or to change it into the harshness of the earth.

But our first parents, through Satan's lying suggestion, turned from Your will and led [themselves] into their own will, and, against Your command, tested good and evil, and permitted themselves to lust according to sense and their own possessiveness, by which Your wrath and anger was awakened in them and destroyed the heavenly image and transformed them into an earthly image like that of the beasts.

Thus, O holy God, You have given us Your commandments and laws, and presented to us in them the heavenly, divine form of perfect obedience, [both of] what we have been, and [of] what we have become in the fall. You demand of us that, in our wills and with all our powers and senses, we are to depend on You alone and work with You alone. Indeed, You demand from us as a noble guarantee the soul that You have breathed into us out of the internal power of Your Name and will. You will that the soul that flowed out from Your power stay in Your Name and power, and work with You, and not use any other strange name, will or lust, but only that Name alone from which it has flowed, so that it hangs fully in its own *centrum* and directs its desires only into Your love, and undertakes no dominion of its own except Your love and activity so that it may be Your instrument through which You rule all the beings of this world. It is to bring its trust to no other force or power and to make nothing as its own possession, and form or fashion nothing, for it is a beam of the Almighty and is to rule perfectly over all things, as God Himself, and yet not with its own possessiveness, but in and with God. [It is to] use the body as its tool that is to be the servant of Your creatures; You have given it everything for its pleasure and joy, and put all things under it.

All this, O great God, You place before us in Your commandments, and demand it of us, according to Your stern righteousness and eternal truth, for the avoidance of eternal punishment, so that whoever does not keep all Your commandments and laws and stay in Your order will be cursed and separated from Your face, and never see Your majesty in eternity, nor come to Your rest.

O great, holy God, You who are a burning fire, what am I to say before You, a poor, miserable man, who is full of disobedience, his own lust and will, who can have no proper love nor inclination toward You? What am I to answer You when You place before me Your judgement, and test my heart and soul?

O dear God, I can do nothing! I stick fast in the slime of vanity to the deepest interior of my soul. Your wrath flames up in me. In me, all evil beasts, with their passions, live.

Ah Lord, my lust in soul and body have formed themselves in these, and before You I am a worm, not a human being; with such a conception I cannot come before Your face, much less to Your holy Name, or to the *centrum* of my soul out of which it sprang. I am ashamed of myself in this spectre before Your face and in myself I have no righteousness before

You. I have become faithless and have broken off from Your will and directed [myself] into [my] own will. Now I stand before Your face as the prodigal son who became a swineherd, and have lost the beautiful cloak of Your power, and eat every hour the husks of vanity with the devil's swine, and am not worthy to be called Your image and likeness. For I cannot be obedient to You out of my own powers. In myself, outside of Your grace, I am only a source of Your anger and wrath.

Yes, I rejoice in Your great mercy that You turned toward us again in Your holy Name, out of which my soul has flowed; yes indeed, You opened the gates of Your eternal unity, and flowed into my soul, which has destroyed Your anger and broken the *monstrum*. Yes, by such influences You have implanted the internal holiness and sweetness of the Name JESUS into my soul, which my soul and humanity has taken up. It has become obedient to You in my stead, and fulfilled Your commandments and stern laws with full love and obedience.

Now I come to You, with thankfulness, O holy God, and pray to You to increase Your given love of Your grace poured into me so that I might be obedient to You in this new gracious love, and fulfill Your commandments and laws with the obedience and love of Jesus Christ.

My Lord Jesus has planted me again in Your Name, out of which my father Adam uprooted me. Therefore I now come in Him and I comfort myself in Him that I am in Him and live within Your obedience (in His indwelling and internal ruling grace and love) and that in Him I can rule over sin, death, devil, world and all creatures, and have become again Your proper image and possession in Him.

Now, O dear God, rule only through this love of Your grace poured into me and do in me as You will. Kill my evil creatures in my flesh daily, and bind Yourself eternally with my soul and mind as You did in the humanity of Jesus Christ. I eagerly will to abandon the evil beasts of the flesh to the earth to your restitution; only, reclothe my soul and mind, and lead my mind to Your obedience, so that it neither seek nor desire any other God or name, but only the holy Name JESUS that fulfills Your commandment within me. Amen.

The Second Commandment

You shall not misuse the Name of the Lord your God; for the Lord will not let him be unpunished who misuses His Name (Exodus 20:7).

Prayer

53. O dear God, this commandment reminds me correctly how You have poured Your holy Name into my soul and mind. Yes, out of Your Name has it sprung, and You have given me authority to rule over all things with Your Name so that out of my mouth by Your power it is to flow forth and rule all things: Yes, I was to form and fashion holy figures and images with my mouth and expression; even as You, O eternal God, have formed and fashioned everything through Your holy Name, You have given Your Word with Your holy Name into my soul and mind so that I, as a form and image of Your will, am to express Your wondrous works also. What You, O great God, have formed bodily and creaturely through Your Word, I was to form spiritually for Your praise and fashion it within Your wisdom, and not to form in my mouth a strange image contrary to Your creation and order. [I am] rather to remain in Your activity, and rule over all things with Your word in my mouth and heart, as Scripture gives witness: The Word is near to you, even in your mouth, and in your heart (Deuteronomy 38:14; Romans 10:8). Again: The kingdom of God is within you (Luke 17:31).

This, Your holy Word, by which You made heaven and earth, You have given into our mouth so that by our mouth You might create and form [Your praise] in our mouths.

After man had led himself into his own lust, and turned his will from You, then he began in Your anger with his mouth to form earthly and hellish figures such as curses, oaths, lies, anger,[45] false evil serpent-forms, wolves, bears, lions, dogs, cats, adders, serpents and all kinds of such poisonous animals, and to form the Name of God in them under the appearance of divine form and truth, and[46] in false magic and deception, thereby casting forth and honouring foreign images as gods, and introducing and forming Your Name in idolatrous images.

All this You present to us in this commandment, and You demand us, in Your strict righteousness, to serve[47] Your Name in holiness; to form [it] to Your praise and in Your praise, in purity and truth; and not to make a form of our words without Your will and work. Rather, [you] wish us to speak, will and form with You, to avoid eternal punishment, as Your commandment says: Cursed be he who does not keep all the words of this law (Deuteronomy 27:26).

O great God, what am I now to say here before You? How many times do we bring Your Word and power into our mouths by false formations, when we swear, curse and bring in false lust, and make a pretty, hypocritical image on our lips, [and] sell and offer [them] to each other as the truth, which are internally nothing but a serpent full of lies and poison? Thus do we form Your Word in its proper appearance in the image of a serpent and the devil's image. Again, by this we curse and thus beget a living figure of the devil and hell. Again, we use it for derisive mockery and we form our beast in it. All that we love in the world, however false it may be, we form, by means of our mouths, as Your Name and power. Again, in swearing, when we take your might to be [our] witness, and also in magic, torments and sickness, yes in all hellish figures we form it with our mouth. Yes, men for their belly's sake, and [for the sake] of temporal pleasure and pride, direct Your revealed Word and will into a strange form, which they themselves do not know, only so that the truth might remain hidden and they, in such strange forms, themselves might be honoured as gods. They make laws and commandments for their own honour and pleasure, and bind them by the oath of Your Name, and yet no one keeps them in his heart.

Ah God, how much of poisonous wrath and evil of our own throats do we bring in Your name? For, in our prideful sense, we slander, and suppress one another with Your Name, and lead them into tyrannical power, and do nothing with Your Name but what the fallen devil [also] does.

All this You show to us in Your commandment, when You said: We shall not misuse it [Your Name]. This is misusing it, when we make it into a false expression and image.

O great God, what am I to say here before You? You demand Your Name from me in the holiness of Your praise. Where am I to put all these devilish images that we poor men form before You in our house of sin? Before You they are vain abominations, for which Your law curses me and judges me to eternal death.

O holy God, I have nothing by which I may come to You excepting only Your great mercy, for, according to the inmost character of Your Love, Your holy Word became man, and as Your first-given Word, which formed itself in our lives, came to help us, so that He[48] might renew us, and kill all those devil's images and redeem the poor soul and mind from such images and[49] serpents.

For this I eternally thank You, and, in the highest Name JESUS, I pray to You, You eternally outpouring Love; come to me as a help, and bring Your Word, which became man, into my soul and mind, and remain in me, so that I might remain in You. Awaken in me the fire of Your great love. Ignite it, O Lord, so that my soul and mind may see these evil beasts and kill them by means of proper, true repentance and Your power, so that I might continually bring and use in myself the holy Name JESUS for Your praise, and thanks, and no longer bring forth evil beasts in Your Word, which [only] belong to Your judgement.

O living breath of God, I do fully give myself to You as a possession. Do what You will with me. Amen.[50]

The Third Commandment

Remember the Sabbath day, that you keep it holy, etc.[51] (For in six days the Lord made heaven and earth, and the sea, and all that is in it, and He rested on the seventh day [Exodus 20:8-11].)

Prayer

54. O dear God, this commandment reminds me of my internal, proper, divine rest in Your love and power; that in You my will is to rest from the possessiveness of its own will; that You, eternal God, wish to work with Your power in my will; that You are the true Sabbath in which all my energies are to work in an eternal rest and be and remain holy in You.

But O, this was that true Paradise in which You placed our first parents, in which they were to keep Your holy Sabbath, or to hallow Your active power. That is, they were to love it properly and not to bring in any strange lust of false desire, and not to darken this holy Sabbath of Your indwelling power with their own desire, and not to lead the serpent's cunning[52] and falsehood into it, but to will, act and live with You so that You alone might be the acting, willing and doing in me.

Ah, dear God, in this commandment You set before me a figure in which I see Your order and will. You demand from me the ability to live in Your[53] order, in Your will, as You created me in Adam. However, my father Adam turned his will away from You and led it to his own lust and desire, and led this paradisaical work in Your rest into a fiery, antagonistic, proud, covetous, envious and wrathful activity, and profaned Your Sabbath and his, and led the serpent's false work and willing into it. Because of this You threw him out of such rest and paradisaical activity, and cursed his false work. Since he works with the devil and hell, and walks in vain restlessness, he has an eternal enmity against [Your] holy Sabbath.

In this commandment You show us how You made all things in six characteristics of eternal nature (as (1) the desire, (2) the movement, (3) the perceptivity, (4) the fire, or life, (5) the light of[54] love, (6) the understanding or[55] knowledge of the powers), but in the seventh property, in the essential unity and wisdom, You brought it to rest. In this [rest] all Your works are to come to rest in Your active love, in which You wish to work with Your love.

This would have been then a proper Paradise on earth in the elements since Your outpoured love would have had complete power in all, but the devil and man have corrupted this. Because of this You, righteous God, cursed the work of the man's false will, and withdrew Your Sabbath from him so that now all things stand in vain sorrow and need, in plunder,[56] murder, killing and antagonism. This my father Adam gave me as an inheritance, so that I now walk and work in Your wrath and continually break and profane Your Sabbath in me, and misuse Your Name that gave itself to me with my life in my willing and working. However, because man grew blind in such knowledge, You have set before him in Your commandments a figure and form to which You created him, and in which order he stood. [You] commanded him to keep Your Sabbath holy in such form and order, and cease from all his work on the seventh day, meaning that You are the Sabbath in which all things rest.

You also present to him[57] the eternal rest where all things (that which has flown to the eternal from the eternal) are to rest in Your Sabbath; and You have set Your curse and wrath against those who do not keep Your order, and who do not rest in[58] You on Your Sabbath but work only in You.

O eternal God, what am I to say concerning[59] You? My conscience convinces me that we do not properly keep Your Sabbath holy, for on it man pursues all godless pomposity and disordered life. A false lust is added to vain things,[60] for the devil works in many in Your wrath and keeps his own sabbath in opposition [to Yours]. The rich man keeps it in luxury and in the pleasure of the flesh, and the poor man in sorrow and care, or, indeed, in the lust of the flesh as well. We allow Your word to call us and to invite us, and hold the sound we hear to be Your Sabbath. You call us to Your Sabbath, but the mind and the soul do not observe it. We go over it like doves who do not hear Your voice. The will has turned itself from You and acts in its own will, in the devil's lust, and satisfies itself in Your statement that it is Your Sabbath. Yet the soul does not want to be still before You and turn its ear and desire to You, so that You might work in it. O Lord, the devil has brought his sabbath to the human race, and has so blinded them that they no longer know Your holy Sabbath. For this reason You threw our father Adam and our mother Eve out of Your holy Sabbath, and set them into the image [of it]. Nevertheless, You brought Your holy Sabbath in the Name of JESUS, again into humanity, so that again He might work in us and we in Him, and [so that] He might destroy the devil's sabbath of falsehood, lies and vanity and restore Paradise; if we only turn ourselves to You and take this Sabbath and by this work give ourselves completely up to Your grace. You, O eternal God, will build in Christ Jesus a new Sabbath and make a dwelling place in us, and again sanctify Your formed Word [in] our mind and soul and set it in Your eternal Sabbath as in the rest of Your unity.

O eternal God, I give my soul and mind to You in Your holy and new Sabbath, Jesus Christ, and I direct all my powers, my will and senses, to You. Take and lead me into Your new Sabbath, for I cannot with my own powers reach it unless You lead me into it, because in Your son Jesus Christ You have called me to come [because] You wish to revive me (Matthew 11:28). I come to Your eternal supper of the eternal covenant in Christ Jesus invited by Your Word, and ask You to make my soul holy in the Sabbath of Your Son Jesus Christ. Bring it into eternal rest, and give it the food of His proper Sabbath, His holy flesh and blood, so that my soul might again make Your Sabbath holy, and You alone might work in it as Your image.

Break the devil's sabbath and false work in me, and give me an obedient heart that continually hungers after Your Sabbath. And let Your Word keep its Sabbath in me, so that my soul might hear what You, in Your work, speak in me, so that I might be obedient to You and place all my trust in You alone.

O eternal Love, Jesus Christ, how majestic is Your Sabbath in the soul when it turns itself to You so that You press through it with Your sweet love, in which Paradise is again unlocked for it. Let my soul dwell eternally in Your Sabbath. Build in me the new Jerusalem, as the city of God, in which Your Sabbath is made holy. Redeem me from evil. Amen.

The Fourth Commandment

You shall honour your father and your mother so that it goes well with you and you might live long in the land which the Lord your God has given you (Exodus 20:12).

Prayer

55. O eternal God, You set before us in our bodily parents an image of our eternal Father and our eternal mother. You are our Father from whom we have received our life; and Your Word is our mother that bore us out of Your creation and formed us after the image of Your revelation. Our soul and mind is, O God, Father, Your image, and our body is an

image of Your outflowing Word. This Word is our eternal mother in whose body we are begotten and nourished. These we are to honour, and to humble ourselves before them, and to be obedient to them. As we are to honour our external, bodily parents, so also [we are to honour] our eternal [parents] out of which ground we have sprung.

O eternal Father, we have been disobedient to You and have given ourselves to the care of a strange mother. We have taken the world as mother; we have been faithless to the inner mother, Your power in Your Word. Now we must suck poison and death from the breasts of the strange mother. Yes, she carries us in her body of oppositions, bearing and corrupting us again in Your anger, and nourishing us, during the time of this whole external life, with vain misery, care, weariness and need, in suffering and thirst; she holds us captive within her so that we cannot see our proper eternal mother. Our soul cries for her, but Your wrath holds us captive within it so that we must serve the strange mother.

O God, how long will You forget us in our misery? Take us again as Your children and bear us again in our eternal mother, and give us an obedient will so that we may not eternally turn away from You.

Give us also an obedient heart toward our bodily parents so that we might love and honour them according to Your order. Since You through them have brought us forth into this world, and to the light of day, help us that we may be obedient to Your commandment.

O dear God, out of grace You have given us a new mother, Your holiest Word in Your Love; and have sent it in our humanity to bring us forth as Your children and heirs in Your eternal power. You pour into us again as the milk of Your holy being in love. Draw us to You, and open in us the proper mouth of faith, so that we continually hunger and thirst for her [the Word as Mother], and are renewed in Your power. For the old body from the earthly mother does not count for anything with You. It cannot possess Your kingdom, for that which is brought forth of flesh and blood or of the will of man (John 1:13) cannot reach Your divine sonship, but only He who is begotten of God [can do so]. Therefore do I pray to You, O eternal Father, bear me anew through the new mother of Your grace and mercy in Jesus Christ, and allow me to grow and increase in Him, to become a living and holy fruit in Your kingdom, so that beside the holy angels, I might be eternally obedient to You, and eternally rejoice in You. Amen.

NOTE: So far had the spirit of prayer begotten itself in the author for holy direction when he came to the end of his pilgrimage, and, in November of the same year, entered into the rest of the saints. However more is to be found in the first *Book of Repentance*, which the author also calls his *Prayer Book*.

THE FOURTH TREATISE
ON
TRUE RESIGNATION
(1622)

How a man must daily die in self with his own will and how he is to bring his desire to God; what he is to pray for and desire from God, and how he is to sprout forth out of the death of the sinful man into a new mind and will in God.

Chapter One

1. We have in Lucifer, and also in Adam, the first man, true examples of what self does when it receives external light as its own property so that it is able to enter into its own dominion in reason. One also sees [this] in learned men;[1] when they get the light of eternal nature as their own possession, nothing results but pride, which all the world seeks and desires as the best treasure. It is indeed the best of the treasures of this world, if it is properly used.

2. Since self, as reason, is held captive in the strong prison as in God's wrath as well as in earthliness, and is firmly bound, it is dangerous for man to bring the light of knowledge into self as if [it were] a possession of self.

3. The anger of eternal and temporal nature will immediately please itself in it, [and] from this, self and one's own reason will climb up in pride, and break [themselves] off from true, resigned humility toward God, and no longer wish to eat of paradisaical fruit but [will eat] of the characteristic of self, as of that life's dominion in which good and evil stand. Thus Lucifer and Adam did, who both entered again, with the desire of creaturely self, into that cause from which creatures are born and become creatures, Lucifer into the *centrum* of angry nature, into the *matrix* of the fire, and Adam into the

earthly nature, into the *matrix* of the external world, into the lust of evil and good.

4. This resulted in both of them because they allowed the light of understanding to shine in the self in which they could mirror themselves and view themselves in being, through which the spirit of the self went into the *imagination*, as into a desire toward the *centrum* so as to raise themselves up, [and to] become great, mighty and cunning. Just as Lucifer sought the fire-mother in his *centrum*, and thereby thought to rule over God's love and all the host of angels, Adam desired to test the mother in the essence out of which good and evil arose, and led his desire into it in order to be cunning and wise.

5. Both Lucifer and Adam were captured in their false desires, in the mother, and broke themselves off from the resignation out of God and were captured by the will's spirit with the desire in the mother, and gained immediately dominion over the creature. As a result Lucifer stayed in the angry dark, inert fire-source, and the same fire was revealed in his will's spirit by which the creature in desire became an enemy to the love and meekness of God.

6. Thus Adam was also immediately grasped by the earthly mother that is evil and good [and that] is created into one being out of God's love and wrath, and the earthly characteristic immediately gained dominion in Adam. From this it came about that heat and cold, envy,[2] wrath and all false opposition and evil[3] against God were revealed and ruled in him.

7. But if they had not directed the light of knowledge into self, the mirror of the knowledge of the *centrum* and of the cause of creatures, in which *imagination* and lust arise, would not have been revealed.

8. To this extent this still brings danger to enlightened children of God today so that, when the sun of the great look

of God's holiness shines on many—by which life steps forth triumphant—reason mirrors itself in it and the will enters into self, that is, into its own search, and wishes to probe the *centrum* out of which the light shines and to overcome it in its self.

9. From this come miserable pride and one's own darkness, so that one's own reason (which is but a mirror of the eternal) thinks it is more [than it is], that whatever it wishes to do, God's will will do it in itself, and that it is a prophet. Yet it is only its self, moving in its own desire, in which the natural *centrum* of the creature immediately sweeps itself into the height and enters into its own desire of falsehood against God, so that the will enters into darkness.

10. Then the flattering devil comes to him and seeks the *centrum* of the creature and brings his false desire into it so that the man in his own selfhood is as drunken and convinces himself that God moves him thus. By this, the good beginning, in[4] which the light of God[5] was shining in the creature, is corrupted and the same light of God is dimmed within him.

11. Yet the external light remains shining in external nature in the creature, for one's own self lifts itself up[6] in it and thinks then that it is still the first light from God. But no, in this (as in the darkness of self in the external light of reason) the devil lifts himself up again by his sevenfold desire after he has had to leave the first light that is divine. Of this Christ says: When the unclean spirit goes out of a man,[7] he walks through dry places, seeks rest and does not find it. Then he takes to himself seven spirits that are more wicked than he is, and returns again into his first house; and discovers it is cleaned with brooms and dwells in it, and this is then worse with the man than it was before (Matthew 12:43-45).

12. The decorated house is the light of reason in self. For if a man brings his desire and will into God, and enters into abstinence from his evil life, and desires God's love, this same [love] appears to him with its wholly friendly joyful look,

through which the external light of reason is ignited; then everything becomes light. Then the devil cannot stay. He must leave. So he searches out the mother of life's cause, the *centrum*. But it has become a dry, impotent place. The wrath of God, as the *centrum* of nature, is in its own characteristic impotent, thin and dry and cannot gain dominion. Satan searches through this place [to see] whether he can find any door open where he can enter with his desire and seek the soul, so that it will lift itself up.

13. And when the willing spirit of the creature swings up with the rational light into the *centrum*, as into the self, and enters its own delusion, it once again leaves God's light. Now the devil finds an open door into it [the will], and[8] a beautifully decorated house, rational light, as a dwelling, and he takes the seven forms of the life characteristics, which have gone out from God into the self like a hypocrite. Then he turns inward and sets his desire to the trust of his self and into a false imagination. When the willing spirit sees itself in the forms of the life characteristics in the external light, then it sinks into it as if it were drunk and then the stars grasp it and lead their mighty constellation into it to search out the wonders of God in it and to be able to reveal themselves in them. All creatures long for God, and even if the stars are not able to grasp God's spirit, they would much rather have a house of light in which they can find pleasure than a locked house in which there is no stability.

14. Thus this man goes on as if he had become drunk with the constellation. He conceives great wonderful things and has a continual leader in the constellations. The devil always notes where a gate is open for him, by which he may ignite the life *centrum* so that the willing spirit in its pride, in its presumption (or even in greed), may travel to the heights.

15. Out of this, one's own honour stands forth so that the rational will wishes to be honoured. For he thinks that he has the meat of salvation since he has a rational light, and that

he can set in order the locked house, which God easily can unlock. He thinks that honour belongs to him since he has reached rational understanding, and he will nevermore realize that he, the devil, rejoices in his desire in the seven life-forms of the *centrum* of nature nor what kind of abominable errors he has set up [in the reason].

16. Because of this reason, the false Babel has come forth in the Christian Church on earth where men order and direct by rational conclusions, [and] have dressed up and established as a beautiful virgin that child of drunkenness with its self and its own lust.

17. But the devil has entered into the seven life-forms of the *centrum* for his habitation, into the self of his own reason, and he leads his will and desire continually into the adorned virgin who has been taken up by the constellations. He is her beast upon which she, very well adorned in her own life-forms, rides (as is to be seen in Saint John's Revelation). Thus she has taken the external brightness, the rational light, of God's holiness, and she thinks that she is the beautiful child in the house, but the devil dwells in her.

18. And so it goes with all those who were once enlightened by God and left true resignation and have weaned themselves from the true mother's teats, from proper humility.

A True Christian's Processus, How He Is To Go

19. Reason stops me and says, "It is proper and good that a man reach God's light as well as the light of external nature and reason, so that he might order his life wisely, according to Holy Scripture."

20. Yes, it is proper, and nothing is more useful for a man nor can he do anything better. It is a treasure above all the treasures of this world when one comes to and reads the

lights of God and of time, since it is an eye of time and of eternity.

21. But listen to how you are to use it. The light of God opens itself first in the soul. It shines forth like a light from a candle and ignites immediately the external light of reason. Not that it gives itself completely to reason as to the external man in his dominion; no, external man sees himself in the piercing appearance as an image before a mirror. He learns to know himself immediately in the self that is good and useful to himself.

22. Now, when this occurs, then reason, as the creaturely self, can do nothing better than not to see itself in self's creature, and not to enter into the *centrum* with the will of its desire, and seek itself. Otherwise it breaks itself off from God's being (which rises with it in the light of God, of which the soul is to eat and be refreshed) and eats the external light and being by which it draws the poison into itself again.

23. The will of the creature with all reason and desire should completely sink into itself, like an unworthy child that is not worthy of this high grace, taking to itself no knowledge or understanding, nor praying for nor desiring any knowledge from God in the creaturely self. Rather, it is only to sink itself unaffected and simply into the love and grace of God in Christ Jesus, and [being] dead to its desires, give itself completely to the life of God in love, so that He might use it as His instrument in whatever way or however He wishes.

24. One's own reason is not to make any speculation either about divine things or human grounds, nor is it to will or desire anything except God's grace in Christ alone. As a child continually longs for its mother's breast, so the hunger is continually to enter into God's love, and to permit itself to be cut off from such hunger by nothing. When external reason triumphs in the light, and says, "I have the true child," the will of the desire must bow to earth, and bring itself into the

deepest humility and most absurd ignorance, and say to it, "You are foolish, and have nothing but God's grace. In this you must wrap yourself with great humility, and be completely nothing in yourself. All that is about or in you, you must see and consider[9] in itself as nothing more than God's instrument, and lead desire into God's mercy alone, [away] from all one's own knowing and willing, counting it all as nothing also and holding no notion of returning either sooner or later to it again."

25. When this occurs the natural will becomes impotent and the devil can no longer sift it with his false desire. The places of his rest become completely dry and feeble to him.

26. Then the Holy Spirit takes the life-forms from God and leads forth His dominion, that is, He ignites the life-forms with His love-flames. Then[10] the haughty science[11] and knowledge of the *centrum* of all being rises according to the internal and external constellations of the creature, into a subtle driving fire of great lust, to sink itself into the same light and to consider itself unworthy and nothing beside it.

27. Thus one's own desire presses into the nothing as [into] only the might and activity of God that He wills in it. And the Spirit of God presses through the desire of the resigned humility. Thus the human self looks to the Spirit of God in the trembling and joy of humility and thus it may look upon all things in time and eternity, for it is near all things.

28. When the Spirit of God goes like a fire of love's flame, the willing spirit of the soul goes under itself and says, "Lord, honour be to Your name and not to me. You have the might to take power, might, strength, wisdom and knowledge [Revelations 5:12]. Do what You will. I can do nothing; neither can I know anything. I do not wish to go anywhere except where You lead me as an instrument. Act in and with me as You will."

29. The spark of divine power falls and glimmers into such humble complete resignation like a kindler into the *cen-*

trum of the life-forms, into the soul fire, which Adam made a dark coal, and [begins to] glow. Since the light of divine power has been ignited in it, the creature must go forward as an instrument of the Spirit of God, and speak what God's Spirit tells [it to]. It is then no longer its own possession but [is] an instrument of God.

30. But the soul's will must ceaselessly even in this fiery drive sink itself into the nothing, as into the deepest humility before God. As soon as it desires to go in the smallest part[12] into its own speculation, Lucifer grasps for the *centrum* of the life-forms and winnows it so that it enters self. It must remain in resigned humility just as a fountain depends in its source, and must[13] ceaselessly draw and drink from God's fountain, and[14] never desire to leave God's way.

31. For, as soon as the soul eats of self and of reason's light, it walks in its own delusion. Then that thing, which it sees as divine, is only the external constellation that intoxicates it as soon as it is grasped. Then it walks in error until it again gives itself completely into resignation, and acknowledges itself again as a dirtied child, dies once again to reason, and thus again gains God's love. This is now harder to do than it first was for the devil brings serious doubts into it. He is not eager to leave his robber's castle.

32. This can be clearly seen in God's saints from [the beginning] of the world. How many were moved by the Spirit of God and yet went from resignation into self, into their own reason and will, in which Satan again threw them down into sin and God's wrath, as may be seen in David and Solomon, as well as in the patriarchs, prophets and apostles. They often made great errors when they went from resignation into self, into their own lust and reason.

33. Therefore it is necessary for God's children to know what they are to do with themselves if they wish to learn[15] the way of God. They must break and throw off the thoughts, and desire nothing nor wish to learn[16] anything. Then they

will discover themselves in true resignation, that God's spirit leads, teaches and guides the human spirit, and that man's own will for its own lust must be completely broken and given to God.

34. All speculation concerning the mysteries of God is a very dangerous thing by which the willing spirit can be trapped. As long as the willing spirit follows the Spirit of God, it has strength in its resigned humility to see all the wonders of God.

35. I do not say that man is not to study and learn in the natural arts. No, this is useful to him, but his own reason is not to be the beginning. Man is to order his life, not only through the external light of reason—this is all very good—but he is to sink into deepest[17] humility before God and set The Spirit and will of God at the beginning of all his studies so that the light of reason sees through God's light. And, even though reason knows much, it is not to take this as its own possession but give the honour to God who alone is knowledge and wisdom.

36. The more reason sinks into absurd humility before God, and the more unworthy it holds itself [to be] before God, [so much] more it dies to its own desire; and [so much] more it is pierced through by God's Spirit, who brings it to the highest knowledge, so that it may see the great wonders of God. God's Spirit acts only in resigned humility, which neither seeks nor desires itself, which in itself desires to be simple before God. This [it is] that God's Spirit grasps and leads into His wonders. He is pleased only by those who fear Him and bow before Him.

37. God has not created us for self-dominion but as instruments of His wonder by which He Himself wishes to reveal His wonders. The resigned will trusts God and hopes for all good from Him, but self-will orders itself for it has broken off from God.

38. All that the self-will does is sin and opposed to God. It is beyond the order in which God created it, has gone into disobedience, and wishes to be its own lord.

39. When the self-will dies to self, it is free of sin. Then it desires nothing but that alone which God desires from His creation. It desires to do only that for which God created it, that which God desires to do through it. If it itself is and must be the activity, it is only the instrument of the activity with which God does what He wills.

40. This is indeed the proper faith in man that he die to self, to [his] self-desire, and that he direct his desires in all his wishes into God's will, taking nothing for his own possession, but considering himself in all his acts as God's servant and worker, and thinking that all he does and desires, God [in fact] does.

41. In such a way, God's Spirit leads him into proper trust and honesty toward his neighbour, for he thinks, "I do not do my thing for myself, but for my God who has called and directed me to it as a servant in His vineyard." He always listens to the voice of His Lord who orders in himself what he is to do. The Lord speaks to him and orders him to act.

42. But the self does what external reason wishes in the constellations, into which lust the inward flying devil goes with his desires. All that self does is outside of God's will. It all occurs in the fantasy so that the wrath of God may take away its pleasures.

43. No work outside of God's will can reach God's kingdom. It is all only a useless carving in the great laboriousness of man. Nothing pleases God except what He Himself does through the will. There is only one God in the being of all beings, and all that works and labours with Him in the same being is one Spirit with Him.

44. However, that which works in its self in self-will is outside of His dominion [and] in itself. It is[18] indeed in His

almighty dominion with which He orders all life, but not within the holy, divine dominion; instead, [it is] in the dominion of nature by which he directs evil and good. Nothing is called divine that does not work and walk in God's will.

45. All plants, says Christ, which my Father has not planted will be rooted out and burned in the fire (Matthew 15:13). All works of man that are done outside of God's will shall be burned in the last fire of God, and will be given to God's wrath, to the abyss of darkness, for [its] everlasting delight. For Christ says:[19] He who is not with me is against me, and he who gathers not with me, scatters [Luke 11:23]; that is, he who does not work and act with a resigned will in trust in Him only wastes and scatters. This is not acceptable to Him. Nothing pleases God except what He Himself wills in His Spirit and does through His own instruments.

46. Therefore, whatever occurs through the conclusions of human self, without divine knowledge and will, is all fable and Babel and is only the work of the constellations and the external world and is not known by[20] God as His work, but it is only a mirror of the contending wheel of nature where[21] good and evil contend with one another. What good builds up, evil breaks down; and what evil builds up, good breaks down. This is the great sorrow of useless laboriousness, all of which belongs to the judgement of God, to the [final] separation of antagonism.

47. Therefore, he who works and builds up in such laboriousness works only for God's judgement. For there is nothing perfect and permanent, it must all become *putrefaction* and be separated, for whatever is done in God's wrath will be taken from him [the doer] and kept in the *mysterium* of His desire for the Judgement Day of God when evil and good are to be separated.

48. However, if a man is converted and leaves self and enters into God's will, even the good that he did in self will be freed from the evil that he has done, for Isaiah said: Though

your sins be blood-red, if you turn and repent, they shall be snow-white as wool (Isaiah 1:18). The evil will be swallowed in the wrath of God and the good will go forth like a plant out of the wild earth.

Chapter Two

1. Whoever thinks to do something perfect and good that he thinks he will rejoice in and enjoy forever, let him leave self, his own self-desire, and enter into resignation with God's will and work with God.

2. Even though the earthly desire of self clings to him in flesh and blood, if the soul's will does not take it, self cannot make any work. For the resigned will always breaks the self's essence again and again, so that the wrath of God cannot reach it. Even if it does reach it, which is not completely impossible and might happen, nevertheless, the resigned will brings forth its power in it, standing before God as a figure, or a work of victory, and is able to inherit the sonship.

3. Therefore, when reason is ignited in the desire of the self, speech and action are not good. Desire prefers to work in the wrath of God by which man gains trouble, for his works are [then] brought into God's wrath and held in [it] for the great Judgement Day of God.

4. All false desires, by which a man intends by subtlety to injure his neighbours [or] to draw the world's manifold [goods] away from his neighbour to himself, will all be taken into God's wrath and belong to that Judgement when all things will be revealed and each [person] will stand in the *mysterium* of the revelation of all power and being, before [all] eyes as good and evil. All premeditated evil belongs to the Judgement of God.

5. This one[22] who is converted goes from it again, but the work belongs in the fire. Everything is and must be revealed at the end. Because of this God led His working power

into a being, so that it might reveal the love and wrath of God and be in each play,[23] to the honour and miracle of God.

6. Each creature is to know this: that it is to remain in that in which God created it or it will walk into the opposition and enmity of the will of God and bring itself into torment. No creature, so created out of darkness, has pain from the darkness,[24] even as a poisonous snake has no pain from its poison, the poison being its life. If it loses its poison, however, so that a good thing is brought within it and becomes revealed in its essence,[25] this will become its pain and death. Thus also evil is pain and death to good.

7. In Paradise man was created in God's love, and as he led himself into wrath, as into poisonous torment and death, this contrary life became pain to him.

8. If the devil had not been created out of the angry *matrix* in hell, and had he not had the divine *Ens*,[26] he would have had no pain in hell. However, since he was created in heaven, and carried the source of darkness in himself and brought himself completely into the darkness of the world, light is now painful for him, that is, [he has] an everlasting despair concerning God's grace and continual enmity in that He cannot endure Him in himself[27] and has cast him out. Thus he is hateful to his mother who bore him, and also hateful to his father out of whose essence and being, that is, eternal nature, he came forth. [They] held him captive as an apostate out of his own *locus* and please themselves in him with his wrath and angry characteristic. Because he will not help to direct God's joyous drama he must now direct in God's wrathful drama and be an enemy to God.

9. God is all. He is darkness and light, love and wrath, fire and light. But he calls Himself only God according to the light of His love.

10. There is an eternal *contrarium* between darkness and light. Neither grasps the other, and neither is the other. And yet there is only one being, but separated by the source and

by the will. Yet is is not a divided being, but one *principium* divides it so that each is in the other as a nothing. But it is there, although not revealed[28] in the characteristic of that which it is.

11. The devil stayed in his place of ruling, but not in the one in which God created him; rather [he stayed] in the one into which he himself went, not into the work of creation, but into the groaning birth of eternity in the *centrum* of nature, toward the anger for the birth of darkness, anguish, torment and characteristics. Indeed [he is] a prince in this *locus* of the world, in the first *principium*, in the kingdom of darkness, in the abyss. In the kingdom of the sun, stars and elements he is no prince or lord, but only in the realm of anger as in the root of evil of all being, and yet he has no dominion to act with this.

12. In all things there is good that keeps and locks the evil in itself. Thus he [the devil] can only go to and rule the evil when it raises itself up in evil desires and leads its desire into wickedness. This an inanimate creature cannot do, but man can do this easily through the inanimate creature when he leads the *centrum* of his will, with his desire, out of the eternal *centrum* into them. This is *incantation* and false *magia*. Into this evil, into which man brings the desire of his soul, which is also out of the Eternal, like a false will, the devil's will may also come.

13. The cause of souls and angels is one out of the Eternal, but, in the time of this world (and its being),[29] the devil has nothing (no more power)[30] but only in the *turba magna*, in which he ignites the eternal anger in himself. There he is busied as in war and strife and in great thunderstorms without water. In fire he can go only as far as the *turba* goes, but no further. He also lives in the lightning bolt, as in the *turba*, but he cannot guide it for he is not lord in it, but servant.

14. Thus the creature awakens with the desire of evil and good, life and death. The human and angelic desire

stands in the *centrum* of the eternal, uncreated nature without beginning, in which it is ignited in evil or good, and whose work it performs.

15. Now God created every thing in that wherein it was to be: angels in heaven and men in Paradise. Now, if the desire of the creature departs from its own mother, it enters into opposition and enmity, and it is tormented in them with opposition, and a false will rises up in a good [one]. From this the good will enters again into its nothing, as into the end of nature and creature, and leaves the creature to its own evil. This is to be seen in Lucifer and also in Adam. Had not God's love-will come again to him, and again gone from grace into humanity, there could not have been a good will in man.

16. Therefore all speculation and study concerning God's will without change of heart is nothing. When the mind is trapped in its own desires of the earthly life, it cannot grasp God's will. It walks only in self from one way to another and yet finds no rest. For self-desire always leads to restlessness.

17. When it completely sinks into God's mercy, desires to die to its self, and desires God's will as leader and understanding, so that it might know and believe itself as a nothing that wills nothing except what God wills, when the wrath's desire in the earthly flesh with the devil's *imagination* comes and attaches the soul's will, the resigned desire cries out to God: *Abba*, dear Father, redeem me from evil [Luke 11:4]. [It] works (even though it might happen that the earthly will in God's anger through the devil's temptations becomes too strong) only in itself, as also Saint Paul says: When I sin, it is not I who do it, but sin that dwells in my flesh (Romans 7:20). Again: I serve the law of God with my mind, but with the flesh the law of sin (Romans 7:23).

18. Saint Paul does not intend that the mind is to will with the flesh's will, but that sin is as strong in the flesh as the aroused wrath of God [is] in the self, that it is, often by force [or] by false approval of godless men or by means of a glimpse

of worldly pomp, led into a lust so that the resigned will is completely deafened and is soon ruled by force.

19. As soon as sin is worked in the flesh, wrath wishes to enjoy it and grasps for the resigned will. The resigned will cries out to God for redemption from evil so that God will forgive it its sins and guide it into the *centrum* into death so that it die.

20. Saint Paul says further: There is now no condemnation for those who are in Christ Jesus (Romans 8:1), those who are called according to God's intention, that is, who are in that intention of God into which God called man, are called back again into the same calling so that they stand again in that intention of God in which He created man in His likeness, in an image after Himself. As long as self-will remains in self, it is not in the intention and calling of God. It is not called, since it has gone from its own *locus*.

21. When the mind turns again to its calling, into resignation, the will is within the calling of God, in the *locus* in which God created it. Then he has the strength to become God's child, as it is written; He has given us the strength to become God's children [John 1:12]. The strength that He gave is His intention in which He created man in His image. This God brought again into humanity in Christ, giving strength to that strength to step on the head of sin in the flesh, the will and desire of the serpent; that is, the resigned will in Christ steps on the head of his desire and kills past sins again. This given strength becomes death to death, and a strength of life to life.

22. Therefore no one has an excuse that he cannot will. Yes, as long as he sticks[31] fast in self, in his own self-desire, and only serves the law of sin in the flesh, he cannot [will], for he is held and is sin's servant. However when the *centrum* of the mind is changed and is turned into God's obedience and will, then he can [will].

23. Now, the *centrum* of the mind is out of eternity, out of

God's great might; it can go where it will. What is from the Eternal has no law. But the will has a law to be obedient to God, and the will is born from the mind and is not to turn itself away from that in which God created it.

24. Thus God created the will of the mind in Paradise to be a playmate in the divine kingdom of joy, out of which it is not to have turned itself. But now, since it has turned itself out of there, God has again led His will into the flesh and in this newly[32] introduced will, gave us strength to bring our wills into it, to ignite a new light in it, and to become His children again.

25. God hardens no one, but the self-will, which clings in the flesh's sins, hardens the mind. It brings the vanity of this world into the mind so that the mind remains closed.

26. God, insofar as He is and is[33] called God, can will no evil; for in God there is only one single will and that is eternal love, a desire for similarity, as for power, beauty and virtue.

27. God desires nothing but what is like His desire. His desire accepts nothing except that which itself is.

28. God accepts no sinner in His power unless the sinner leave sin and enter into God with his desire. Those who come to Him He will not cast out [John 6:37]. He has given an open gate to the will in Christ, saying: Come to me all you who are burdened with[34] sin, and I will revive you. Take my yoke upon you [Matthew 11:28-29], that is, the cross of enmity in the flesh that was Christ's yoke who bore it for all man's sins. The resigned will must take this on itself within the evil, earthly, sinful flesh, and in patience, in the hope of redemption, bear it after Christ. With the resigned soul's will, in Christ's will and spirit, it is always to tread on the serpent's head and break and kill the earthly will in God's wrath, nor [is it] to be at ease or rest in a soft bed when sin has been committed and think, "I will repent once again for this."

29. No, no; in this comfortable bed the earthly will grows strong, fat and lascivious. But as soon as the breath of

God stirs itself in you, and points out your sin, then the soul is to sink itself into the suffering and death of Christ, firmly wrapping itself in it, and take Christ's sufferings as its possession, being (with Christ's death)[35] lord over the death of sin and breaking and killing it[36] in Christ's death.

30. Although unwilling, [sin] must [die]. Struggle against the pleasure-seeking, earthly flesh; do not give it what it wishes, let it fast and hunger until appetite ceases. Hold the flesh's will to be your enemy and do not do what the desire in the flesh wishes. Thus you will lead the death of the flesh into death. Do not attend to the scorn of the world. Think that they only scorn your enemy because he is become a fool to them. Hold him also yourself to be a fool whom Adam awakened in you and gave you as a false inheritance. Cast out the maid's son from the house, as a strange son whom God gave you in the beginning, in Adam, not in the house of life, for the maid's son is not to inherit with the freewoman's son (Galatians 4:30).

31. The earthly will is only the maid's son. The four elements were to have been servants to man but Adam led them to sonship. God therefore said to Abraham as He revealed the covenant of promise in him:[37] Cast away the maid's son, for he is not to inherit with the freewoman's [son, Genesis 21:10]. The freewoman's son is Christ, whom God, of His grace, brought to us in the flesh as a new mind, where the will, that is, the eternal will of the soul, might fetch, and drink the water of eternal life, concerning which Christ says: Whoever drinks of this water that He will give us, for him it will be a fountain-source springing into eternal life (John 4:14). This source is a renewal of the soul's mind, the eternal star of eternal nature, the characteristic of the soul-creature.

32. Therefore I say, any pretence to God, whatever name it may be given, by which man might pretend to approach God, is[38] a fruitless, useless thing outside of a regenerated mind.

33. There is no other way to God than a new mind that turns from evil and enters into regret for its past sins, departs from iniquity, wills it no more, but wraps its will in Christ's death, and kills off the sins of the soul with earnestness in Christ's death, so that the soul's mind no longer will sin. Even though all the devils tormented it and brought their desires into its flesh, the soul's will must stand silent in the death of Christ, shelter itself [therein], and will nothing other than the mercy of God.

34. No hypocrisy and external comfort helps in any way, where man, while still remaining firm in self, wishes to cover with Christ's payment the rogue of sin in the flesh and remain in the self. Christ said: Unless you are converted, and become as children, you will not enter the kingdom of heaven (Matthew 18:3). So much must there be a new mind, like [that] in the child who knows nothing of sin. Christ further says: You must be born anew or you cannot see the kingdom of heaven (John 3:3). An entirely new will must arise out of Christ's death. Yes, it must be born out of Christ's entrance into humanity and arise in Christ's resurrection.

35. If this is to occur the soul's will must first die in Christ's death, for in Adam it took up the maid's son, sin. This one [sin] he must first cast out from the will, and the poor captive soul must in earnest wrap itself, with all that it is, in Christ's death, so that the maid's son, sin in it, dies in Christ's death. Yes, sin must die in the soul's will or else there can be no vision of God. The earthly will, in sin and in[39] God's wrath, shall not see God but Christ who came in the flesh [shall see God]. The soul must put on Christ's spirit and flesh. In this earthly tent it may not inherit God's kingdom; even though sin's kingdom hangs on eternally to it [the flesh], it must rot in the earth and [then] is to rise in new power.

36. There is no hypocritical forgiveness or one of mere words. We must not be externally accepted children, but

children internally reborn out of God, in a new man, given over to God.

37. All hypocrisy by which we say, "Christ has paid and made satisfaction for sin; He has died for our sins," is all false deception[40] (an empty useless comfort) if we also do not die to our sins in Him and draw on His merit in new obedience and live in it.

38. He who is antagonistic to and an enemy of sin has Christ's suffering for comfort. He who neither eagerly sees nor hears nor tastes [it], who is its enemy, who continually wishes the right and to do it if he only knew what he is to do, such a person has put on Christ's spirit and will. But the external hypocrisy, the externally accepted sonship, is false and useless.

39. Work done in the external flesh alone does not make sonship, but the work of Christ in the spirit, which is powerful with its external work and shows itself as a new light and reveals the sonship in the external work of the flesh, is and makes sonship.

40. For if[41] the eye is the light of the soul [Luke 11:34], the whole body is the light in all its members. Anyone who boasts of sonship, and permits the body to burn in sin, or lies captive in heavy darkness, yes, in the fetters of the devil, is not capable of sonship. If he does not find the earnest will for good deeds in love burning in him, all his attempt [at sonship] is only[42] a rational pretense from his self that may not see God unless he is born anew and shows himself in the power of sonship. There is no fire without light. If the divine fire is now in the mind it will certainly shine forth and do that which God will have [it do].

41. But you say, "I have a will for it. I would eagerly do it. But I am held back. I cannot."

42. Yes, dear dirtied stick, that is true. God draws you to sonship, but you do not wish [it]. Your soft pillow in evil is

much dearer to you. You place the joy of earthly evil before God's joy. You still stick fast completely in self, and live according[43] to the law of sin that holds you. You do not wish to die to the pleasures of the flesh and therefore you are not in the sonship. God draws you to it but you yourself do not wish it. Oh, how good it would have seemed to Adam if, with this will, he could have been taken into heaven, and set the evil child, full of falsehood, on God's throne. Lucifer wishes to have it so, but he was thrown out.

43. The dying of the evil will is painful; no one wishes it. All of us would eagerly like to be children, if one would take us in with this covering, but it cannot be so in any way. This world passes away; so too the external life must die. What [good], then, is sonship to me in a mortal body?

44. Whoever wants to inherit sonship must also put on a new man who can inherit sonship and is like to the Godhead. God wishes to have no sinner in heaven, but[44] only simple newborn children who have put on heaven.

45. Therefore it is not so easy a thing to become or[45] be a child of God, as one tells us. It is very easy to him who has put on the sonship, whose light shines, and who has his joy in it. However, to convert the mind and to break self[46] there must be strict, irremissible earnestness and such a resolution that, although body and soul were to spring apart, yet the will would remain firm and never again enter into self.

46. This must be striven for until the dark, hard, locked *centrum* springs apart and the spark in the *centrum* ignites so that immediately the noble lily-branch (as out of the divine grain of mustard seed [Luke 13:19], as Christ says begins to sprout forth. There must be earnest prayer with great humility, and for a time one must be a fool to one's own reason, and [one must] consider one's self foolish until Christ becomes a form in this new incarnation.

47. Then, when Christ is born, Herod comes immediately and wishes to kill the child [Matthew 2:16], and tests it outwardly by persecution and inwardly by temptation

[to see] if this lily-branch will be strong enough to break the devil's kingdom that is revealed in the flesh.

48. This Serpent-destroyer is led into the wilderness after he has first been[47] baptized by the Holy Spirit. He is tempted [to see] whether he will remain in resignation in God's will. He must stand fast, so that if it would so happen, he might forsake all the earthly,[48] yes, even the external life, for the sake of sonship.

49. No temporal honour or goods must be preferred to sonship, but he must with his will abandon all this and not look on it as his own, and [he must] see himself only a steward of the same, who serves his Lord in obedience. He must leave all the possessions of this world, not that he may not own anything or possess it, but his heart must leave it and not bring his will into it nor look on it as his own. Otherwise he has therein no might to serve the needy with it.

50. Self serves only[49] temporal being, but resignation rules over all that is under it. Self must do whatever the devil in flesh's pleasure and pride of life would have, but resignation steps on these with the feet of the mind. Self despises what is absurd, but resignation lies down in the dust with the lowly, and says, "I want to be simple, and understand nothing, so that my reason will not lift itself up and sin. I want to lie down in the forecourts of my God at His feet, so that I may serve my Lord howsoever He wishes me to. I do not want to know anything so that the commandments of my Lord lead me and guide me, and I do only that which God does and wishes through me. I want to sleep in my self until the Lord awakens me with His spirit. And if He does not want [to awaken me], I will rest eternally in stillness in Him and await His command."

51. Dear brothers, man now prides himself in his faith, but[50] where is faith? Faith at present is a history. Where is the child who believes that Jesus was born? If there was one and he believed that Jesus was born, then he would draw near the child JESUS,[51] receive and nourish Him. Ah, [these things]

are now only historical faith and pure scientific knowledge, and more than that, a tickling of conscience: that the Jews killed Him; that He has left this world; that He is not Lord of the earth in the animal man; that man may do as he will; that he need not die to sin and evil lust. Self, the evil child, rejoices that it may live in fatness and make the devil fat.

52. This indicates that proper faith was never sicker and weaker since Christ's day, than now. Yet the world shouts loudly, "We have found true[52] faith," and fighting over [this] child has never been more evil since man has been on earth.

53. If you are Zion, a reborn and newly found child— show your power and virtue and set forth the child JESUS out of you[53] so that man might see that you are His wet-nurse. If not, then Christ's children[54] will say that you have found only the child of history, only the cradle of the child.

54. Where do you have the child JESUS, you rebel with the historical and false appearance of faith? How will that child JESUS one day visit you in the Father's characteristic, in your own *turba*, which you have fattened. He [the Child] calls you in love, but you will not hear for your ears are closed up by covetousness and pleasure. Therefore, the sound of trombones with a tremendous peal of thunder will one day break upon your[55] *turba* and wake you [to see] if you once more will seek for and find the child JESUS.

55. Beloved brethren. It is a time of seeking, finding, and of earnestness. He whom it strikes, it strikes. He who watches shall hear it and see it, but he who sleeps in sin and in his fat days of the belly says, "All is peace and quiet; we hear no sound from the Lord." But the Lord's voice has sounded in all the ends of the earth and a smoke rises up, and in the midst of the smoke there is a great brightness of light. Amen. Halleluja. Amen.

Rejoice to the Lord in Zion, for all mountains and hills are full of His majesty. He shoots up like a green branch; who shall hinder it. Halleluja.[56]

THE FIFTH TREATISE
ON THE NEW BIRTH
THAT IS

How a man, who is in earnest regarding holiness, must allow himself to be led out of the twisted and antagonistic Babylon through Christ's Spirit so that he might be born anew in Christ's Spirit and live alone in Him.

(1622)

Preface of the Author

1. Although in my other very deep writings I have explained this [matter] fully enough, and described it in its ground, everyone does not have them at hand, nor is everyone's notion [of the topic] to be understood. I have therefore written a short summary on this new birth to be of use for the simple children of Christ and at the request of good friends, if anyone may wish to learn to know himself.

2. Whoever desires to search the deep ground out of which this flows, and has the gifts to understand, let him read the book on *The Three Kinds of Lives of Man*; also the three books *On the Incarnation and Birth of Jesus Christ*; again *The Book of the Six Points*; *On the Mysterium Magnum*; *On the Three Worlds*, and how they stand in one another as one but make three *principia*. That is, three births or beginnings, etc.; also the book *de Tribus Principiis*. There he will find all that he can ask, as high as the mind of man is able to move, [as] also in the *Forty Questions on the Soul*.

3. I have written this for the hearts hungering and thirsting after God's fountain, my fellow-members in the spirit of Christ. To the scorners, however, I have not written, for they have their own book in themselves by which they drive

Christ's children under the cross, and Christ's children must be their servants against their will, even though they do not understand.

Chapter One

1. Christ says, Except you be converted, and become as little children, you shall not see the kingdom of God (Matthew 18:3). And He again said to Nicodemus: Except one be born again out of water and the spirit, he cannot enter into the kingdom of God for what is born of the flesh is flesh; and what is born of the spirit is spirit (John 3:5-6). The Scriptures clearly testify that fleshly, natural man gains nothing from the Spirit of God. To him it is foolishness and he cannot grasp it.

2. However, although we all have flesh and blood [and] in addition are mortal, as is evident, at the same time the Scripture says that we are also a temple of the Holy Spirit that lives in us (I Corinthians 6:19), and that the kingdom of God is within us (Luke 17:21), yes that Christ must win a form in us (Galatians 4:19), and that He wishes to give us His flesh as food and His blood as drink, and further it says: He who does not eat the flesh of the son of man has no life in Him (John 6:53). Because of this we must consider earnestly what kind of man is in us who can be like to and capable of the Godhead.

3. This cannot be said concerning mortal flesh, which will become earth and lives in the vanity of the world, and which continually lusts against God, that it is the temple of the Holy Spirit, much less that the new birth occurs in this earthly flesh, since it dies and disappears and is, moreover, a continual house of sin.

4. However, since it remains true that a true Christian is born of Christ, and that the new birth is a temple of the Holy Spirit who dwells in us, and that only the new man born of Christ enjoys the flesh and blood of Christ, it is not a simple thing to be a Christian. Christianity [moreover] does not

[simply] stand in the history that we only know and which knowledge we take to ourselves so that we say "Christ died for us and has broken death in us and made it into life. He has paid the debt for us. We need only to comfort ourselves with this and firmly believe that it has happened."

5. Since we in ourselves find that sin in the flesh is living, desirous and active, that it might work, the new birth out of Christ must be something else that does not work along with the sinful flesh and that does not will sin.

6. Saint Paul says: There is no damnation to them who are in Christ Jesus (Romans 8:1). And further: Should we who are Christians be found sinners? Far be it [from us] (Galatians 2:17). (In Christ) we have died to sin. Moreover the man of sin is not a temple of the Holy Spirit, and yet there is no man who does not sin, for the Scripture says: God has locked them all under sin (Romans 11:32). Again, Before you no man living shall be justified. You shall judge sin (Psalms 143:2). The just man falls seven times a day (Proverbs 24:16), but still this is not to be understood that the righteous man himself falls and sins, but merely his mortal, sinful [aspect].

7. For the righteousness of a Christian is in Christ: He cannot sin. Saint Paul says: For our walk is in heaven, from whence we wait for our Saviour Jesus Christ (Philippians 3:20). If our walk is in heaven, heaven must be in us. Christ dwells in Heaven. If we are His temple, the same heaven must be in us.

8. If then sin in which the devil has access to and in us seeks us, hell must also be in us, because the devil dwells in hell. Where he always is, he is in hell and cannot leave it. And, if he takes a man, he lives in the man, in hell, as in God's wrath.

9. Now we are to consider man, what and how he is; that a true Christian is not only a historical new man; that it is not enough that we believe in Christ and confess that He is God's Son and paid for us. No externally imputed righteous-

ness that we only believe has happened [has any value]; only an inborn, a childlike [righteousness] counts. Just as the flesh must die, so also the life and the will of sin must die, and must become as a child that knows nothing and groans only for the mother who bore it. So too a Christian's will must enter completely into its mother, as into the Spirit of Christ and into self and become a child of self-willing and abilities. There will and desire are only ordered to the mother, and it must rise out of death with a new will and obedience in the Spirit of Christ in righteousness and no longer will sin.

10. For the will that allows vanity in itself and desires it is not reborn; and yet at the same time a will that sins and looks to vanity remains in the reborn [man]. Thus it is proper to consider the human image, how the new birth occurs, since it does not occur in mortal flesh, but truly takes place in blood, in water and spirit, as Scripture says [John 1:13; 3:5].

11. Thus we must properly consider what kind of person is in us who is a member of Christ, and a temple of God, and who dwells in heaven; and then also what kind of person it is who dwells only in the external world, and what kind of person it is whom the devil rules and forces. He [the devil] cannot rule and force the temple of Christ, nor is he concerned for mortal flesh. Yet there are not three persons in one man, but only a single [one].

12. If we wish to consider this now, we must consider time and eternity, how they are in one another, light and darkness, good and evil, but especially the human origin and cause.

13. This is thus to be considered: We see the external world of stars and four elements, in which man and all creatures live. This neither is nor is called God. God certainly dwells in it, but the external world does not grasp Him. We also see how light shines in darkness and darkness does not grasp the light (John 1:5), yet one dwells in the other. We also have an example of this in the four elements, which in their

origin are only one element that is neither hot nor cold, dry nor wet, and yet, by its movement, it divides itself into four characteristics, into fire, air, water and earth.

14. Who would believe that fire brings forth water, and that the origin of fire could be in water, if we did not see it with our eyes in lightning storms, and also discover in living things that the essential fire in the *corpus* dwells in the blood, and that the blood is its mother and that fire is the father of blood?

15. As God now dwells in the world and fills all and yet possesses nothing, so the fire dwells in water and does not possess it; and so the light dwells in the darkness and does not possess the darkness; the day in the night, and the night in the day; time in eternity and eternity in time. Thus also man is created. According to the external humanity he is the time, and in time, and time is the external world, which is also the external man; and the internal man is also eternity, spiritual time, and the world that also consists of light and darkness, as in God's wrath according to the eternal darkness. Whichever is revealed in him, in it his spirit dwells, either in darkness or in light. Both are in him, light and darkness; each dwells in itself, neither possesses the other.

16. When one enters into the other, and wishes to possess the other, the other loses its right and governance. The suffering loses its governance; for if the light is revealed in the darkness the darkness loses its darkness and is not known. So also, on the contrary, if the darkness rises in the light, and gains control, the light is extinguished with its control.

17. This is also to be noted in men. The eternal darkness in the soul is hell, a source of anguish, which is called God's wrath; and the eternal light in the soul is the kingdom of heaven, where the fiery, dark anguish has been changed into joy.

18. For just as the nature of the anguish is the cause of melancholy in the darkness, so also in the light it is a cause of

the exalted and moving joy. The suffering in the light and the suffering in the darkness are only one suffering, only one nature, even as the fire and the light are only one nature, yet they give a dominating difference in the suffering. One dwells in the other and begets the other, and yet is not the other; fire is painful and destructive, [yet] light is giving, friendly, powerful and joyous, a loving joy.

19. So also we are to consider man: He stands and lives in three worlds. The first is the eternal dark-world, the *centrum* of eternal nature, which begets the fire, the source of suffering; the second is the eternal light-world, which begets eternal joy and is the divine dwelling place in which the spirit of God dwells, in which the spirit of Christ takes on human being, and drives out the darkness so that it must be a cause of joy in the spirit of Christ to be in the light; the third world is the external visible [world], the four elements and visible stars. Each element has a star according to its own characteristic in itself out of which desire and characteristic rise, just as in a mind.

20. Understand it thus: The fire in the light is a love-fire, a desire for meekness and joy, and the fire in the darkness is a fire of anguish, and is painful, antagonistic, and contrary in its essence. The fire of light is a good taste, but the taste in the dark essence is completely contrary and antagonistic. In fire the forms all stand in great anguish.

Chapter Two

1. Here we are now to consider how man was created. Moses rightly says: God created man to His image; yes to the image of God created He him (Genesis 1:27). We understand this out of the eternal and the temporal birth, out of the internal spiritual world that He breathed into him in the created, [external] image, and then out of the internal, spiritual world's being that is holy.

2. For just as there is a nature and essence in the external world, so also there is a nature and essence in the internal, spiritual world that is spiritual, out of which the external world is breathed out and born out of light and darkness and is created into a beginning and time. Out of the internal and external world's being man was created in a likeness according to birth and made out of the birth of all being. The body is a *limbus (limus)* of earth and also a *limbus (limus)* of the heavenly being. Earth has been breathed out or spoken out of the dark-[world] and [out of] the light-world. Out of this, man was created in the *verbo fiat*, that is, in eternal desire, formed and created in an image out of time and eternity.

3. The image was within the internal, spiritual element out of which the four elements come out and are born. Paradise was in a single element, for the characteristics of nature, out of the fire-, dark- and light-worlds, were all in the same concordance, mass and weight [Wisdom of Solomon 11:21]. None was more particularly revealed than the other. Thus there was also no frailty in them; for no characteristic might overpower the other; there was no strife or opposition between the powers and characteristics.

4. Into this created image God breathed the spirit and breath of reason from all the worlds, as a single soul, which, in the inner dark- and fire-world, is in the eternal, spiritual nature, according to which God names Himself a strong, jealous God and a destructive fire.

5. This is now the eternal creaturely great soul, a magical fire's breath, in which the fire is the cause of life out of the great might of change. In this characteristic is God's wrath, as well as the eternal darkness, insofar as fire gives no light.

6. The other characteristic of the breath of God is the source-spirit of the light, out of the great fiery love's desire, out of great meekness, according to which God calls Himself a loving, merciful God. In this [characteristic] the true spirit of reason and life stands in power.

7. Just as a light shines out of each fire, and the power of reason is known in the light, so [God's] light-breath hangs onto God's fire-breath [and] is breathed into the human image.

8. The third characteristic of the breath of God was the external air with its air constellation in which was the external being and body's life and constellation. This He breathed into his nostrils. As time and eternity depend on each other, and time is born out of eternity, so also the internal breath of God depends on the external. This threefold soul was once breathed into man; each being of the *corpus* took the spirit according to its own characteristic. Thus the external flesh took external air with its constellation for its own rational and growing life, for the revelation of the wonders of God. The light's body, or the heavenly being, took the breath of light as the divine power, which breath is called the Holy Spirit.

9. Thus the light pierced through the darkness, the dark fire-breath, and also the external air-breath in its constellation, and took governance from all the characteristics so that neither the anguish of the fire-breath in the internal soul's characteristic nor heat and cold, nor all other characteristics of the external constellations might or could be revealed. The characteristics of all three worlds in soul and body stood in equal concordance and weight. The internal, holy, ruled through the external, as through the external powers of the external life, the external constellations, and the four elements.

10. This was the holy Paradise. Thus man stood in heaven and also in the external world, and was a lord over all creatures of this world. Nothing might have destroyed him.

11. So also was the earth until the curse of God. The holy characteristic of the spiritual world also sprang through the earth and bore the holy paradisaical fruit that man could eat in such a magical paradisaical way, and needed neither

teeth nor intestines in the body. For just as light is lost in darkness, and fire swallows water and still is not filled with it, so man has a *centrum* in his mouth, according to the manner of eternity. And in such a magical manner he could bear [one] like to himself without tearing and opening his body and spirit. Even as God bore the external world and did not tear Himself, but made the fashioned characteristics and qualities in His desires, as in the *verbo fiat* and revealed them out of the *verbo fiat*, and directed them into a figure according to the birth of the external spiritual world; so man also was created in such an image and likeness according to time and eternity, but in an eternal immortal life that was without antagonism and opposition.

12. However since the devil had been a prince and *hierarcha* in the place of this world, and because of his pride was cast into the dark, anguished, painful, hostile characteristic and suffering, into the anger of God, he did not wish for man the honour that he was created in his place in the spiritual world, and so he lead [his] *imagination* into the created image of man and made the lusting for the characteristics of the dark world, as for the external world, to rise up in man, and the similarity to leave the same concordance and to overpower the other. Then did the characteristics each reveal itself in itself, and each lusted after its likeness. Those out of the dark-world's birth as well as those out of the light-world's birth, each wished to eat out of the *limbus (limus)* of the earth, according to its hunger.

13. Thus evil and good were revealed in Adam. Because the hunger of the characteristics entered into the earth, out of which the characteristics of the body had been drawn, the *fiat* drew such a growth out of the earth out of which the characteristics in their awakened vanity could eat.

14. This was possible, since in Adam there was the spirit of the strong and great magical might from time and eternity

out of which the earth with its characteristics was exhaled. Thus the *fiat*, as the strong desire of eternal nature, drew the essence of earth.

15. Thus God let the tree of the knowledge of good and evil grow according to the awakened characteristics of Adam. The great might of soul and body had caused it. Therefore man had to be tested to determine whether he would stand in his own powers before the tempter, the devil, and before the anger of eternal nature, whether the soul would [remain] standing in the same concordance of characteristics, in true resignation under God's spirit, as an ordered instrument of the harmony of God, an instrument of God's kingdom of joy, on which God's Spirit would play. All this was here sought by that tree. To this end came God's stern commandment and said, You shall not eat of it, for on the day that you eat of it you shall die (Genesis 2:17).

16. However since God knew that man would not stand firm, that he already imagined and lusted for good and evil, God said: It is not good that man be alone; we will make him a helper who will be with him [Genesis 2:18]. He well saw that Adam could not beget magically, since his lust had gone into vanity.

17. This Moses now says: And He allowed a deep sleep to fall on him and he slept (Genesis 2:21), that is, since he did not wish to remain in obedience in the divine harmony, to stay still in those characteristics that he possessed as an instrument in the Spirit of God, He allowed him to fall from the divine harmony into his own harmony, into the awakened characteristics, into evil and good. There the soul's spirit went in.

18. In his sleep [he] died to the angelic world (quality) and fell into the external *fiat*, and it now occurred to the external image according to God's generation. Then his angel-form and might lay on the ground and fell in helpless-

ness. Then through the *fiat* God made from him woman, out of the *venus matrix*, that is, out of that characteristic which Adam had the begetter in himself; out of one body two, and he divided the characteristics of the *tinctures*, as into the element of watery and fiery constellations, not completely in being but in spirit, as the characteristics of the watery and fiery souls and yet it was only one. However the characteristic of the *tinctur* was divided. The self love-desire was taken from Adam and formed in the woman after his likeness. Therefore man now greatly desires the woman's *matrix*, and the woman desires the man's *limbus*, as the fiery element, the cause of the true soul in which the fire's *tinctur* is understood. These two were one in Adam and in this the magical birth consisted.

19. As Eve was made from Adam in his sleep, so were Adam and Eve ordained for the external, natural life. They were given the members for animal reproduction along with earthly intestines in which they could bag vanity and live as beasts. Because of these the poor soul, captured in vanity, shames itself today that it received such a bestial monstrous form in its body, as is obvious. From this has arisen human shame so that man is ashamed of his members and also of his naked form, and must borrow his clothing from earthly creatures, since he has lost his angelic [cloak] and has been changed into a beast. This cloak indicates well enough to him that he is not at home with this awakened vanity (with the soul in it) in that heat and cold come to him, for vanity with its false cloak must again leave the soul and die.

20. When Adam woke from sleep, he saw his wife and knew that she came out of him. He had not yet eaten of vanity with the mouth, only with the *imagination*, of desire and lust. It was Eve's first desire that she wished to eat of the tree of vanity, of evil and good, which the devil in serpent's form fully persuaded her: Your eyes shall be opened and you shall

be as good as God Himself (Genesis 3:5).

21. This was lie and truth. He did not say to her that she would thereby lose the divine light and power. He only said that her eyes would be opened, that she could taste, test and know evil and good, as he had done. Nor did he say to her that heat and cold would be awakened in her and that the characteristic of the external constellation would rule mightily in the flesh and mind.

22. It was only his intention that the angelic image, as the being of the inner spiritual world, might fade in them, so that they would [have to] live under gross earthiness and the stars. He knew well that when the external world died, the soul would be with him in darkness. He saw that the body would die, which he also had from God's suggestions. Thus he intended in his falsely assumed form to be a lord in the *locus* of this world for eternity. Therefore he led man astray.

23. Then, as Adam and Eve now ate into their bodies the fruit of good and evil, the *imagination* of the body received vanity in the fruit. Now was vanity in the flesh awakened and the dark world received governance and dominion in the vanity of earthiness. Immediately, the beautiful heavenly image, of the heavenly, divine world's being faded. Here Adam and Eve died to the kingdom of heaven and woke in the external world; the beautiful soul was corrupted to the love of God as to the holy power and characteristic and angry wrath awoke in its place in her, the dark fire-world, and she became in one part of her soul, in the inner nature, a half-devil and in the other part, the external world, a beast. This is the goal of death and the gates of hell, because of which God became man that He might break death, and change hell into the great love again, and destroy the vanity of the devil.

24. Let it be said to you, you human children. It is also told to you in the sound of [the last] trombones that you are now to leave shameful vanity, for this same fire burns [within you].

Chapter Three

1. Now when Adam and Eve fell into this misery, the anger of nature awoke in each characteristic and impressed in its desire the vanity of the flesh and the anger of God into itself. Then the flesh became gross and harsh, as any other animal, and the noble soul was caught in the essence by it. They looked at themselves, and saw that they were beasts in their bodies and saw their bestial organs for reproduction, and the stinking intestines in which the desires of the flesh enclosed the vanity (nausea). They were ashamed of this before God, and they crept under (behind) the trees in the Garden of Eden. Heat and cold also fell upon them.

2. Here the heaven in man trembled before the terror. Even as the earth trembled in anger when this wrath was broken on the cross by the sweet love of God, so wrath trembled before the great love of God.

3. Because of this awakened vanity in man, God cursed the earth so that the holy element no longer pressed through external fruit, and bore the fruit of Paradise. There was no creature that could then have enjoyed this nor was this of any more value to the earthly man. God did not wish to cast the noble pearl before beasts [Matthew 7:6]. Since an ungodly person is in his body nothing other than a gross, brutal beast, even if he is a noble essence, he is completely poisoned and a loathsomeness (vanity) before God.

4. When God saw that His beautiful image was corrupted, He revealed Himself before it and comforted it, and promised Himself to it as an eternal possession so that, with His great love in the humanity [which He had] taken on, He would, by His love, break the power of the serpent-characteristics, the vanity in the anger of God. That was the treading of the head [Genesis 3:15] so that he might break dark death and overpower wrath with His great love. [He] presented this covenant of His future incarnation in the life's

light. On this covenant the Jewish sacrifices were ordered as to a goal where God with His love had promised Himself. The Jewish faith went into sacrifice and God's *imagination* went into the covenant. The sacrifice was a figure of the restitution of that which Adam had lost.

5. God thus reconciled His wrath in the human characteristic, by the sacrifice, to the goal of the covenant. In this covenant the holiest Name JESUS, out of the holy Name and mighty power JEHOVAH, had embodied itself, so that He wished to stir and reveal Himself again in the heavenly world's being that died in Adam, and ignite it again in the holy, divine life.

6. The covenant's goal was continued from Adam and his children, from man to man, and went from one to all. Sin and also the awakened vanity went from one to all, and finally consisted of the promise of the covenant in the root of David in Mary the Virgin, who was in the internal kingdom of hidden humanity, the corrupted being in God's kingdom, the Daughter of the covenant of God, and in the external [kingdom] according to natural humanity, she was raised by her real bodily father, Joachim, and her real mother, Anna, out of their body and soul essences and being, like all other children of Adam, a true daughter of Eve.

7. In this Virgin Mary, in the promised goal of the covenant, of which all prophets had foretold, the eternally speaking Word, which has created all things according to its highest and deepest love and humility, moved in the Name of JESUS, and brought the living, divine heavenly being into the heavenly part of Adam's corrupted humanity to which he had died in Paradise, into Mary's seed. Understand [that this is] in the love *tinctur* as in the characteristic in which Adam should have reproduced himself in a magical, heavenly manner, as in the true woman's seed of the heavenly being that was corrupted in Paradise. When the divine light was put out in the same heavenly essence, God's Word as the divine

power of divine reason brought the heavenly, living being and awakened the corrupted being in Mary's seed and bore it to life.

8. God's being in which God dwells and works and the corrupted human being became now one person. The holy divine being anointed the corrupted. Therefore this person is called CHRIST, the anointed of God.

9. And this is the dry rod of Aaron that sprouted forth there and bore almonds; (and the correct high priest); and this is the humanity of which Christ said (John 3:13): He was come from heaven and was in heaven, and that no man could come to heaven except the Son of Man who is come from heaven, and who is in heaven. In that He says, He is come from heaven, He understands heavenly essence, heavenly corporeality, for the power of God does not need any coming. It is overall completely measureless and undivided. But essence needs coming. Power needs only to move itself and be revealed in being.

10. However the being entered into the human being and took on the human, and not only the part of the human being that was corrupted in Adam, but the whole human essence in soul and body, according to the three worlds.

11. The awakened and impressed vanity that the devil, with his *imagination*, brought into the flesh by which the flesh worked sin, he did not take on. He did take on the awakened life-forms, in that they came out from the same concordance, each in its own desire.

12. In this lay our sickness and death that He was to drown with his heavenly, holy blood. Here He took to Himself all our sins and sickness, even death and hell in the anger of God, and broke the devil's kingdom in the human characteristic. The anger of God was the hell in which Christ's spirit entered as He now poured heavenly blood into our external human (blood) and tinctured it with love, and changed that same hell in the human characteristic into heaven and led and

ordered the human characteristics again into the same concordance in the divine harmony.

Chapter Four

1. Here we now understand what our new birth properly is, how we can be and remain a temple of God and still, (this time) also according to the external humanity [be] sinful, mortal men. Christ broke and opened in the human essence the gates of our internal, heavenly humanity that were locked in Adam. Nothing now lies in this except that the soul lead its will out of the vanity of the (corrupted) flesh and direct it into these open gates in the spirit of Christ.

2. There must be great and mighty earnestness, not only a learning and knowing, but a hunger and thirst for Christ's spirit. Knowledge alone is no faith, but the hunger and thirst for that which the "I" desires, which I consider in myself, and take and grasp possessively with this consideration, that is faith.

3. The will must leave the vanity of the flesh and freely give itself to the suffering and death of Christ and to all the scorn of vanity (which scorns him because he has left his own house in which he was born), and will no more in vanity but desire only the love of God in Christ Jesus.

4. And in such hunger and desire [it] impresses on him the spirit of Christ, with His heavenly corporeality; that is, his great hunger and desire grasps the body of Christ, as the heavenly being, within its corrupt image in which the Word of the power of God is the working life within.

5. The soul's hunger leads its desire through the smashed characteristic of the heavenly part of its humanity corrupted in Adam. The sweet love-fire in the death of Christ smashed this when death in the proper heavenly humanity was broken. The soul's hunger through its desire grasped the holy heavenly Being, as the heavenly corporeality (Christ's

heavenly corporeality that fills the Father to all parts, and that is near to all, and is through all) within its corrupted corporeality. And by this the corrupted heavenly body is resurrected in the power of God in the sweet Name JESUS.

6. And this same awakened heavenly, spiritual body is Christ's member and a temple of the Holy Spirit, a true dwelling of the Holy Trinity, as Christ promised when He said: We will come to you and make our dwelling in you (II Corinthians 6:16). This same essence of this same life eats Christ's flesh and drinks His blood, for Christ's sake, as the Word, which in the humanity of Christ makes itself visible outside and within our corrupted humanity, by the external man of this world's being, eats its holy being in its fiery being. Each spirit eats from its [own] body.

7. Thus when the soul now eats of this sweet, holy, heavenly food, it then ignites itself in the great love in the Name JESUS. From this its anguish-fire becomes a great triumph, and the true sun rises for it, in which it is born to the will of another. Here is the wedding of the lamb, which we deeply wish that that which uses the name and calls itself Christianity might once experience so that it might go from history to being.

8. The soul does not gain the pearl of holy power in the time of its life, since it has yet the external, bestial flesh characteristic in the outer man as its possession. The power of Christ, which ties itself [to the soul] in the marriage of the lamb, sinks into heaven's image, as into the being of the heavenly man that is Christ's temple, and not into the fire-breath of the soul, which, during this whole time is bound fast with its lust-breath to the external kingdom, to the bonds of vanity, and is in great danger.

9. Indeed it very often gives its love beams into the soul, from which the soul receives its light. But the fire-breath does not give itself at this time to Christ's spirit but only to the breath of light that was extinguished in Adam. In this is the

temple of Christ, for it is the true, holy heaven.

10. Understand us correctly, [concerning] what and how the new birth is and occurs. The external, earthly, mortal man is not reborn in this time, neither [is] the external flesh nor the external part of the soul. They both stay in the vanity of their will awakened in Adam. They love their mother in whose body they live, which is in the dominion of this external world in which the sin's birth is revealed.

11. The external man in soul and flesh—understand [this as] the external part of the soul—has no divine will, [and thus] does not understand anything of God, as the Scripture says: The natural man takes nothing from the Spirit of God (I Corinthians 2:14).

12. But the fire-breath of the inner world, once it is enlightened, understands it. It has a great groaning, complaining, hungering and thirsting for the sweet fountain, Christ. As a hungry branch on the Christ-vine it refreshes itself through hunger and thirst in the sweet fountain, Christ, for His new body of heavenly being. This is the true faith.

13. This is the cause that the fiery soul at this time cannot come to perfection, because it stands bound fast to the external bonds of vanity by which the devil continually shoots his poisonous beams on it, and sifts it, so that it often bites and poisons itself. From this there rises up great sorrow and anguish, so that the noble Sophia hides Herself in Christ's fountain in the heavenly humanity and cannot come near to vanity.

14. She knows how it went with Her in Adam when She lost Her pearl, which, out of grace, was given again to the internal man. (Therefore she is called Sophia, as the bride of Christ.)

15. Then She faithfully calls to the fiery soul as to Her bridegroom, and admonishes it to repentance, and to an unburdening of and departure from the abomination of vanity.

Then strife begins in the whole man. The external, fleshly man seethes against the internal, spiritual, and the spiritual against the fleshly, and so man stands in strife, full of difficulty, care, anguish and need.

16. The internal [man] says to the fire-soul, "O my love, turn and leave vanity or you will lose my love and the noble pearl." The external reason, the bestial, (earthly) soul, says, "You are foolish in that you wish to be the world's fool and scorn. You need the external world for your life. Beauty, might and majesty are the best for you. In these you can have joy. Why do you wish to lead yourself in anguish, need and scorn? Follow after pleasure that will be good for the flesh and mind."

17. With such filth a proper man is often dirtied. The external man dirties himself, just as a pig in the filth, and darkens his noble image. The more vain the external man becomes, the darker the internal man [becomes] until he finally completely dies. Thus it occurred by the beautiful tree of Paradise, and it will be difficult to obtain it again.

18. When the external light, as the external soul, once is enlightened so that the external light of reason is ignited by the inner light, the external soul eagerly gives a hypocritical appearance and sees itself as divine, even though the pearl has gone.

19. Thus it is with many, and the pearl-tree in Christ's garden is often spoiled, of which Scripture makes a hard knot: that those who have once tasted the sweetness of the future world, and [have] again fallen away, will with difficulty see God's kingdom (Hebrews 6:4-6).

20. Although it is true that the gates of grace still stand open, yet the appearance of light of the external soul of reason keeps [men] away so that they think they have the pearl, but they live only in the vanity of the world and dance as the devil pipes.

Chapter Five

1. Here a Christian is to consider why he calls himself a Christian and is truly to consider whether he is one. Because I may learn to know and understand that I am a sinner, and that Christ has killed my sins on the cross and shed His blood for me, this in no way makes a Christian out of me. The inheritance is only for the children. A maid in the house knows well what the wife would eagerly have. This does not therefore make her an inheritor of the wife's goods. The devil also knows that there is a God [James 2:19]. That does not therefore make him an angel again. However, if the maid in the household marries the wife's son, then she can truly come to the inheritance of the wife's goods.

2. Thus also it is to be understood in our Christianity. The historical children are not the inheritors of the goods of Christ, but the legitimate children who have been born anew out of Christ's spirit [are]. God said to Abraham: Cast out the maid's son, for he is not to inherit with the son of the free-woman (Galatians 4:30). He was a scorner and only an historical son of the faith and spirit of Abraham, and as long as he was such he was not in the proper inheritance of the faith of Abraham. Therefore God had him cut off from his goods.

3. This was a figure of the future Christianity. The promise of Christianity occurred to Abraham. Therefore the figure was at the same time described in the two brothers, Isaac and Ishmael: how Christianity would keep itself and that two kinds of men would be in it, true Christians and mouth-Christians. The latter, under the title of Christianity, would be scorners like Ishmael and Esau who was the image of the external Adam, [while] Jacob [was] the image of Christ and of His true Christianity.

4. So, each one who wishes to call himself a Christian is to cast out of himself the maid's son, that is the earthly, evil

will, always killing and breaking [this evil will] and not taking control of the inheritance, nor giving the pearl as a plaything to the bestial man so that he does not continually drive himself into the external light in the flesh's lust. With our father Abraham, he is to lead the son of our proper will to Mount Moriah and offer it up to God in obedience [Genesis 22], always eagerly wishing to die to sin in Christ's death, allowing no rest in Christ's kingdom to the beast of vanity, nor permitting [himself] to become lewd, proud, covetous, envious or evil. These characteristics are all Ishmael's, the maid's son's, whom Adam [Abraham!] bore in his vanity by the wanton whore of the false maid, by the devil's *imagination*, out of the earthly characteristic of the flesh.

5. The scorner and the titular Christian is the whore's son, who must be cast out for he is not to inherit Christ's inheritance in the kingdom of God (Galatians 4:30). He is no use, and only Babel, a confusion of the one language into many languages. He is only a talker and arguer about the inheritance and wishes to talk and argue to it with his mouth-hypocrisy and appearance of holiness, but he is only a blood-thirsty murderer of Abel his brother who is the true heir.

6. Therefore we say what we know, that a man who wants to call himself a Christian is to test what kind of characteristics drive and rule him; whether the spirit of Christ drives him to truth and righteousness and to love of neighbour so that he would eagerly do good if he only knew how he could. Thus when he discovers that he has a hunger for such virtue, he can certainly think that he is drawn. Then he is to direct it into work, not only to will and not to do. The Father's love to Christ consists of willing, but true life consists of doing.

7. The proper spirit acts properly. However if [there is] a will to act and action does not follow, the proper true man is in a vain lust that holds action back and he is only a hypocrite,

157

an Ishmaelite. He speaks one thing and does another, and shows that his mouth is a liar. What he teaches he does not do himself, and only serves the bestial man in vanity.

8. If one says, "I have the will and wish eagerly to do good, but I have earthly flesh that holds me [back] so that I cannot [act]; nevertheless, I shall be blessed by grace because of the merit of Christ. Since I console myself indeed with His suffering and merit, He will take me out of grace, without any merit of mine, and forgive me my sins," he acts like one who knows of good food for his health and does not eat it, but who eats instead the poison from which he becomes ill and dies.

9. What does it help the soul if it knows the way to God and does not wish to take it, but goes instead on a way of error, and does not reach God? What does it help the soul if it consoles itself with the sonship of Christ, [with] His suffering and death, and is itself hypocritical, but cannot enter into the childlike birth so that it is born a true child out of Christ's Spirit, out of His suffering, death and resurrection? Certainly and truly, this tickling and hypocrisy about Christ's merits aside from the true inherited sonship is false and a lie, [regardless of] who teaches.

10. This consolation belongs to the repentant sinner who is in strife with sin and God's wrath when the temptations come that the devil sets on the soul. Then the soul is to wrap itself completely in the suffering and death of Christ in His merit.

11. Christ alone has truly merited salvation for us, but He has not merited it as a merit that is given as a payment out of His merits so that He gives us the sonship out of His merit externally and thus takes us into the sonship. No; He is Himself the merit. He is the open gate through death, through which we must go. He does not take beasts into His merit, but those who turn and become as children.

12. The same children that come to Him are His payment; He has merited us. He also said thus: Father, the men

were Yours and You gave them to me, and I gave them eternal life (John 17:6). But now the life of Christ will be given to no one except him [who] comes to Him in the Spirit of Christ, in His humanity, suffering and merit, and is born in His merits, a true child of merit. Out of His merits we must be born and put on Christ's merit in His suffering and death, not externally with hypocrisy, not only with consolation and remain a foreign child in a foreign essence. No, the foreign essence does not inherit the sonship, but the inborn essence inherits it.

13. The same inborn essence is not of this world, but [is] in heaven. Of it Saint Paul says: Our walk is in heaven (Philippians 3:20). The childlike essence walks in heaven, and heaven is in man. If heaven is not open in man and he only stands before heaven hypocritically and says, "I am truly outside, but Christ will take me in my grace; His merits are indeed mine," such a man is according to the internal man in vanity and sin and with the soul in hell, as in God's wrath.

14. Therefore learn to understand properly what Christ has taught us and has done. He is our heaven. He must win a form in us if we are to be in heaven. Thus the inner soul-man is then with the holy love of Christ, as in the new birth, in heaven and the external, mortal [man] is in the world. Of this Christ says: My sheep are in my hands. No one can tear them away from me. The Father who gave them to me is greater than all (John 10:27-29).

Chapter Six

1. Dear brothers: We wish to speak with you faithfully, not out of a hypocritical mouth to please the Anti-christ, but out of our pearl, out of Christian essence and knowledge, not from husks and histories, but out of a childlike spirit, out of Christ's knowledge, as a branch of the vine of Christ, out of the measure of the opened knowledge in us in God's counsel.

2. Now man binds us to histories, to the stone churches, which in their value would be indeed good if man also brought Christ's temple into them.

3. Man teaches [that] his absolution is a forgiveness of sins; again, that the Lord's Supper takes sins away; again, that the Spirit of God is poured in by the office of preaching.

4. All this would have its way (value) if it were properly explained and if man did not hang onto the husks. Many a man goes to church for twenty or thirty years, hears sermons, uses the sacraments, allows himself to be absolved and is still [just as bad a] beast of the devil (and of vanity) as the rest. A beast goes into the church and to the Lord's Supper, and a beast goes from there again. How does he who has no mouth wish to eat? How does he who has no hearing wish to hear? Can one enjoy food whose mouth is locked shut? How does he expect to drink who is far from the water? What does it help me that I go into the wall-church and fill my ears with an empty breath, or, go to the Lord's Supper and feed only the earthly mouth that is mortal and corrupting? Can I not give it as well a piece of bread at home so that it is satisfied? What does it help the soul, which is an immortal life, that the bestial man keeps the patterns of Christ's service, but that it cannot reach the treasure of the service? Saint Paul says concerning the Lord's Supper: You receive it to your condemnation because you do not distinguish the Lord's body (I Corinthians 11:29).

5. The covenant stands; it is moved in its practice. Christ offers us His Spirit in His word as in the preached word, His body and blood in the sacraments, and His absolution in brotherly reconciliation.

6. What does it help if a beast belongs there and has no hearing of the internal, living word, or has no container in which it can lay the word so that it can bring forth fruit? Of these Christ says: The devil tears the word from their hearts, so that they do not believe and become holy (Luke 8:12). Why? Because the word finds no place in the hearing where it can be held.

7. So also regarding absolution: What does it help that one says to me, "I announce to You the forgiveness of your sins," but the soul lies completely locked in sin? He who says this to a locked-up soul is in error, and he who receives this without God's voice in him also deceives himself.

8. No one can forgive sins but God alone. The preacher's mouth does not have forgiveness in its own power: The Spirit of Christ in the voice of the priest does have it if he is also a Christian. However, what help is it to those who heard Christ teach on earth when He said: Come to me all you who are weary and heavy laden and I will revive you [Matthew 11:28]? What did it help those who heard it and were not weary? Where was the revival? Since they had dead ears and heard only the external Christ but not the word of divine power they were not revived. So much does his hypocritical absolution help the bestial man; so much do the sacraments help him.

9. This is now just as clear in the sacraments as [it is] in the office of preaching. The covenent is announced. The nourishment of the soul occurs, but in the characteristic in which the soul's mouth is, as the external beast receives bread and wine; it could eat this at home also. The fiery soul receives the testament according to its characteristic as in the wrath of God; it receives the eternal world's being but according to the dark-world's characteristic. As the mouth is, so also is the food belonging to the mouth. It receives it for itself as judgement, in the [same] manner in which the godless will see Christ in the last judgement as an earnest, strict judge, and the saints, as a loving *ImmanuEL*.

10. Against the godless God's wrath stands clear in His testaments but toward the saints the heavenly corporeality and the power of Christ stand clear in the holy Name JESUS. What does the holy help the godless who cannot enjoy it? What is there here to take away his sin? Sin is only announced and revealed.

11. For the saints, there is no removal of sin in the sac-

raments, nor through them forgiveness. But it goes thus: When Christ rises, Adam dies in the serpent's essence. When the sun rises, the night is swallowed up in day, and there is no more night. The forgiveness of sins is thus: The Spirit of Christ eats of His holy being; the inner man is the grasper of holy being. He takes what the Spirit of Christ brings into him, Christ's flesh and blood as God's temple. What happens to the beast? Or what happens to the devil, or the soul in God's wrath? They eat of the heavenly love in that heaven in which they dwell, in the abyss.

12. So [it is] also with the office of preaching: The godless [man] hears what the external soul preaches to the external world. He takes it as a history. If there is stubble or straw in the sermon, then he sucks vanity out of it, and the soul sucks false poison and murder of the devil out of it. With this it tickles itself, [in] that it hears how it can direct mankind. If the preacher is also dead, and sows poison and insults out of his affects, the devil teaches and the devil hears. This same teaching is taken by the godless hearts and brings forth wicked fruit out of which the world has become a murder-den of devils so that both in the teacher and hearer there is nothing but vain scorn, slanders, haughtiness, word arguments and antagonism about what is in the husks.

13. But in the holy teacher, the Holy Spirit teaches and in the holy hearer Christ's Spirit hears through the soul and the divine home of the divine sound. The saint has his church in himself where he hears and teaches internally. Babel has the stone-heap into which it goes with hypocrisy and flattery, permitting itself be seen with beautiful clothes, pretending to be devout and pious. The stone church is its god in which it puts its trust.

14. The saint however has his church with him and in him at all places. He goes and stands, he lies down and he sits, in his church. He is in the true Christian church in the temple of Christ. The Holy Spirit preaches to him out of each creature; in everything that he sees, he sees God's preacher.

15. Here the scorner will say that I despise the stone church where the congregation comes together. To this I say, "No," but I only point to the hypocritical whore of Babylon who pursues her whoring with the stone church, and calls herself Christian when she is a whore-brat.

16. A proper Christian brings his holy church along into the congregation. His heart is the true church where man practices the worship of God. If I should go to church for a thousand years and to the sacrament every week, [and] also permit myself to be absolved every day, and did not have Christ in me, it would all be false and useless talk, a carving in Babel, and there is no forgiveness of sins.

17. The saint does holy works out of the holy power of his mind. The work is not the reconciliation [with God] but it is the building that the true Spirit builds in His being. It is his dwelling just as fable is the dwelling of the false Christian where his soul goes in hypocrisy. The external hearing goes into the external and works in the external, and the internal hearing goes into the internal and works in the internal.

18. Pretend, cry, shout, sing, preach, teach as you will. If the internal teacher and hearer is not open, all is Babel and fable, a carving where the external world-spirit makes a model or carving according to the internal. With this it pretends as if it had a holy worship service, but often the devil is mightily active in the middle of such worship, and by his *imagination* tickles the heart with those things that the flesh would eagerly have. This often occurs to the children of God according to the external man who do not take care about themselves. So does the devil sift them.

Chapter Seven

1. A proper man who is born again in Christ's Spirit, who is in the simplicity of Christ, no longer has any argument over religion with anyone. He has in himself enough strife with the bestial, evil flesh and blood. He always thinks that he

is a great sinner and is frightened before God since his sins stand revealed and are the judgement, for the *turba* encloses them in him. By this the wrath of God charges him as guilty in his own sight, but Christ's love presses through and drives it out as day swallows night.

2. The sins of the godless however rest in the sleep of death, sprout up in the abyss, and bring forth fruit in hell.

3. The Christianity in Babel argues over knowledge, how man is to serve, honour and know God, what He is in being and will, teaching simply [that] he who is not one and the same piece with them in knowledge and thought is no Christian but a heretic.

4. Now I eagerly wish to see how one is to bring all these sects together into one, which would call itself the Christian Church, because all of them now are despisers and each group denounces the other and decries it as false.

5. A Christian however has no sect. He can dwell among the sects, even appear in their services, and yet hang on to none. He has only a single knowledge and that is Christ in him. He seeks only one way, which is the desire always eagerly to act and live correctly. He puts all his knowing and willing into the life of Christ. He sighs and always wishes that God's will might happen in him, and that His kingdom might be revealed in him. He kills the sins in the flesh daily and hourly, for the woman's seed as the internal man in Christ continually tramples the head of the devil's vanity (Genesis 3:15).

6. His faith is a desire for God that he has wrapped in certain hope; in this he dares to test the words of promise. He lives and dies in it and yet he never dies according to his proper man. Christ thus says: Whosoever believes in me shall never die [John 11:26], but has pressed from death to life. Again: There will be streams of living water flowing from him, [John 7:38] as good doctrine and works.

7. Therefore I say that all is Babel that bites and argues with the other over the letter. The letters all stand in one root, which is the Spirit of God, even as various flowers all stand and grow on the earth beside one another. None bites at the other because of colour, smell and taste. They allow the earth and sun, the rain and wind and also heat and cold to do with them as they will. Each grows according to its own essence and characteristic. So it is also with the children of God. They have many gifts and much knowledge, but all of one Spirit. They rejoice with one another in the great wonders of God and thank the Highest in His wisdom. Why should they argue long about Him in whom they live and are, and of whose being they themselves are?

8. It is the greatest folly in Babel that the devil has made the world argue about religion so that they argue about self-made ideas, about the letter. The kingdom of God does not consist of any idea but of power and love. This Christ said to His disciples, and left it with them at last, that they were to love one another as He loved them, so that each man might know that they were His disciples [John 15:17; 13:35]. If men so endeavoured for love and righteousness as they do for ideas, there would be no strife at all on earth. We would live as children in our Father, and would need no law nor order.

9. God is served by no law, but by obedience alone. Laws are for the wicked who do not wish love and righteousness. They are driven and compelled with law. We all have one single order, which is that we hold all our being silent before God and give our wills to Him and allow His Spirit to work in us, playing and making what He wills. What He works and reveals in us we give to Him again as His fruits.

10. If now we do not argue over the many fruits, gifts and knowledge, but confess to one another as children of the Spirit of God, what would judge us? God's kingdom does not lie in our knowing and supposing, but in the power.

11. If we did not know half as much, and were more childlike, but had only one brotherly will among one another, and lived as children of one mother, as twigs on one tree that all take sap from one root, we would be much holier.

12. Knowing is only for the purpose (that we learn) since we have lost the divine power in Adam, and are now inclined to evil, so that we learn to know that we have evil characteristics in us and that evil acts do not please God, so that we, by that knowing, may learn to act properly. If we have the power of God in us however, and desire with all our powers to act and to live correctly, knowing is only our game, in which we enjoy ourselves.

13. True knowing is the revelation of the Spirit of God through the eternal wisdom. He knows what He wishes in His children. He pours out His wisdom and wonders through His children as the earth [does] many flowers. If we now dwell beside one another in Christ's Spirit as humble children and each one enjoy the other's gifts and knowledge, then who will judge us? Who judges the birds in the forest who praise the Lord of all being with many voices, each one out of its essence? Does God's Spirit punish them for not bringing their voices into a harmony? Does not all their sound come from His power, and do they not play before Him?

14. Therefore those people who argue about knowledge and about God's will, and therefore despise one another, are more foolish than the birds in the forest and the wild beasts who have no proper reason. They are of less use before the Holy God than the meadow-flowers that are silent before the Spirit of God and let Him reveal divine wisdom and power through them. Yes, they are worse than the thistles and thorns among the beautiful flowers that are silent. They are as the ravenous beasts and birds in the forest that frighten other birds out of their singing and praise of God.

15. In sum, they are the devil's growths in the wrath of God, who by their pain must serve the Lord. With their

misery and persecution they drive out the sap through the essence of the children of God so that they move them by the Spirit of God with prayer and earnest cries, in which the Spirit of God moves itself in them. By this, desire is practiced, and also the children of God practice [it], so that they sprout and bear fruit. God's children are revealed in trouble, according to Scripture: When You chasten them, they cry in anguish to You [Isaiah 26:16].

Chapter Eight

1. The whole Christian religion consists in this: [firstly] that we learn to know ourselves, what we are, whence we have come, how we have gone from unity into disunity, evil and unrighteousness that we have awakened in ourselves; secondly, where we were in unity when we were the children of God; thirdly, how we now are in disunity, in strife and antagonism; fourthly, where we are to go out of this fragile life (being); where we wish to go both with the immortal and with the mortal.

2. In these four points consists our whole religion: to come out of disunity and vanity, and to go again into the one tree from which all of us, in Adam, came, which is Christ in us. We dare not strive about anything, nor have any strife. Let each one practice how he may enter again into the love of God and of his brethren.

3. Christ's testaments are throughout nothing other than a brotherly bond by which God in Christ binds Himself with us and we with Him. All teaching should teach this [as should] all willing, living and doing. What teaches or does otherwise is Babel and fable, only the carving of pride, a useless judgement, a false object of the world, and the hypocrisy of the devil by which he blinds the simple.

4. All that teaches outside of God's Spirit and has no divine understanding, and still sets itself up in the kingdom of

God as a teacher and wishes to serve God by teaching, is false, and serves only the idol-belly and his proud and haughty thought in that he wishes to be honoured and called holy. He carries an office chosen by human children who have ordered him hypocritically for favour. Christ said: Whoever enters not by the door of the sheepfold, that is, through Him, but climbs in some other way, is a thief and murderer, and the sheep do not follow him, for they know not his voice (John 10:1-5).

5. He does not have the voice of the Spirit of God, but only the voice of his art, of his learning. He teaches and not God's Spirit. But Christ says: Every plant that my heavenly Father has not planted is to be rooted up (Matthew 15:73). How will [he] who is godless plant heavenly plants when he has no seed in the power in him? Christ said clearly: The sheep do not hear his (the false shepherd's) voice, they do not follow him (John 10:5).

6. The written word is merely an instrument by which the Spirit leads. The word that is to teach must be living in the literal word. The Spirit of God must be in the sound of the letters, otherwise no one is a teacher of God, but only a teacher of the letter, a knower of history, and not of the Spirit of God in Christ. Everything with which man wishes to serve God must occur in faith, in the Spirit that makes the work complete and acceptable to God. What a man begins and does in faith he does in the Spirit of God, which works along in that work. This is pleasing to God, for He has made it Himself, and His power is in it. It is holy.

7. What is made in the self without faith is only a figure or husk of correct Christian work.

8. If you serve your brother and do it only out of hypocrisy, and if you give grudgingly to him, you do not serve God, for your faith does not arise from love in hope, in your gift. You do indeed serve your brother, and he thanks God and blesses you on his part. However, you do not bless him since you give in your gift to him a grudging spirit that does not

come from God's Spirit in the hope of faith. Therefore your gift is only half-given and you have only half the reward for it.

9. So it is also to be understood with the receiving. If one gives in faith in divine hope he blesses his gift in his faith. He who receives it however without thanks and grudges in the spirit, curses it in the enjoyment. Thus for each one his own [self] remain [in it]: what he sows, that he also reaps.

10. So also in the teaching office: What one sows, he also reaps. If one sows the good seed of Christ's Spirit, it takes root in the good heart and bears good fruit. In the ungodly, however, who are not capable of it, the wrath of God is declared. If one sows argument, despising, evil intentions, all ungodly men receive it and it also takes root and bears such fruit that one mocks, slanders, reproaches and misleads the other.

11. Out of this the great Babel is born and awakened when man out of pride argues over the history of the justification of the poor sinner before God, and makes the simple err and seethe so that one brother despises the other because of the histories and changes of letters and gives him over to the devil.

12. Such slanderous brats do not serve God, but the great building of disunity. Since a corrupted search still lies in all men, in the earthly flesh, they awaken abominations in the simple children of God and make God's people, with the children of evil, to slander and are only the architects of the great Babel and the world and [are] as useful as the fifth wheel of a wagon, except that they raise up the building of hell.

13. Therefore it is very necessary that the children of God earnestly pray and learn to know this false building and leave it with their spirit, and not to help build it, and themselves persecute the children of God and thereby keep themselves out of God's kingdom and be misled. As Christ said to Pharisees: Woe unto you, Pharisees, for you go over sea and land to make one a Jewish believer, and when he is made, you make of him two times [more] the child of hell than yourselves

(Matthew 23:15). This occurs the same in the present mobs and sects, and in the criers and teachers of argument.

14. Therefore all the children of God who think they are members of Christ must leave such abominable arguing and blood-duels, brother-quarrelling—of which I have surely warned them out of those gifts that God has truly revealed in me—and look only simply to love and righteousness toward all men.

15. If one is a good tree he is also to bear good fruit. Even if he must then suffer pigs to eat his fruit, he is to remain a good tree and wish to work continually with God, and not allow any evil to overcome him. Thus he stands in God's field and bears fruit for God's table, which he shall enjoy forever. Amen.

END

THE SIXTH TREATISE
ON THE SUPERSENSUAL LIFE
[THAT] IS
A CONVERSATION OF A TEACHER
AND STUDENT
(1622)

How the Soul may come to divine contemplation and hearing; and what its childhood in the natural and supernatural life is; and how it goes out of nature into God and again out of God into the nature of self; also what its holiness and damnation is.

1. The student said to the master: "How may I come to the supersensual life so that I can see God and hear Him speak?" The master said: "If you can sweep up for a moment into that in which no creature dwells, you can hear what God speaks."

2. The student said: "Is that near or far?" The master said: "It is in you. If you could be silent from all willing and thinking for one hour you would hear God's inexpressible words."

3. The student said: "How can I hear when I remain silent in thinking and willing?" The master said: "When you remain silent from the thinking and willing of self, the eternal hearing, seeing and speaking will be revealed in you, and God will see and hear through you. Your own hearing, willing and seeing hinders you so that you do not see and hear God."

4. The student said: "With what shall I see and hear God, since He is above nature and creature?" The master said: "When you move silently then you are that which God was before nature and creature, [that] out of which He created your nature and creature. Then you will hear and see with that with which God saw and heard in you before your own willing, seeing and hearing began."

5. The student said: "What holds me back from coming to this?" The master said: "Your own willing, hearing and seeing, and that you strive against that out of which you came. With your own will you break yourself off from God's will, and with your own seeing you see only in your will. Your will stops your hearing with the self-interest of earthly, material things and leads you into a ground and overshadows you with that which you will so that you are not able to come to the supernatural, supersensual life."

6. The student said: "Since I stand in nature, how might I come through nature into the supersensual ground without destroying nature?" The master said: "For that three things are necessary. The first is that you give your will to God and sink into the ground of His mercy. The second is that you must hate your own will and do nothing to which your own will drives you. The third is that you throw yourself in patience under the cross of our Lord Jesus Christ so that you might bear the temptations of nature and creature. When you do this God will speak in you and will bring your resigned will into Himself, into the supernatural ground, and you will hear what the Lord speaks in you."

7. The student said: "Then must I leave the world and my life so that I might do this?" The master said: "As you leave the world you will come into that out of which the world was made. As you lose your life and come into the impotency of your abilities you will stand in Him for whose sake you left it, in God out of whom it came into body."

8. The student said: "God created man in the natural life so that he might rule over all the creatures on earth and be Lord over all life in this world. Therefore he must possess it as his own." The master said: "If you only rule externally over the creatures, you are, with your willing and ruling, bestial, and stand only in a formed and transitory lordship. Moreover, if you lead your desire into bestial essence you will be infected and trapped and receive a bestial way of life, but if you have

left the way of images you are above the images and rule in the ground over all creatures out of which they were created and nothing on earth can harm you, for you are like all things and nothing is unlike you."

9. The student said: "O dear Master, teach me how I might come nearest to this, [so] that I might be like all things!" The master said: "Indeed [I will]. You must think on the words of our Lord Jesus Christ when He said, Unless you be converted, and become as children, ye shall not see the kingdom of God (Matthew 18:3). If you want to become like all things you must leave all things and turn your desire from them and not desire nor seek to gain as your own possession what is something. For as soon as you grasp the something in your desire, and allow it into yourself and take it as a possession, the something is a thing with you, and works with you in your will. Then you are responsible to protect it, to take it to you as your own being. If you take nothing into your desire, you are free from all things and, at the same time, you rule over all things for you have nothing in your acquisition and you are a nothing [to] all things and also all things are a nothing [to] you. You are as a child, which does not understand what a thing is, and even if you do indeed understand it, you understand without the movement of your perceptivity in the way in which God rules all things and sees and yet no being grasps Him. However, you said that I should teach you how you may come to this. Look to the words of Christ, when He said: Without me you can do nothing (John 5:5). By your own ability you cannot come to such rest so that no creature disturbs you. When you give yourself completely into the life of our Lord Jesus Christ, and completely give over your will and desire to Him and without Him wish nothing, you stand with your body in the world of characteristics, and with your reason under the cross of our Lord Christ, but with your will you walk in heaven and you stand at the end from which all creatures come and to which they again go. Then you may see

everything externally with the reason, and internally with the mind, and with Christ, to whom all power in heaven and on earth are given, to rule over all things" (Matthew 28:18).

10. The student said: "O Master! Those creatures that live in me hold me so that I am not able to give myself, no matter how eagerly I wish to." The master said: "As your will goes out from the creatures, so the creatures in you are abandoned and are in the world, and if only your body is with the creatures, you walk spiritually with God. When your will leaves the creatures, the creatures die in it and live only in the body in the world. If the will does not bring itself into them they are not able to move the soul. Saint Paul says: Our walk is in heaven (Philippians 3:20). Again: You are the temple of the Holy Spirit that dwells in you (I Corinthians 6:19). Thus the Holy Spirit lives in the will, and creatures in the body."

11. The student said: "If the Holy Spirit lives in the will of the mind, how can I protect myself so that He will not turn from me?" The master said: "Hear the words of Our Lord Jesus Christ, who said: If you remain in my words, my words remain in you [John 8:31]; that is, if you remain with your will in the words of Christ, His word and Spirit will remain in you, but if your will goes into the creatures, you have broken yourself away from Him, and you can protect yourself in no other way than by remaining continually in resigned humility and by giving yourself up to the most constant repentance, so that you are ever sorrowful that creatures live in you. If you do this, you stand in daily dying to the creature, and in daily ascension with your will."

12. The student said: "O dear Master! Teach me how I might receive such constant repentance." The master said: "When you abandon that which loves you and love that which hates you, you can ever stand in it."

13. The student said: "What is that?" The master said: "Your creatures in flesh and blood that love those who love

174

you because your will cares for them. These the will must leave and hold as enemies. You must learn to love the cross of our Lord Jesus Christ, with the world's scorn, and take this as daily practice in repentance. Then you will have continual cause to hate yourself with those creatures and to seek the eternal rest in which your will might rest as Christ said: In me you have rest, but in the world you have anxiety" [John 16:33].

14. The student said: "How can I keep myself strong in such temptation?" The master said: "If once each hour you can sweep up, out of all creatures, over all sensual thought, into the purest mercy of God, into the suffering of our Lord Jesus Christ, and give yourself into it, you will receive power to rule over sin, death, the devil, hell and the world. Then you can stand strong in all temptation."

15. The student said: "What might happen to me, poor man, if I should gain with my mind that place where no creature is?" The master said very pleasantly to him: "O dear student, if it was possible that your will might be able to break away from all creatures for one hour and rise up where no creature is, it would be dressed over with the highest brightness of God's glory and would taste in itself the sweetest love of our Lord Jesus Christ that no man can describe. It would discover in itself the inexpressible words of our Lord Jesus Christ concerning His great mercy. It would feel in itself that the cross of Our Lord Christ had been changed in itself into a tender goodness and that it would rather win this than all the world's honour and goods."

16. The student said: "What would happen to the body since it must live in the creatures?" The master said: "The body would be placed into the imitation of our Lord Christ who said: His kingdom is not of this world [John 18:36]. It would begin to die both internally and externally: Externally it would die to the world's vanity and evil deeds and be in opposition [to] and antagonistic to all haughtiness; internally

it would die to all evil inclinations and proclivities. It would receive a mind and will that would continually be directed to God."

17. The student said: "But the world would hate and despise him because he would have to contradict it and live in a different way and act differently." The master said: "He would not concern himself with this as if harm had come to him, but he would rejoice in that he is worthy to be like the image of our Lord Christ and should fully and eagerly carry our Lord's cross after him, so that the Lord might pour His sweetest Love into [him] because of this."

18. The student said: "What would happen to him if the wrath of God grasped him internally and the evil world externally as happened to our Lord Christ?" The master said: "Let it happen to him as to our Lord Christ. When He was scorned by the world and the high priests and was crucified, He commended His soul into the hands of His Father and went from the anguish of the world into eternal joy. Thus he will press from all the world's scorn and anguish, into the great Love of God and be revived and held by the sweetest Name JESUS. He would see and discover in himself a new world that would press through God's wrath, into which he would wrap up his soul and consider every thing the same. Whether the body be either in hell or on earth, its mind would still be in the greatest love of God."

19. The student said: "How would his body be supported in the world, and how would it support its dependents if the world's disfavour fell on him?" The master said: "He would receive a greater favour than the world can give because he would have as friends God and all His angels who would protect him in all need. God is thus his blessing in all things and even if it seems as if God did not [wish to bless], it is only a test and a love-pull so that he is to pray to God all the more and to commit all his ways to Him."

20. The student said: "But he will lose all his good friends and no one will be with him who will stand by him!" The master said: "He receives the heart of all friendship as his possession and loses only his enemies who earlier had loved his vanity and sin."

21. The student said: "How does it happen that he gains his good friends as his own?" The master said: "He gains as brothers and members of his own life all souls who belong to our Lord Jesus. God's children are all one in Christ; Christ is in all. Therefore he receives them as corporeal members in Christ, for all have the heavenly goods in common and live in the one love of God like branches of a tree from one sap. Yet he can not lack external natural friends as our Lord Christ [did]. Even if the high priests and authorities of the world, who do not belong to Him and are not members and brethren, might not love him, yet all those will love him who are capable of His word. Thus, those who love truth and righteousness will love him and associate with him, as Nicodemus, who loved Jesus because of the truth, [came to] Jesus by night, and externally feared the world. Thus he will have many good friends who are not known to him."

22. The student said: "But it is hard to be despised by all the world!" The master said: "What now seems hard to you, you will later learn to love the most."

23. The student said: "How will it be or occur that I shall love that which despises me?" The master said: "Now you love earthly wisdom. However when you have been clothed only in heavenly [wisdom] you will see that all the world's wisdom is only foolishness, and that the world hates only your enemy, mortal life, which you yourself also hate in your will. Then you will also begin in such scorn of the mortal body (life) to love."

24. The student said: "How can these two things agree, that a man hate and love at the same time?" The master said:

"What you love for yourself, you love, not as yours, but as the given love of God. You love the divine ground in yourself by which you love God's wisdom and miracles, as well as your brothers. That which you hate for yourself, you do according to yourself in which evil hangs onto you. You do this in that you eagerly wish to completely break the 'I' and it wishes to become for you a completely divine ground. Love hates the 'I' because the 'I' is a dead thing and [the two] cannot stand together, for love possesses heaven and dwells in itself, but the 'I' possesses the world with its being and also lives in itself. Just as heaven rules earth, and eternity rules time, so love rules over the natural life."

25. The student said: "Dear master, tell me why must love and suffering, friend and foe, live together? Would not love alone be better?" The master said: "If love did not consist in suffering, it would have nothing to love. However, since its being that it loves, as the poor soul, stands in suffering and pain, it has reason to love its own being and to rescue it from pain so that it might be loved again. Neither can it be known what love is if it did not have [something] that it might love."

26. The student said: "What is love in its power and virtue, and in its height and greatness?" The master said: "Its virtue is the nothing, and its power is through everything. Its height is as high as God and its greatness is greater than God. He who finds it finds nothing and everything."

27. The student said: "Oh dear master, tell me how I am to understand this!" The master said: "When I say, 'Its virtue is the nothing,' you are to understand that when you leave all creatures and become a nothing to all nature and creatures, you are in the Eternal One, which is God Himself, and you will discover the highest of virtues, love. When I say, 'Its power is through everything,' then you discover in your soul and body that when the great love is lighted in you it burns as no fire can. You will also see in all of the works of God how love has poured out into all and is the inmost and outermost

ground in all things: inwardly according to the power and outwardly according to the form. When I say further, 'Its height is as high as God,' you are to understand in yourself that it leads you in the self as high as God Himself is, as you can see in our dear Lord Christ according to our humanity, which the love brought to the highest throne in the power of the Godhead. But when I also said, 'Its greatness is greater than God,' this is also true for where God does not dwell, there love enters. When our dear Lord Christ stood in hell, hell was not God, but love was there and broke death. Also when you are in anguish, God is not that anguish; but His love is there and leads you from anxiety into God. When God hides Himself in you, love is there and reveals Him in you. And when I further say, 'He who finds love finds nothing and everything,' this is also true, for he finds a supernatural, supersensual abyss that has no place as its dwelling and finds nothing that can be compared to it. Therefore one compares it with nothing because it is deeper than everything. Therefore it is a nothing to all things because it is incomprehensible. Because it is a nothing, it is free of all things and is that single good that one cannot tell what it is. When I finally say, 'He finds everything who thus finds it,' this is also true. It has been the beginning of all things and rules all things. If you find it you will come into the ground out of which all things proceed and in which they stand, and you will be in it a king over all the works of God."

28. The student said: "Dear master! Tell me where does it dwell in man?" The master said: "Where a man does not dwell there it has its place in man."

29. The student said: "Where is that place where man does not dwell in himself?" The master said: "That is the resigned soul brought to the ground. Where the soul dies to its own will and itself wills nothing more than what God wills, there it dwells. For insofar as the self-will is dead to itself, it takes for itself the place, where earlier the self-will sat. There

is now nothing [there], and where nothing is, God's love works alone."

30. The student said: "How may I grasp it without dying to my will?" The master said: "If you want to grasp it for yourself it will flee from you. But if you give yourself wholly and completely to it, you are dead to your own will and it will then be the life of your nature. It does not kill you but makes you alive according to its life. Then you live, yet not you, but its will for your will is its will. Then you are dead yet live to God."

31. The student said: "How [is it] that so few men find it but so many eagerly wish to have it?" The master said: "They all seek it in something as in formed meaning in a desire, for they nearly all have their own natural lust. Though it offers itself to them it can find no place in them, for the imaginativeness of self-willing has put itself in their place. It flees them for it lives only in the nothing, therefore the self-will cannot find it."

32. The student said: "What is its office in the nothing?" The master said: "Its office is to press ceaselessly into the something, and when it finds a place in the something that stands silent, it takes it and rejoices in it with its fire-flaming love more than the sun in the world. Its office is to ignite fire ceaselessly in the something and burn the something and moreover immolate itself with it."

33. The student said: "O dear master, how am I to understand this?" The master said: "If love were to ignite a fire in you, then you would feel how your 'I' burns itself and how greatly it rejoices in your fire so that you would sooner allow yourself to be killed than go again into your something. Moreover, its flame is so great that it will not leave you. Even if it soon costs you your mortal life, it goes with you in its fire into death. If you should go to hell, it would break hell for your sake."

34. The student said: "Dear master, no longer can I bear being wrong. How can I find the nearest way to it?" The master said: "Go where the going is hardest. Whatever the world rejects, take for yourself. Whatever it does, do not do. Go against the world in all things and you will come on the nearest way to it."

35. The student said: "If it should happen that I were to walk contrary to all things, I would indeed stand in need and unrest and be known as foolish." The master said: "I do not tell you to harm anyone. Only the world loves deception and vanity and walks on the wrong way. If you would be opposed to its way in all things, you must walk only in the right way, for the right way is opposed to all its [the world's] ways. You say, however, that you will stand in useless anguish. This occurs according to the flesh. It gives cause for continual repentance and in such anguish love is most loving in its fire-incitement. You say also that you will be known as foolish. That is true for the way to the love of God is foolishness to the world, but wisdom to God's children. When the world sees such love-fire in God's children, it says they are foolish; but to the children of God, this is the greatest treasure, for no life can express, nor can mouth describe, the fire of the inflaming love of God that is whiter than the sun, sweeter than any honey, more powerful than any food or drink, and lovelier than all the joys of this world. He who reaches this is richer than any king on earth, nobler than any emperor can be, and stronger than all might."

36. The student questioned the master further: "Where does the soul go when the body dies, be it holy or damned?" The master said: "It can take no journey unless the external mortal life, and the body too, separate themselves from it. Earlier it had heaven and earth within it, as it is written: The kingdom of God comes not with external show; nor can one say, See here! There it is! for look, the kingdom of God is

within you (Luke 17:20-21). Whichever, hell or heaven, is revealed in it [the soul], of that it consists."

37. The student said: "Does the soul not go into heaven or hell just as a man goes into a house or as a man goes through a hole into another world?" The master said: "No, there is no entrance in such a way, for heaven and hell are present everywhere. There is only the changing of the will either into God's love or [into] wrath. This takes place in the time of the body, as Saint Paul says: Our walk is in heaven (Philippians 3:20). And Christ also says, My sheep hear my voice, and I know them, and they follow me, and I give unto them eternal life, and no one shall tear them from my hand" (John 10:27-28).

38. The student said: "How does this entrance of the will into heaven or hell occur?" The master said: "When the will gives itself into the ground of God, then it sinks outside of itself, outside all grounds and places to where God alone is revealed, where He works and wills. It itself becomes a nothing according to its own will. God works and wills in it and God lives in its resigned will by which the soul is made holy and comes to divine rest. When the body breaks up, the soul is pressed through with divine love and is illuminated with God's light, as fire glows through iron by which it loses its darkness. This is the hand of Christ. When God's love completely dwells through the soul and is a shining light and a new life in it, it is in heaven, a temple of the Holy Spirit, and is itself God's heaven in which He lives. The godless soul does not wish to go in this life in divine resignation of its will, but it only goes toward its own lust and desire in vanity and error, in the devil's will. It takes to itself only evil, lies, pride, covetousness, envy and wrath, and resigns its will to these. This vanity is revealed and works in it and presses through the soul completely and totally, as fire does iron. It cannot come to divine rest for God's wrath is revealed in it. When the body is separated from the soul, eternal regret and despair begin. It

finds that it has become such a vain, anxious abomination and it is ashamed that it should try to press toward God with its false will; indeed, it cannot, for it is held captive by anger and is itself vain anger in which it has locked itself up by its false desires that it has aroused in itself. Since God's light does not shine in it, and His love does not stir it, it is in great darkness, and a painful, anguishing fire-source and carries hell in itself and cannot see the Light of God. Thus it dwells in itself in hell and dare have no exit. Whatever it is in, it is in hell and even if it could raise itself many hundreds of thousands of miles, it would still be in such a source and darkness."

39. The student said: "How [is it], then, that the holy soul cannot perfectly discover such light and great joy in this time, and that the godless cannot feel hell, since both are in man, although only one works in man?" The master said: "The kingdom of heaven works in the saints and is active and discovered in their faith. They feel God's love in their faith by which the will gives itself up to God. But the natural life is wrapped in flesh and blood and stands in the opposition of God's wrath, wrapped by the vain lust of this world that continually presses through the external, mortal life. On the one side is the world, on the second the devil, and on the third the curse of God's wrath. These press through and sift the flesh and blood of life. Therefore the soul often stands in anguish when hell thus presses in it and wishes to reveal itself in it. However, it sinks into the hope of divine grace, and stands as a beautiful rose among thorns until the kingdom of this world falls away from it in the death of the body. Then, when nothing more hinders it, it will be properly revealed in God's love. At this time it must walk with Christ in this world: Christ redeems it from its own hell in that he presses through it with his love and stands by it in its hell and changes its hell into heaven. But you say: 'Why does the godless not feel hell at this time?' I say: 'He feels it in his false conscience but he does not understand it, for he still has earthly vanity

with which he is enamoured and in which he has joy and pleasure.' Moreover, the external life still has the light of external nature in which the soul has pleasure, so that pain might not be revealed in it. When the body dies, the soul can no longer enjoy such temporal pleasure, and the light of external nature is also put out in it. Then it stands in eternal thirst and hunger for such vanities with which it enamoured itself here, and it cannot reach anything except a false, self-centered will. It had too much of the one [false will] in this life and cannot allow itself to be content. Of the other [vanity] it had too little, so it is in eternal hunger and thirst for vanity, evil and frivolity. It would ever eagerly do more evil, but it has nothing in or with which it can bring it about. Thus the completion occurs only in itself. Such hellish hunger and thirst cannot be completely revealed in it until the body, with which it thus loved in pleasure and which it tied to that after which it lusted, dies."

40. The student said: "Since heaven and hell are thus in strife with each other within us at this time, and God is thus near to us, where do the angels and devils dwell in such a time?" The master said: "Where you according to your own self and will do not dwell, there the angels dwell over and in you. Where you dwell according to your own self and will, there the devils live in and over you."

41. The student said: "I do not understand that." The master said: "Where God's will wills in a thing there God is revealed. In such a revelation the angels also dwell. And where God does not will in a thing with the thing's will, there God is not revealed to him, but He dwells only in Himself, without that thing's cooperation. Then self-will is in the thing without God's will and there the devil dwells and everything that is not God."

42. The student said: "How far are heaven and hell from each other?" The master said: "As day and night, as everything and nothing. They are in each other and each is to the

other as a nothing and yet they cause each other joy and pain. Heaven is through the whole world, and outside the world it is over all without any division, place or position, and works through the divine revelation only in itself. And in that into which it comes, or in that in which it has become revealed, there God is revealed. For heaven is nothing other than a revelation of the Eternal One where everything works and wills in silent love. And hell is also in and through the whole world also dwelling and working only in itself and in that in which hell's foundation is revealed, as in self and false willing. The visible world has both of these in itself. Man, however, is according to his temporal life only in the visible world, and therefore during this time he does not see the spiritual world. The external world with its being is a cover for the spiritual world, just as the soul is covered with the body. When the external man dies, then the spiritual world in the soul is revealed, either according to the eternal light with the holy angels, or according to eternal darkness with the devils."

43. The student said: "What is an angel then, or the soul of man, that they can thus be revealed in God's love or His wrath?" The master said: "They are from the same cause, a piece from the divine knowledge of His will, sprung from the divine Word and led into an object of divine love. They are from the ground of eternity out of which light and darkness spring. As in the possessiveness of self-desire is darkness, so light is in the same willing with God. For if the will of the 'I' of this soul wills with God, there is God's love in action; in the self-possessiveness of the soul's will God's will works painfully, and is a darkness so that the light might be made known. They are nothing other than a revelation of divine will, either in light or darkness, of the spiritual world's characteristics."

44. The student said: "What then is the body of man?" The master said: "It is the visible world, an image and being of all that is in that world. The visible world is [also] a revela-

tion of the inner spiritual world out of eternal light and out of eternal darkness, out of spiritual working. It is an object of eternity with which eternity has made itself visible, since the self-will and the resigned will work with each other as [do] evil and good. One such being is the external man, for God created the external man from the external world and blew into him the inner spiritual world for his soul and rational life. Therefore the soul, in the external world's being takes up and uses evil or good."

45. The student said: "What will happen after this world, when with all its things it shall have ceased [to be]?" The master said: "Only material being will end, the four elements, the sun, moon and stars; but the inner spiritual world [will be] completely visible and revealed. However, whatever is done in this time through the spirit, be it evil or good, each act will separate itself into either eternal light or into eternal darkness according to its spiritual way. That which is born of each will press back into its similarity again. Darkness will then be called hell, as an eternal forgetfulness of the good; and light will be called the kingdom of God, as an eternal joy and eternal praise of the saints now redeemed from such pain. The Last Judgement is the ignition of the fires according to God's love and wrath. In it all the *materia* of all being will pass away and each fire will draw to itself its own nature, each being its own similarity. Everything that is born in God's love draws the love-fire of God into itself, in which it will burn according to the manner of love, giving itself to the same being. However, what is done in God's wrath according to darkness draws painfulness to itself and destroys the false being. Then the painful will remains only in its own image and form."

46. The student said: "In what *materia* or form will our bodies be resurrected?" The master said: "The human body sown on earth as a natural, gross and elemental body is like the external elements at this time, and in this same gross body

[there] is a subtle power, as there is a subtle good power in the earth that may be compared to the sun and agrees with [it], which at the beginning of time sprang out of divine power, out of which the good power of the body was taken. This good power of the mortal body is to come again, to live or remain eternally in a beautiful, transparent, crystalline, material characteristic in spiritual flesh and blood. Just as the good powers of the earth, so too the earth will also be crystalline and the divine light will shine in all being. And as the gross earth will pass away and not be restored, so also the gross flesh of man will pass away and not live eternally. However, before judgement, everything will be separated by fire, both the earth and the ashes of the human body. Then, when God moves the spiritual world once more, each spirit will again draw its own spiritual being to itself: The good spirit and soul will draw its good being to itself, and the evil one its evil. One must understand, however, only an essential material power, since being is but naked power, like material *tinctur* since grossness disappears in all things."

47. The student said: "Shall we not arise in our material bodies and live in them eternally?" The master said: "When the visible world passes away, all that was external, that came out of it, passes away as well. The world remains. Only a heavenly, crystalline manner and form of the world remains. Only the spiritual earth remains in man, for then man will be exactly like the spiritual world that is now hidden."

48. The student said: "Will there be man and woman in the spiritual life or children or kindred? Will they associate with each other as happened here?" The master said: "How have you become fleshly minded? There shall be neither man nor woman, but all shall be like God's angels, androgynous virgins, neither daughter, son, brother, nor sister, but all one sex in Christ, all of one [piece] like a tree with its branches, and yet separate creatures; but God all in all. Then there will be spiritual knowledge of what each has been and what he has

done but there will be no more possessiveness, or desire to possess such being."

49. The student said: "Shall they all enjoy the same eternal joy and glorification?" The master said: "Scripture says: Such as a people is, such is their God [II Kings 17:29]. Again: With the pure You will be pure; with the twisted, twisted (Psalm 18:26-27). And Paul said: They will differ one from another in the resurrection, as sun, moon and stars (I Corinthians 15:41). Know then how they will indeed all enjoy divine work, but their power and enlightenment will be very different. Everything will be done to each with power according [to his life] in this time, in his anguished work, for the anguished work of the creature in this time is an opening and a generation of divine power by which God's power becomes moving and working. Those who have worked with Christ during this time, and not in the fleshly lust, will have great power and beautiful glorification both within and outside of themselves. The others however, who only wait upon a calculated satisfaction and who in the meantime served their belly-god, and yet finally were converted and came to virtue, will not have so great a power and enlightenment. Therefore, there will be a difference with these, as between sun, moon and stars, or as the flowers of the field in their beauty, power and virtue."

50. The student said: "How, or by whom, is the world to be judged?" The master said: "By divine movement in the person and Spirit of Christ who through the Word of God that became man will separate all that does not belong to Christ, and will completely reveal His kingdom in the place where this world stands, since the movement of separation happens everywhere at the same time."

51. The student said: "Where will the devils and the damned be cast, since the place of the whole world is to be glorified as the kingdom of Christ? Will they be driven to a place beyond this world, or will Christ reveal His Lordship outside this world's location?" The master said: "Hell will

remain in the place of this world in all its parts, but it will be hidden in the heavenly kingdom as the night in the day. The light will eternally shine in the darkness and the darkness cannot grasp it [John 1:5]. Light is the kingdom of Christ. The darkness is hell, in which the devil and the godless dwell. They will thus be suppressed by the kingdom of Christ and become a footstool in scorn."

52. The student said: "How will all peoples be brought before the Judgement?" The master said: "The eternal Word of God from which all spiritual, creaturely life has come shall move itself at that hour according to love and wrath in all life that is from eternity, and draw the creature before the Judgement of Christ. Through such a movement of the Word, life will be revealed in all its works and each one shall see and discover in himself his own sentence and judgement. The judgement will be revealed to the soul immediately on the death of the human body. The Last Judgement is only a reappearance of the spiritual body and a separation of the world when in the being of the world and in the body evil is to be divided from good. Each thing [is to return] to its eternal entrance and preserver. There is a revelation of the hiddenness of God in all being and life."

53. The student said: "How will sentence be made?" The master said: "See the words of Christ, who will say to them on his right, 'Come, you blessed of my Father, inherit the kingdom prepared for you from the beginning of the world: For I was hungry and you fed Me; I was thirsty and you gave Me drink; I was a stranger and you took Me in; I was naked and you clothed Me; I was sick and in prison and you visited Me and came to Me.' And they will answer him, 'When did we see You hungry, thirsty, naked, sick and in prison and served You?' And the King will answer and say to them, 'What you did unto one of the least of these My brothers, you did to Me.' And He will say to the godless on the left, 'Depart from Me, you cursed, into eternal fire prepared for

the devil and his angels: For I was hungry, thirsty, a stranger, naked, sick and in prison, and you did not serve Me.' And they will also answer Him and say to Him: 'When did we see You so and did not serve You?' Then He will answer them, 'Verily I say unto you, what you did not do to one of the least of these My brothers, you did not do to Me.' And these [evil persons] shall go into everlasting punishment, but the righteous [shall go] into life eternal" (Matthew 25:34-36).

54. The student said: "Dear master, tell me why Christ says, 'What you have done unto the least of these you have done to Me; and what you have not done to them, you have not done to Me'? How did man do this to Christ so that it happened to Him?" The master said: "Christ lives essentially in the faith of those who have given themselves completely to Him. He gives them His flesh as food and His blood as drink and thus possesses the ground of their faith in the interiority of man. Therefore a Christian is called a branch on his vine, and is called a Christian because Christ dwells in him spiritually. Whatever a man does to such a Christian in his corporeal needs he does to Christ Himself, who dwells within him for such a Christian is not his own, but he and his possessions are completely given to Christ. Therefore this happens to Christ Himself. He who draws his hand from these needy Christians, and does not serve them in need, rejects Christ from himself and despises Him in His members. When a poor person who belongs to Christ requests [something] of you and you deny him aid in his need, you have denied it to Christ Himself. And when one injures such a Christian he injures Christ Himself. When one scorns, insults, reviles and casts off such people he does this all to Christ Himself. However he who receives, feeds, gives drink to, clothes and helps those in need—he does this to Christ and His own body's members. Yes, he does it to Him Himself, if he is a Christian, for in Christ we are only one, like a tree in its branches."

55. The student said: "How will those fare on the day of such Judgement who thus torment the poor and wretched, sucking their very sweat from them, oppressing them, drawing them down with force, viewing them as something to trample, so that they themselves may be important and may destroy their sweat in proud and vain voluptuousness?" The master said: "All these do it to Christ Himself, and they belong to His stern judgement. They thus lay their hands on Christ, persecute Him in His members, and, in addition, help the devil to expand his kingdom, and by such oppression draw the poor away from Christ so that he [the devil] seeks an easy way to fill his belly. Yes, they do nothing else than what the devil himself does, who ceaselessly opposes Christ's kingdom [and His] love. All those who do not turn with whole heart to Christ, and serve Him, must enter into hellish fire in which such vanity is."

56. The student said: "How will these fare in this time who strive against the kingdom of Christ, and who because of this persecute, shame, slander and revile each other?" The master said: "All these have not yet known Christ, and they understand only in a figure how heaven and hell struggle for victory with each other. All the heights of pride in which man strives about meanings is an image of self-interest. He who does not have faith, and humility, and stands [not] in Christ's Spirit, is armed only with God's wrath and serves only for the victory of the image of self-interest as the kingdom of darkness and the wrath of God. For all self-interest on the Day of Judgement will be given to darkness, as well as all those useless arguments by which they seek not love but only the image of self-interest that exalts itself in their interpretations. By these interpretations the princes are led to cause wars, and by these ideas they attack and storm lands and people. These belong to the separation of the wrong from the right in the Judgement. Then all meanings and images will cease and all

the children of God will walk in the love of Christ and He will [dwell] in us. All in this time of struggle [who] are not eager for the Spirit of Christ, and do not desire to promote love, but seek in strife only for their own need, are from the devil and belong in the darkness and will be cut off from Christ, for in heaven all serve God, their Creator, in humility."

57. The student said: "Then why does God allow such strife in this time?" The master said: "Life stands by strife so that it may be revealed, experienced and discovered, and so that wisdom may become separated and known. [Strife] serves for the eternal joy of victory. In the saints of Christ great jubilation will arise because Christ has overcome the darkness and all the self-interest of their natures in them, and they are released from strife. This will eternally bring them joy when they know how the godless are rewarded. God therefore lets all things stand with a free will so that the eternal Lordship for love and wrath, and for light and darkness, may be revealed and known, so that each life may cause and awaken its own judgement itself. That which is to the godless a delight and a joy in this world will be changed into eternal pain and shame. Therefore the joy of the saints must rise in death as the light of the candle possesses another world. As light has a completely other characteristic than fire, and gives itself, but the fire takes and consumes itself, so the holy life of mercy sprouts forth through the death in which self-will dies, and then God's love-will alone rules and acts in all things."

"Thus the Eternal One took perceptivity and divisibility, and by perceptivity led itself forth again through death into the mighty kingdom of joy, so that there might be an eternal play in the endless unity, and an eternal cause [to bring about] the kingdom of joy. Thus pain must be a ground and cause of motion."

"And in this there lies hidden the *Mysterium* of the hidden wisdom of God."

"Whoever asks receives, whoever seeks finds and to him who knocks it shall be opened" (Matthew 7:7).

"The grace of Our Lord Jesus Christ, and the love of God, and the communion of the Holy Spirit be with us all. Amen" [II Corinthians 13:14].

THE SEVENTH TREATISE
THE PRECIOUS GATE
ON DIVINE CONTEMPLATION
(1620)

What Mysterium Magnum [*is*], *and how all is from, through and in God; how God is so near to all things and fills all.*

Chapter One

What God is; and how man is to know His divine being in His revelation.

1. REASON says: I hear much said of God, that there is a God who has created all things, who also upholds and bears all things, but I have seen no one, nor heard of anyone, who has seen God, or who could tell where He dwells, or is, or how He is. For when it [reason] looks at the being of the world and considers how it fares for the pious as for the evil, and how all things are mortal and fragile; moreover how the pious can find no Saviour who might redeem them from the anguish and opposition of evil, and thus must go with anxiety into the depths of misery; then it thinks that all occurs as it will, that there is no God who Himself takes up sorrowing [men], since He lets those who hope in Him stick fast in their miseries; and go to the grave with them; and no one has heard of anyone who came again from corruption and said that he has been with God.

2. ANSWER: Reason is natural life whose ground is in a temporal beginning and end, and [which] cannot come to the supernatural ground where God is to be understood. Even if it may so see itself in this world, and discover in its contemplation no other ground, it discovers in itself a longing for a higher ground in which it might rest.

3. It [reason] understands that it came from a super-

natural ground and that there must be a God who brought it into life and willing. It is terrorized by its willing of evil; it is ashamed of its own will, and it judges its own willing of evil as evil. Even if it does evil, it accuses itself and fears a judgement that it does not see. This indicates that the hidden God who has brought Himself into nature, dwells in it, and punishes those of evil ways, and that the same (hidden God) must not be of the nature of perceptivity since reason neither sees nor grasps Him.

4. On the other hand, abandoned reason, which to this point incorrectly [it thought] had been tortured by misery, discovers a desire in itself to abandon itself yet more, and [to] give itself willingly to suffering. [However], it steps into unjust suffering in the hope that what it had created will take it from its misery into itself, and it desires to rest in that which does not suffer. It seeks rest in something that does not have it in itself. It desires the death of its "I" and yet does not desire to be a nothing, but desires only to die to torment so that it might rest in itself.

5. Therefore it gives itself to suffering so that the governance of painfulness might kill its suffering and [that] it might in its life through the death of its self-death enter without suffering into a painless [life], for [it lives] a painful life.

6. In this one correctly understands the hidden God, how he reveals Himself in the mind of man, punishes injustice in his conscience, and, by suffering, draws unjust suffering to Himself; and how rational life, as the natural life, must through suffering overcome a desire to turn itself back again into that out of which it came, and how it must desire to hate its self and to die to the natural will so that it may reach a supernatural [will].

7. REASON says: Why has God created a painful, suffering life? Would it not have been better in this world [condition] without suffering and anguish, since He is the ground

and beginning of all things? Why does He tolerate the disobedient will? Why does He not break evil so that good alone remains in all things?

8. ANSWER: No thing may be revealed to itself without contrariety. If it has no thing that resists it, it always goes out from itself and does not go into itself again. If it does not go into itself again, as into that out of which it originally came, it knows nothing of its cause.

9. If the natural life did not have any contrariety, and was without a goal, it would never ask for its ground out of which it came. The hidden God would thus remain unknown to the natural life. Moreover if there were no contrariety in life there would be no perceptivity, nor willing nor working, nor understanding, nor knowledge, for a thing that has one will has no divisibility. If it does not discover a contrary will that causes in it a drive to movement, it remains still. For one single thing does not know more than one [thing]; and if it is in itself good, it knows neither evil nor good, for it has nothing in itself that makes it perceptive.

10. Thus we can also philosophize concerning God's will, saying: If the hidden God, who is only one being and will had not led Himself by His will out of Himself, and had not led Himself out of eternal knowledge into the *temperamentum* into a divisibility of wills, and had not led the same divisibility into [His] incomprehensibility, to a natural and creaturely life, and if this same divisibility in life did not consist of strife, how then would the hidden will of God, which in itself is one, have been revealed to itself? How can there be knowledge of self in one single will?

11. However, there is divisibility in this single will so that the divisibility leads itself into the *centra* and into self-will, so that a self-will is in the separated [will], and thus uncaused and innumerable wills rise in one will as branches from a tree. We thus see and understand that in such divis-

ibility each separated will leads itself into its own single form, and that the strife of wills is for the form, that one form in divisibility is not as the other, yet all stand in one ground.

12. A single will cannot break itself apart in pieces, as the mind does not break in pieces when it separates itself into a good and evil willing, but the outgoing of the *sensus* separates itself into an evil and good willing and the mind remains completely within itself and suffers, because an evil and a good will have arisen and dwell in him.

13. REASON says: What is good or useful in the fact that with the good, evil must be?

ANSWER: Evil, as a contrary will, causes the good, as will, to press again toward its own cause, toward God, and to become desirous again of the good, as the good will. For a thing that is good only in itself, having no anguish, desires nothing, for it knows nothing better in itself or for itself after which it can lust.

14. Thus we can philosophize and say concerning the single good will of God, that He in Himself can desire nothing for He has nothing in or before Himself, that can give Him anything and therefore He brings Himself out of Himself into divisibility, into *centra*, so that contrariety arises in the outflow, as in [those which] flowed out, so that the good might become perceptive, working and willing in the evil, that is, desiring to divide itself from evil and desiring to go again into the single will of God.

15. But since the outflowing of the single, eternal will of God continually goes out of Himself for His own revelation [of Himself], so the good also as the divine power out of the Eternal One, flows out with such an outflow, and goes along with divisibility, into the *centra* of the manifold.

16. Thus the continuous outflow of the will causes the good in it with its movement to long again to remain still, and it becomes desirous to press into the Eternal One again. In

such pressing into itself, the One becomes moving and desirous, and in such working consists of perceptivity, knowledge and will.

17. God, insofar as He is called God, can will nothing but Himself. He has nothing before or after Him that He can will. If He does will something, that same thing has flowed out from Him and is His own counter-stroke in which the eternal will wills something in itself. If the something were only one [thing], the will would have no destructiveness in it. For this reason the ungrounded will separated itself in the beginning and grasped itself in being so that it might work in something, just as one has a similitude of a man in his mind.

18. If the mind did not flow out from itself, it would have no thoughts. If it had no thought, it would have no knowledge of itself, or of other things, and could have no creativity nor working. But the thoughtful outflow from the mind (which is a counter-stroke of the mind in which the mind discovers itself) makes the mind willing and desiring, so that the mind directs the thoughts into something, as into a *centrum* of an "I," in which the mind works with the thoughts and reveals and sees itself in working with the thoughts.

19. If there were no *contrarium* in these *centra* of the thoughts in the counter-stroke, all *centra* of the thoughts that flowed out would be only one in all of the *centra*, only a single will that always did only one thing. How then would the wonders and powers of divine wisdom be known in the mind (which is an image of divine revelation) and be brought [before it] in figures?

20. However if there is a *contrarium*, a light and darkness, in [these *centra*], this *contrarium* is contrary to its self, and each characteristic causes it to lead the other into desire to wish to strive against the other, and to rule [it]. In this desire the thoughts and the mind are led into a natural and creaturely ground, to their own willing, as to a ruling in its some-

thing, as with its *centrum* over all *centra*, as a thought of the mind over the others.

21. From this strife and anguish, as well as the contrary will, originate in the mind so that the whole mind is caused by this again to go into a breaking of the thought and of self-willing, as of the natural *centra*, and to lead itself out of the pain of the contrary will and strife, out of anguish, and to wish to sink into eternal rest, as into God out of whom it sprang.

22. Out of this arise faith and hope, so that the anguished mind hopes for redemption, and yearns for its cause again, as toward God.

23. Thus we are also to understand the divine revelation. For all things have their first beginning from the outflow of the divine will, be it evil or good, love or sorrow. Since the will of God is not a thing, neither nature nor creature, in which is neither pain, suffering, nor contrary will, from the outflow of the Word, as through the outgoing of the un-grounded mind (which is the wisdom of God, the great *Mysterium* in which the eternal understanding lies within the *temperamentum*) flowed forth understanding and knowledge. This same outflow is a beginning of the willing by which the understanding divided itself into forms. Thus the forms, each in itself, became desirous of having a counter-stroke for their likeness. This same desire was an incomprehensibility to self or to individuality, place, or to something. Out of this something the *Mysterium Magnum*, as the unnatural power, became natural and grasped for itself the something for a self-will.

24. This self-will is the ground of its own self, and surrounds itself as a desiring will. Out of this the magnetic *impression* for sharpness and hardness took its origin and was the ground of darkness and painful perceptivity out of which contrary will, anguish and flight (perceptivity) had their origin. This is the ground of nature out of which the multitude

of characteristics comes so that in this contrariety one will arises out of the other, separating itself from pain, just as the thoughts separate themselves from the mind, just as the mind with the thoughts consists of continual anguish, working, willing and breaking.

25. In such a divine outflow, in which the divine power breathes forth out of itself, leads and has led itself into nature and creature, two [facts] are to be known: first, the stern understanding of the one good will that is a *temperamentum* and thus brings itself only into perceptivity and working for the revelation of power, colours and virtue, [so] that power and virtue appear in divisibility and form, and the eternal knowledge may be revealed and come into knowledge. Out of this the groaning of angels, souls and creatures came, as well as the powers and dominions together with the visible world.

26. Secondly, we are to understand the original will of nature as the incomprehensibility of the *centra* in which each *centrum* in the divisibility surrounds itself into the place of the "I" and of self-willing, as an individual *mysterium* or mind surrounds itself, out of which originates the dissimilarity of willing. In these two, a *contrarium* arises for there are two in one being.

27. In the first place, the internal, from the origin of the divine power, desires only a counter-stroke of its likeness, as a good in which the good, divine, outflowing will works and reveals itself. Secondly, the self-begotten natural self-will, from the place of the self of the dark *impression* of sharpness, also desires a likeness as a counter-stroke through its own incomprehensibility. Through this grasping within, it makes itself material and desires nothing other than its own corporeality, as a natural ground.

28. In these two we can understand good and evil wills in all things. In it is also correctly understood how the internal, spiritual ground of all being originates in divine power,

and also how in all things natural self-desire originates; how all *corpora* of visible, perceptive being originate from the desire of nature.

29. From this we are now clearly to note that, as natural self-desire, which had a beginning, makes itself material and a counter-stroke of itself in which it works, so also the divine ground and will makes for itself with its incomprehensibility of love a counter-stroke and spiritual being in which the divine holy will works, and leads the divine power into forms and divisibility for the revelation of divine power and majesty.

30. In this world's being two beings are always to be understood in one thing: first, an eternal, divine, spiritual [being]; second, a created, natural and breakable [being] in the self-will. Hence, two wills lie in one life. The first is a created, natural will in which the will is its own *astrum*, unites with all external, natural, elemental and sidereal qualities. The second is an eternal, spiritual will, or eternal, spiritual being, which is the incomprehensibility or ungraspable being of the divine will. With this the divine will also makes a counter-stroke and being for itself, in which it works. These two beings are to be understood as in two *principia*, the first, divine, in the heavenly [*principium*], and the second temporal, in the earthly.

31. Just as the heavenly divine *(principium)* depends on the earthly, so the earthly depends on the heavenly, and yet neither is the other, for the heavenly has spiritual being that is only an essential power, that presses through the earthly and yet only possesses its *principium* and gives power to the earthly being so that it receives another will and longs for the heavenly. This longing is a desire to leave the vanity of nature, as Scripture says: All creatures beside us long to be free from the vanity to which they are cast under, against (over) their wills (Romans 8:19-22).

32. Understand [this] correctly. The outgoing desire of the divine energy toward nature out of which nature and self have arisen longs to be free from the natural self-will.

33. This same desire is burdened against its will with the *impression* of nature because, since God has brought it therein, it is to be redeemed from this burdening vanity of nature, and brought into a crystalline, clear nature. Then it will be revealed why God has locked it in a time and cast it under painfulness to suffer, namely: so that by natural pain the eternal power might be brought into form, character and divisibility for perceptivity; and that creatures as creaturely life in this time might become revealed, and so become a play in the counter-stroke of divine wisdom. Through folly wisdom is revealed, because folly ascribes abilities to its own self, and yet it stands in its ground and beginning and is finite.

34. Thus immortal life is carried into view through folly so that praise to the honour of God may rise in it and the eternal [and] durable might be known in mortality.

35. Thus, the reason in its first question is answered, in that it thinks that all things happen without reason, and that there is no God because He allows the pious to live in pain, anguish and sorrow, and only in the end leads them to the grave, as [He does] the godless. It seems as if God did not concern Himself about anything, or as if there were no God, since reason does not see, know or discover Him. Thus it is told that its own life is only a counter-stroke of the proper life; and that it finds no hunger and desire in itself for that from which it originated in the beginning; that there is only foolishness and game-playing in its own life in which wisdom brings forth its wonders.

36. For it [reason] sees in the wise according to external nature such foolishness and sees how God abandons the foolishness of the wise so that it [foolishness] must stand in shame and scorn before that self-willed foolish cleverness that does not know its own end. Foolish reason thinks that there is

no Saviour and does not understand how the wise man is saved in himself and will be redeemed from inherited foolishness, since his own will enters into its breaking and into its not-willing through the pain and the opposition of the godless and sinks again into its first beginning, as into God's will, and is born anew in it. God is not served in the gross, mortal flesh as if He wished to bring his salvation into the bestial, self-willed life. He is concerned [however] that self-will is broken and sinks again in God. Thus the internal good being is grasped in God's will and more pain is laid upon the mortal body so that the natural self will not again go into a self-desire of self and set itself up as the ruler of the internal ground, and destroy the true image of God.

37. This the earthly reason does not understand because it does not know how God dwells in it and what God's will and being is. It does not know that God dwells through and is close to it and that its life is only foolishness to wisdom by which life wisdom reveals itself so that it may become known what wisdom is. Its will went from God into self, and boasts of its own abilities, and does not see that its abilities are created and finite, that it is only a processed mirror by which wisdom sees itself for a time in the foolishness of the wise man. Finally, by such pain of the godless, the foolishness in the wise breaks so that they begin to hate this frail and foolish life, and begin to die with [their] reason and give [their] will to God.

38. Earthly reason considers this foolishness, especially when it sees that God also abandons the earthly foolishness in the wise, and allows the body of foolishness, in which foolishness saw itself, to descend into the grave without help. Then it thinks [that] this man has not received salvation from God. Since he trusted in Him [Matthew 27:43], his faith must indeed have been false, or He would have saved him, indeed during the time of this life.

39. Moreover, since it does not immediately feel its

punishment, it thinks that it is no longer a serious [matter], and does not know that the more it forms itself in foolishness the greater a source of eternal pain grows within it, so that, when the light of external nature, in which for a time it had strutted in its "I," breaks in it, then it stands in itself in eternal darkness and pain, so that its false, self-desire is a vain, harsh, piercing, hard sharpness and counter-will.

40. At this time it hopes for external aid and leads itself into the pleasure of will and holds this to be its heavenly kingdom. However when the external light is put out in death, it stands in eternal despair, and sees no Saviour within or about it.

41. But at this time the wise man becomes a fool to himself, and he learns to hate his foolishness (which reason holds as cleverness). Thus must his wisdom (which the world holds a foolishness) be foolishness for his reason, at which it [reason] is greatly vexed. God thus also hates the foolish, mortal life in the wise man as the wise man himself hates it so that the true divine life may rule with reason within him. Therefore there is no complaint with God concerning the mortal body of the wise, for he forms the divine *Ens* in him in his spirit and will and allows the body of foolishness to go into the grave with its foolishness, until the day of the separation of all being.

42. The reason does not understand this; therefore it is foolish. And a man is supposed to be man, not according to foolishness but according to God's spirit, and not to judge what is divine according to reason's images for it is written: He who builds on [the foundation of] his flesh (as on the mortal reason of his own), will reap from the flesh destruction; but he who builds on [the foundation of] the spirit (as on God's will) and sets his will in the hope of divine promise, will from the spirit reap everlasting life (Galatians 6:8).

Chapter Two

Of the mind, will and thoughts of human life, how they have
their origin from God's will, and how they are a counter-stroke
as an image of God, in which God wills, works and dwells.

1. REASON says: Because the mind with the senses is a
created, natural life, which stands in time and transitoriness,
how can it be brought to the supersensual divine life in this
time, or how is the divine indwelling [to take place] in life?

2. ANSWER: The life of man is a form of the divine will
and was breathed into the created image of man by the breath
of the divine. It is the formed word of divine knowledge, but
it has become so poisoned by the counter-breath of the devil
and the anger of temporal nature that life's will has formed
itself with the external, earthly counter-stroke of mortal nature, and is come out of its own temperament into the divisibility of characteristics.

3. For this reason it still stands in an earthly image, and
is now seen in its three *principia*. According to its true origin it
stands in the outgoing will of God, in divine knowledge,
which originally was a *temperamentum* in which divine
energy worked sensually. [It was] properly a Paradise or
working of divine powers, in which it is understood as an
eternal formation of divine will. This growth is understood in
the outgoing of the good senses through which divine wisdom
figuratively forms in a divine way, and reveals itself through
such an image of the divine understanding, through the outgoing of the sensual life. This is why it is properly called an
image of God in which the divine will reveals itself.

4. But when this life in the first *principium* was so
breathed upon in its image by the angry devil, the devil suggested to it that it might be useful and good to break off the
outgoing of the senses from the life of the temperament, and
lead itself into its own image, according to the characteristics

of the manifold, to probe dissimilarity, as to know and discover evil and good.

5. Thus the self-will of life agreed to it and led the sense into an outgoing lust, and it led itself into desire for self-will, and pressed and fashioned itself into the self.

6. Immediately the knowledge of the life in the characteristics was revealed. Nature held [the understanding] captive in dissimilarity, and brought forward her dominion. Therefore it was painful and the inner divine ground of the good will and being was put out, that is, [became] nonworking according to the creature. The will of life broke itself off and went into perceptivity, out of unity into the manifold, and strove against the unity as [against] the eternal rest and the one good.

7. When this occurred the divine ground (as the second *principium* in which the divine power with the exhaled will of God has thought itself into the life of images as the counterstroke of God, understand: God's wisdom, as the essential will of God) was corrupted in the false will. For the cause of movement of holy being changed itself to earthliness in which good and evil stand in strife.

8. Understand: The eternal, ungrounded will of life turned itself from the holy, divine *Ens* and wished to rule in good and evil. Therefore, the second *principium*, God's kingdom, was put out. In its place the third *principium* in its own formation, the source of the stars and the four elements, grew up, out of which the body became gross and bestial, and the senses false and earthly.

9. Thus life lost the *temperamentum* as the eternal rest, and with its own desire made itself dark, painful, stern, hard and rough. It became vain restlessness, and it now walks in earthly power in an eternal ground, and seeks rest in fragility and finds none. Fragility is not the likeness of life and life now therefore lifts itself over the being of the world and rules the mortal power of stars and elements as [if it were] its own god

of nature. By such worship it has become foolish and mad, so that it cannot know its own ground and origin in such earthly formation and self-possessiveness, in which its own eternal rest stands and is properly called foolish. It has led itself out of the divine *Ens* and set itself in a fragile being, and wishes to rule that which breaks it and which goes as quickly as smoke.

10. And as that breaks over which it had ruled, life remains in contrariety in the first *principium* in the darkness, and it is nothing other than an ever-enduring, inextinguishable, painful fire-source, as devils and such are.

11. To this captive life God's great love came to help again and immediately after such a fall it breathed into the internal *Ens*, into the extinguished being, the divine characteristic, and gave life to a counter-stroke, [to a] new source-spring of divine unity, love and rest. It entered into the corrupted divine *Ens*, revealed itself in it, created life out of it so that it might put out its own painfulness and restlessness in the *centra* of [its] characteristic.

12. This new source-spring of divine love and unity through its outflow in Christ also embodied itself in the true life of all three principles of the human characteristic. It has entered into the formed *sensus*, into the natural, creaturely, deflected, formed will of life, took on humanity, and broke the "I" and self-willing with the inflow of the single love of God, as with the Eternal One, and led the will of the life again into the Eternal One, as into a *temperamentum*. Thus the will, which the devil had disturbed, broke its self-confinement, for then the devil's introduced will was destroyed and the painfulness of life was brought into true rest and burst the captivity, death. [The will] again restored the divine, sensual, paradisaical sprout of the holy thoughts and works and led the holy life through the confinement of death, and made death and the devil's will a mockery, thus powerfully showing how the Eternal One can be strong over the manifold and individuality; that the might of formation is not a god but that the

might of superformation and nonformation rules all. For the formed is only a counter-stroke of the nonformed will of God, through which the will of God works.

13. But since the great love of God in Christ thus came to human life in an earthly image to the help [of us men] and made an open gate of grace, a divine entrance for us poor men, the situation is now this: that the captured will of life in its earthly formation must again leave the earthly self and self-will, and completely give itself to this embodied grace which pressed in upon all from one, from the first man (Romans 5:18). It must take this grace to itself, and, in the power of such possession and divine entrance, sink with the resigned life-will into the supra-sensual, unconditioned Eternal One, as into the first ground of life's beginning. It again must give itself into the ground out of which life sprang. Thus is it again in its eternal place, as in the *temperamentum*, in (true) rest.

14. REASON says: How can a person do this, since Scripture says (I Corinthians 15:45; Genesis 1:28) [that] the first man was made for natural life, to rule over all the creatures and beings of this world? Therefore life must bring desire in earthly characteristics; [is this not so?]. ANSWER: Human life is set in a counter-stroke of the divine will, in and with which God wills. Earthly creatures are set up as a counter-stroke of human life, in and with which man is to will. With God's will the human will was to rule and will over all natural and creaturely life. It was not to stand in beastly essence, but in divine essence. Even though man was set with his life in nature, yet his nature was *temperamentum*, and his life was a house of the divine will.

15. However since in this time life must now consist of earthly essence, and yet cannot take it for itself, man must look on the threefold manner of life according to the three principles with which man may sweep up to the supersensual being of God—and how this may be done and can occur.

16. Christ said (John 15:5): Without me you can do noth-

ing. No man can achieve the highest ground with his own ability unless he sink his innermost ground of the first *principium* according to life's formation into the embodied grace of God, and according to the same ground become quiet in his own being, and in divine hope leave himself completely to the will of God, in such a way that his own will no longer speaks according to such a ground, except what God speaks and wills through that ground. Here he is at his highest goal.

17. If it were possible for him to remain quiet for an hour or less in his inner self-will and speaking, the divine will would speak into him. Through this inspeaking, God's will forms His will in man in Himself, and speaks into the formed, natural, essential, external life of reason and smashes the earthly formation of the rational will, and enlightens it so that immediately the supersensual divine life and will sprouts in the rational will and centers itself in it.

18. For even as little as the self-will of life, in self and in the will that is turned away from God's will, can stand quiet for a moment from work in nature so that it might sink beyond all nature, so little can the divine speaking, in that life which is resigned to its ground, be quiet from all activity.

19. For if life stands quiet in its own willing, when it stands in the abyss of nature and creature, in the eternal speaking out of God, then God speaks in it.

20. Life then went forth from God's speaking, and came into the body, and is nothing other than the formed will of God. If now one's own self-image and willing are still, divine forming and willing will rise up. For whatever is without will is one thus with the nothing and is beyond all nature, which abyss is God Himself.

21. Since the abyss, as God, is an eternal speaking, a breathing out of Himself, so also the abyss is spoken into the resigned life. The abyss's breathing speaks through the static ground of life. Life has arisen out of divine breathing and is a likeness of the divine breathing. Therefore one likeness begins

the other. As we understand this in the life thoughts, which are also such an outgoing of the breath of the mind, so the mind is an outgoing and counter-stroke of the divine mind of divine knowledge.

22. As God by the breathing-forth of His eternal wisdom and knowledge has revealed Himself by nature and creature, both by the internal holy life (will), by the life of the angels and men, and has led His will of knowledge into formation to reutterance by a formed verbal manner, so [he has done] also by nature and its breathing-forth once more of the creatures of the visible world. [He] has always made that externally spoken by nature subject to the inner ground so that the inner was to rule through the external corporeal and be a spirit of the external.

23. Know thus that the introverted, newborn life form in divine power and might, will also and can rule over the external rational life of the stars and elements. If it does not happen that the internal eternal life in man, in divine power and light, rules over the external, earthly, astral life of mortal lust, and breaks that will of earthly lust (in which the serpent-*monstrum* lies) there is no new birth, or divine will, at work or revealed in that life. Such a person (as long as he stands in the earthly will alone) is no child of heaven. For divine science is changed into an earthly, bestial characteristic by the self-formation of the false will, and is, in its body, an evil beast and, in its soul, a twisted false will that does not will God, [but], after the manner of the devil, stands in its own formation of sensual knowledge.

24. For this reason Christ said (Matthew 12:30): He who gathers not with me, scatters; that is, he who does not work, will and act with the embodied grace of God, which God through Christ has revealed and offered, but who works through natural self-will, scatters, not only the divine order of the senses, but he scatters as well his own works over a false ground.

25. Look at the sun as an example. If a plant does not have sap, then it is burned by the sun's beams. If it has sap, then the sun's beams warm it, [and] because of them it grows. So it is in the life of essence in man. If it has no *Ens* from God's meekness and love as from the Eternal One, it impresses itself into an angry fiery sharpness, so that the mind becomes completely raw, hungry, covetous, envious and prickly. Such false thought and will then go hereafter from life into the body, and into all its beings and work.

26. Thus, such a fiery, covetous, envious manner scatters and breaks all that is good with the sharp *sensus* of life. There is danger to everything with which it has to do, for it brings poisonous beams into it and seeks to draw everything to itself and bring in its poison, the hungry covetousness. However if it happens that this fiery life can eat of the divine love, then it is a similitude of how light presses out and goes from fire. So also the proper life presses out from the fiery manner, with a new spirit and will of divine love from within outward, and is no longer taking as is the manner of fire, but giving. The love-will gives itself, as light from a fire, to all things and works good in all.

27. If the sun no longer shone in the depths of the world, the *spiritus mundi* in the sharpness of the constellations, in the sulphuric, mercurical manner of the four elements, [would be] completely stern, raw, dry, harsh, thick, dark and hard. Then all life in the elements would die, and man would soon see what hell and God's wrath are.

28. So also in a similar way the external man is a *limus* of the external, elemental world. His body stands in the power of sun and stars, and the body, as the earth, is a *coagulation* of the *spiritus mundi*: If it were not able to have the sun's light-love-power in its food, in its *nutrimentum*, it would become completely evil, fiery and deadly, and external life would die.

29. So also in a similar way the soul is a *limus* of the internal, spiritual world out of the *Mysterium Magnum* as out

of an outgoing and counter-stroke of divine power and knowledge. Now if it cannot have the *Ens* of divine love for its food so that it breaks off from the abyss as from resignation, it too becomes sharp, fiery, dark, raw, prickly, envious, antagonistic, contrary and in itself complete restlessness and leads itself into a mortal, perishing and angry source, which is its damnation in which it dies, as happened to the devil, and as happens to all the godless.

30. However, if it [happens] that such a fire-source can again reach divine love, as the essential life of God, and take it into itself, such a fire-source of the soul will be changed into a kingdom of joy, into praise of God, but this is not possible without a changed will, which does not stop its *impression* and limitation. The sun's light cannot work in a hard stone as [it does] metals, in herbs and in trees, for water is grasped and coagulated into a hard *impression* in it.

31. So also it is to be understood with the false self-will of the soul with divine meekness. In such covetous, envious fire-desire the divine meekness does not work. This Christ properly says (John 6:53): The life of man that does not eat that bread which is come from heaven to give life to the world has no life in him. With this He points to the essential love that God revealed in Him by means of a new fountain-source for the revival of the poor dried-up soul. The soul that does not eat of it cannot reach the divine light and is without divine life, as He calls Himself in John 8:12: The light of the world. Again in the Psalms: A light that shines in the darkness and changes the darkness into light (Psalms 112:4).

Chapter Three

*Of the natural ground; how nature is a counter-stroke of divine
knowledge, through which the eternal (single) will, with the
ungrounded, supernatural knowledge, makes itself visible, perceptive, working and willing; what* Mysterium Magnum *is;
how all is through and in God; how God is so near all things and
fills all in all. A most precious gate for the careful consideration
of the God-loving reader.*

In John 1:1-3, it stands [written]: In the beginning was
the Word, and the Word was with God, and the Word was
God. The Same was in the beginning with God. All things
were made by Him; and without Him was not anything made
that was made.

1. The beginning of all being was the Word, as God's
breathing-forth, and from eternity God has been the Eternal
One and remains thus in eternity. But the Word is also the
flowing-out of the divine will or the divine knowledge. For
just as the thoughts flow out of the mind and the mind still
remains a unity, so also was the Eternal One present in the
outflow of the will. It says: In the beginning was the Word,
for the Word as the flowing-out from the will of God, was the
eternal beginning, and remains so eternally, for It is a revelation of the Eternal One, by which and through which divine
power is brought into a knowing of something. [We] understand by Word the revelation of the will of God, and by God
we understand the hidden God, as the Eternal One, out of
which the Word springs eternally.

2. Thus the outflow of the divine One is the Word, and
yet God Himself as His revelation.

3. This outflow flows out of God, and that which flows
out is wisdom, the beginning and the cause of all powers,
colours, virtues and characteristics.

4. Out of such revelation of powers into which the will
of the Eternal One looks flow out the understanding and

knowledge of the everything. The eternal will sees itself in the everything and in wisdom brings itself into a desire for likeness and like image.

5. This same likeness is the *Mysterium Magnum*, the Creator of all being and creatures, for it is the *Separator* of the will's outflow of which it makes the will of the Eternal One divisible. It is the divisibility of will out of which powers and characteristics arise.

6. These same powers are of an outflow of themselves in which each power leads itself into its own will against the same power's virtue. From this the manifoldness of the wills originates as well as the creaturely life of the eternal as of angels and souls takes its origin. No one can say that a nature or creature is understood in this, but [it is] a formation of divine Word and will where the Spirit of God has played in such a form of likeness with His self, in such a counter-stroke in the powers of wisdom.

7. Just as the mind of man in understanding with the senses leads itself into a counter-stroke of like image, and flows out with the same, and grasps itself in images, which images are the thoughts of the mind in which the will of the mind works, thus by desire it brings itself into sharpness, as into a magnetic attraction from which arises joy and sorrow.

8. So also we are to know from the eternal mind of perceptivity that the outgoing of the single will of God has led itself into divisibility through the Word. And divisibility has led itself into possessiveness, into its own lust and desire toward its own self-revelation, from unity into plurality.

9. Desire is the ground and beginning of the nature of the perceptivity of the self-will, for in it the separation of the unity is brought into possessiveness, out of which the separations of the wills are brought into perceptivity of self, in which the true, creaturely, perceptive, angelic soul-life is understood.

10. The will of the Eternal One is not perceptible, without inclination toward anything, for it has nothing to-

ward which it might tend, but only [toward] itself. Therefore it leads itself out of itself and brings the outflow of its unity into plurality and into a taking-on of self, as into a state of nature from which characteristics come. Each spiritual characteristic has its own *Separator*, divider and maker in it, and is complete in itself, according to the character of the eternal unity.

11. Thus the *Separator* of each will, will again bring characteristics out of itself from which the endless plurality rises and through which the Eternal One makes itself perceptible, not according to the unity but according to the outflow of the unity. Only the outflow brings itself so far into the greatest sharpness with the magnetic possessiveness, even into the fire-manner in which fiery manner the Eternal One becomes majestic and a light. The eternal power also becomes desiring and working by this and is [thus] the origin of perceptible life, for in the word of the powers, in the outflow, an eternal perceptible life originates. If life had no perceptivity, it would have neither willing nor working, but pain makes it working and willing. Light, such igniting through fire, makes it joyous, for it is an anointment of the painfulness.

12. Out of this eternal working of perceptivity and thought, which same working has from eternity thus brought itself into nature, as into characteristics, have arisen the visible world and its hosts [which] have been brought into creation. The eternity of such working to fire, light and darkness has led itself into a counter-stroke with the visible world, and ordained the *Separator* in all the powers of outflowing being to be the ruler of nature, with which the eternal will rules, makes, fashions and forms all things.

13. Thus can we in no way say that God's being is something distinct, that it possesses a special place or spot, for the abyss of nature and of creatures is God Himself.

14. The visible world that flowed out with its hosts of creatures is nothing other than the Word [that] flowed out, that led itself into characteristics, for in the characteristics,

self-will arose. With the possessiveness of the will creaturely life arose, which life, at the world's beginning, led itself into a possessiveness, to a creaturely [life] that the *Separator* divided according to characteristics, bringing it into self-will, according to such form. Thus now with the self-will of such a desire the existence, the body, came into being, for each possessiveness from its own likeness and characteristic, by which [means] the *Separator* signatured Himself and made [Himself] visible, as may be seen in all life.

15. In such a counter-stroke of the divine will, we are to understand two kinds of life: first, an eternal, and second, a temporal, mortal [life]. The eternal is in the Eternal and originates out of the eternal Word, and consists of the ground of the eternal, spiritual world, as in the *Mysterium Magnum* of the divine counter-stroke, and it is the sensible, understandable life at the ground of the eternal fire and light.

16. The innermost ground is a spark of the will of God that flowed out through God's breath. It is bound with God's Word to will nothing other than that which the single will of God wills in such outflow.

17. It is nothing other than a house of divine will through which the divine will reveals itself, and is revealed to no individuality of its own will but only as an instrument of the divine will by which the same orders His miracle. It is the *Separator* of the divine will as an instrument of God, in which the divine will has formed itself as a miracle worker of all might and majesty through which He wishes to rule all things. Because of this the divine understanding was also given to it.

18. The other life is a created outflow of the *Separator* of all powers, and it is called the soul of the external world. This life became creaturely in the outflowed characteristics and is the life of all creatures of the visible world by which the *Separator* or Creator of this world forms Itself and makes an image of the spiritual world in which the power of the inner spiritual world forms, images and sees itself.

19. For the spiritual world of fire, light and darkness stands hidden in the visible elemental world and works through the visible world and forms itself through the *Separator* with the outflow in all things, each according to its (kind and) characteristic. As each thing is of a kind and characteristic, so such characteristic receives this [quality] from the *Separator* from the internal spiritual power. The visible being does not receive the visible for possessiveness and its own might, so that the external may thus be changed into the internal. No, this is not so. The inner power forms itself only as we understand it in the power of plants, trees and metals. For the external spirit is only an instrument of this [internal power], as of the inner spirit, by which the inner power forms itself in the external spirit.

20. In such powers of growing things we understand three sorts of *spiritus* in distinct *centra*, but yet only in one *corpus*. The first and external *spiritus* is the rough sulphur, salt and *mercurius*, which is a being of the four elements or of the constellations, according to the stellar characteristic of the roughness. This makes the *corpus* and impresses or fashions itself into a being, or it draws the internal out of the spiritual *Separator* to itself, as well as the external elements from without, and it coagulates itself with them. From this the *signatur* or designation appears out of the *Separator*. The same [*signatur*] forms the visible *corpus*, according to the characteristic of the great power of the *spiritus mundi*, as the constellation of the stars or the characteristic of the planets and the ignited elements.

21. The second *spiritus*, which has its own *centrum*, lies in the oil of sulphur, which one calls the fifth essence as the root of the four elements. This is the softening and joy of the gross, painful, sulphur- and salt-spirit, and takes its *nutrimentum* first from within out of the light of nature, from the outflowing of divine meekness, from the internal spiritual fire and light. And secondly, it takes its *nutriment* externally from the sun, and from the subtle power of the *spiritus mundi*, and it

is the true cause of growing life, a joy of nature, as the sun is in the [four] elements.

22. The third spirit is the *tinctur*, as a counter-stroke of the diving *Mysterium Magnum*, in which all powers lie in equality and [it] is called proper Paradise or divine joy. It is a house of divine power, a house of the eternal soul, out of which all external power sprang in the same manner as air out of the fire.

23. For the *tinctur* is nothing other than a spiritual fire and light in which fire and light from a self (single) being [are] within it. But since it also has its *Separator* in it, as the divine will [that] flowed out to revelation, it is the highest ground out of which the first divisibility of characteristics in the being of this world originated, and according to its own characteristics it belongs to eternity. Its origin is the holy power of God and has its own *centrum* as the innermost ground of the creature, which is indeed hidden to the mortal creature because man has brought a false will against it. Because of this the curse of the earth arose in the fall of man. Yet this high, holy ground in its own *centrum* presses through all the being of this world and flows out into the external powers as the sun into the elements. The creature however cannot touch the *centrum* of this power unless it happens by divine permission or occurs in the new birth.

24. Such revelation one sees in all things living and growing. All things consist of these three *principia* or beginnings. You can see an example of this in a plant of the earth that has its *nutrimentum* from within and [from] without, as from [within] the earth and [as without] from the sun and stars, by which the earth's *spiritus* forms together with the external. When the same plant grows this occurs in such governance [that] this designates (signifies) itself externally in the form and image in the plant, the external *Separator* in sulphur, salt and mercury, for it is the plant's movement and perceptivity and makes itself corporeal.

25. Thus, when I see a plant, then I say truthfully: This is an image of the earth-spirit in which the upper powers rejoice, and they hold it to be their child, for the earth spirit is one being with the upper external powers. And when the plant is grown up, it blooms, and the oleous spirit designates itself by beautiful colours. And with the beautiful smell of the blossom, the *tinctur* designates itself as the third ground.

26. By this man understands that the internal hidden spirit of the elements has revealed itself, and leads itself into the formation of fruit. The earth would have no such smell, nor colours, nor such virtue, if the hidden power of the divine outflowing did not reveal itself.

27. So also it is to be seen with the metals, which externally are a gross *corpus* of sulphur, *mercurius* and salt in which their growth stands, and in their internal ground they are a beautifully transparent *corpus*, in which shines the formed light of nature from the divine outflow. In this lustre one is to understand the *tinctur* and great power, how the hidden power makes itself visible. One cannot say of such power that it is elemental, nor of the power of the blossom. The elements are only the house and counter-stroke of internal power, a cause of the movement of the *tinctur*.

28. The power goes out from the *tinctur* through the movement of the gross elemental spirit, and leads itself into perceptivity as into taste and smell.

29. Smell is nothing other than the perceptivity of the *tinctur* by which the outflow of divine power reveals itself, and thus takes on perceptivity. The sharpness of the smell is indeed elemental, but the true power and virtue, in the sharpness of the smell, is the *tinctur*. Movement of a thing is not the highest ground of power but that out of which the cause of movement comes.

30. The *medicus* uses a fragrant plant for his medication, but the smell, that is, the sharpness of the smell, is not the cure that heals the patient in sickness. Rather the cure is that

from which such balm or smell arises, the *tinctur*, which has formed itself into such a balm.

31. Christ says (Matthew 21:19) to the fig-tree: Wither; but the power by which it was done was not the external audible human word or sound. The power was that out of which the word came. If the external human sound had done it, other men could also do it.

32. Similarly, it is to be understood in faith. The confession or acceptance of a thing is not proper faith, much less [is] knowledge, but faith is that out of which the creed arises, as [it] is the revealed Spirit of God in the inner ground of the soul which by confession [of faith] forms itself into audible word, and makes itself externally visible, and works with the visible elements of the body, and points to itself externally so that man understands that God's Spirit works with it in works of faith even as He works with and through the power of the elemental world, and makes Himself visible through the world's being with a counter-stroke.

33. Thus I can truthfully say of everything that I look at, be it evil or good: Here in this thing the hidden spirit of the *Separator* of all being has formed himself into one characteristic and has made here a counter-stroke or image of itself according to its outflow, either according to evil or good, everything according to the characteristics of nature, according to heat or cold, according to harsh, bitter, sweet or sour, or however it may be. In all such formation externally, there is only such an elemental manner as in such sulphur and salt, but in the internal ground, in the *tinctur*, it is good and useful, and belongs to its likeness, for the *nutrimentum* of life, which according to the astral and elemental manners stands in all characteristics according to the external ground.

34. Each thing, be it plant, grass, tree, beast, bird, fish, worm or whatever it be, always is useful and has come from the *Separator* of all being, as from the word or separated will of

God, by which the *Separator* of each thing's characteristic has made a likeness or image in which it works.

35. For this visible world, with all its host and being, is nothing other than a counter-stroke of the spiritual world, which is hidden in the material, elemental [world] just as the *tinctur* [is] in plants and metals.

36. And just as the *tinctur* forms itself and by its *tinctur* makes itself visible in all things by its outflow so that one can see and know, by colours and smell, what kind of *Separator* was in the *tinctur*, or what kind of divine will flowed from the *Mysterium Magnum*; so also one can know in the visible world, in sun, stars, elements and creatures and creation, the internal ground out of which they sprang.

37. No thing, no being of a thing, came to its place from a distance; but in the place in which it grows is its proper ground. The elements have their cause in themselves out of which they sprang. So also the stars have their *chaos* in themselves of which they consist.

38. Elements are nothing other than formed, moving [being] of the invisible, unmoved [being].

39. So also stars are an outflow of the characteristics of the spiritual world, according to the divisibility of the *Separator*, whose ground is the Word, or the separated will of God.

40. The being and weaving together of the elements are fire, air, water and earth, in which are thick and thin, wet and dry, hard and soft. [These all] are set together in one being. [It is] not that they are from varied origins and sources, for they all come out of only one single ground. This same place from which they came is everywhere. Only think that at one place is greater ignition toward a characteristic than at another, from which the movement was greater and the matter was more in one form and being than in another. In the matter of the earth, as in water and air, so a separation is understood

in each *polus* as it is in each place over the earth. So [from this also it follows that there is] a separation of customs, virtues, dominions, orders and creatures.

41. However, the separations of such characteristics arose in the *Mysterium Magnum* by [means of] the one movement of the powers of all being, for therein the single will of all being moved itself once and led itself out of imperceptivity [and] into the perceptivity and divisibility of powers and made the eternal power working and willing, so that a counter-stroke arose in each power as a self-desire. This same self-desire in the counter-stroke of powers led itself again out of itself to another counter-stroke from which the desire of each outflow became sharp, austere and gross, and coagulated itself in matter.

42. As the outflow occurred out of the inner powers out of light and darkness, out of sharp and dull, out of fire and light, so the various forms of matter came. The further the outflow of a power has stretched itself, the more external and gross its *materia* become, for one counter-stroke came out of the other until finally [they resulted] in the gross earth.

43. We must, however, properly complete the ground of such *philosophia* and indicate from what hard and soft have taken their ground, which we see in the metals. Each *materia* that is hard, as are metals and stones, as well as wood, plants and the like, has in it a very noble *tinctur* and high spirit of power, as is also to be known in the bones of creatures. For the noblest *tinctur* as the greatest sweetness, according to the light's power, lies in the marrow of the bones and, on the contrary [there is] in the blood only a fiery *tinctur*, as in sulphur, salt and *mercurium*. This one understands as follows:

44. God is the Eternal One, as the greatest meekness, in so far as He exists in Himself outside of [His] movement and revelation. His movement, in which He is called the one God in Trinity as a three-in-one being, of which one speaks of

three and yet only of one, and in which He is called the eternal power and word, is the precious and highest ground. It is thus to be considered, how the divine will surrounds itself as to power in place of self, and works in itself, but goes out by its working and makes a counter-stroke of itself, as wisdom, by which the being, ground and origin of all things have sprung.

45. In like manner know this: All that in the being of this world is soft, mild and thin, that is, outflowing and giving of itself [in] its ground and origin, is according to the unity of eternity, for the unity always flows out from itself, as one understands that there is no perceptivity nor pain in the being of thinness, as in water and air, that this same essence is a unity in itself.

46. In what is hard and impressing, [such] as bones, wood, plants, metals, fire, earth, stones and similar materials, lies the image of divine power and movement, and it locks itself before the grossness with its *Separator* (as an outflow of divine desire) as a noble treasure or spark of divine power before grossness. Therefore, it is hard and fiery, because it has its ground of divine incomprehensibility, as where the Eternal One always leads itself into a ground of trinity for the movement of the powers and shuts itself up against the outflow, against the introduction of nature's own will and works, with the power of unity, through nature.

47. So also it is to be understood with the noble *tinctur*. Where it is the noblest, there it is the most surrounded with hardness, for its unity lies in a movement, as in a perceptivity of working and therefore it hides itself again. But in thinness it does not lie in such perceptivity, but it is the same in all things, as water and air are similar to all things and are in all things. However the dry water is the correct pearl-ground in which the subtle power of the working of the unity lies in the *centrum*. To those of us who are worthy of this it is here

indicated that we do not take to ourselves the soft without fiery manner to seek the mystery in it. Understand the mystery thus:

48. The soft and thin originated from the outflow of the unity, from the *Mysterium Magnum*, and is the nearest to the unity. On the other hand, *Mysterium Magnum*, the noblest ground of the divine revelation, lies in the power and working of the fiery hardness, and is a dry unity or *temperamentum* within which lies the divisibility of all powers. Where the powers do not lie in the unity of a will, there the will is divided and no great power is to be understood in the thing. This must be well noted by physicians, for they are not to look to the gross *spiritus* or strong smell, and hold it as the proper balsam. Even though it is truly in it the *tinctur* in it is very mobile and volatile.

49. The *spiritus* of the strong power in smell must be brought into the *temperamentum* as into the unity and not flee from it; for then one might wish to cure and give to the patient salt with the sharpness of fire, [or] soul without spirit.

50. The soul of such balsam is divided in the characteristics. Each gives itself especially in great joy, but in their separation they are too contrary-willed; they do not unify life's enmity and divisions, but they further ignite the division of life.

51. Enclose all of them and make them one, so that they all might have one will in love, and you have the pearl in the whole world. To provoke [them] to wrath makes pride and strife that are known in all things.

52. One can only comfort a prisoner by his freedom, until he puts his will in the hope, and grasps himself in patience. Finally, then, his restlessness goes into hope, into the *temperamentum*, and in such hope he learns humility. Then he rejoices when one tells him of his release.

53. So also, you physicians, note it. This is your pearl. If you understand this, the meaning is within and without.

Chapter Four

On the "in" and "out," how the eternal will of God brings itself outwards into perceptivity and inwards into the one again. So that man can understand to what end the being of this world was created, and what the use of the creaturely ground is; also for what purpose joy and sorrow have been revealed, and how God is close to all things.

1. In John 1:11-13 it stands: He (Jesus Christ) came to His own and His own received Him not. But as many as received Him, to them He gave strength to become God's children, even to them who believe on His name; who were born, not of blood, nor of the will of the flesh, nor of the will of man, but of God.

2. In these words the precise ground of divine revelation lies as the eternal "in" and "out." They speak of how the hidden, divine, eternal Word, the divine power in unity came to its own out into the "out-"flowing, natural, creaturely formed word as into human nature.

3. For the outflowing, formed, creaturely word is the eternally speaking Word's possession. By this is clearly indicated that "His own," the last formed self-will, did not receive [Him]. This formed self-will arose out of its own ground, out of the flesh and blood of its own nature of man and woman, that is in the *Separator* of the "out-"flowing will where the eternal will has locked itself up in its own and wishes to go "out" and will in its own power and might.

4. This did not receive the eternal Word that, as an outflow of divine grace, came again to the lost will because it wishes to be its own lord. To that will which has changed so that it has been newborn in the divine outflow, He has given strength to become God's child. The natural self-will cannot inherit divine sonship, but only this which, united to the unity, is like all things in which God Himself works and wills.

5. In this is clearly to be understood how the internal

ground has turned "out" and made itself visible, and is a possession of God, as an outflow of divine power and will.

NOTE: The precious gate was not further opened by the author, since he was prevented from completing this by the writings that followed. However, what the former editions of the *Mysterium Magnum* have included here belongs, in fact, to the *Clavis* or *Key of the Most Important Points*, and is to be found in Sections 137, 138 and 139 of that work.

THE EIGHTH TREATISE
CONVERSATION[1] BETWEEN AN ENLIGHTENED AND UNENLIGHTENED SOUL
(1624)

How an enlightened soul seeks and comforts the other and leads it along into its knowledge on the pilgrim path of Christ and faithfully is to set before its sight in a mirror the thorny way of this world which goes in the abyss and on which the lost soul wanders.

In an open letter to a soul hungering and thirsting for the fountain of the sweet love of Jesus Christ.[2] By a loving soul of the children of Jesus Christ under the cross of our Lord Jesus Christ.

1. A poor soul wandered out of Paradise and came into the kingdom of this world. The devil met it and spoke to it, "Where are you going, you half-blind soul?"

2. The soul said, "I wish to look upon the creatures of the world that the Creator has made."

3. The devil said, "How do you wish to look on them when you are not able to know out of what essence and characteristic they are made? When you see only a painted image, you are not able to know them."

4. The soul said, "How then can I know them in essence and being?"

5. The devil said, "If you eat of that out of which creatures are made good and evil, your eyes will be opened and you will be like God Himself, and know what the Creator is."

6. The soul said, "I am noble and holy and might die from that, as the Creator has said."

7. The devil said, "Nothing will kill you but your eyes will be opened and you will be as God is, and know good and evil. Moreover you will become mighty, strong and great, as I am. All of the subtleties of the creatures will be revealed to you."

8. The soul said, "If I had the knowledge of nature and creatures I would wish to rule the world."

9. The devil said, "The ground of such knowledge lies in you. Simply turn your will from God into nature and creatures, and a lust toward such tasting will rise in you. Then you can eat of the tree of the knowledge of good and evil; then you will know all things."

10. The soul said, "I shall eat of the knowledge of good and evil so that I might rule over all things in my own might and be my own lord on earth, and thus do what I wish as God Himself."

11. The devil said, "I am a prince of the world. If you wish to rule on earth you must lead your longing toward my image so that you gain the subtlety of my image." Then [the devil] set before the soul the *mercurius* in *vulcanus*, as the fire-wheel of essence, in a serpent-form.[3]

12. When the soul saw this, it said, "This is the might of all things. How may I be like this?"

13. The devil said, "You yourself are such a fiery *mercurius*. If you break your will off from God and direct your desire into this art, your hidden ground will be revealed in you, and you can also do this. But you must eat of such fruit in which the four elements each in itself rules over the other, in which they are in strife, as the cold against the heat and the heat against the cold. Since all characteristics of nature work by perceptivity, you will be immediately like the fire-wheel, bringing all things into your own governance, and possess them as your own."

14. Now when the soul broke its will off from God and directed its desire into the *vulcanus* of *mercurius* (into the fire-wheel, into the self-ability of the mind)[4] there immediately rose up in it the lust to eat of the knowledge of evil and good. It grasped the fruit of the knowledge of good and evil, and ate of it.

15. When this occurred *vulcanus* ignited the fire-wheel of the essence, and awoke all the natural characteristics of the soul and brought it into its own lust and desire. Then arose first the lust for pride to be mighty, great and dominant, to subjugate all things to itself, and to rule with control. It wished to be its own lord, so that nothing might compare with it. It despised humility and equality, considered only itself subtle, wise and clever, and held all as foolishness that did not compare with its own subtlety.

16. Secondly, there arose [in it] a lust for possessiveness, as covetousness, which wished to draw to it and to possess everything. Since the lost lust of pride had turned its will off from God, its life no longer trusted God, but wished to take care of itself, and led its desire and possessiveness[5] to the creatures and to the earth, to metals and trees.

17. Thus the ignited *mercurius* became hungry and covetous, like a fiery life, after it broke from God's unity, love and meekness and drew to itself the four elements and their being and led its self into bestiality in which life was dark, empty, angry, and the heavenly powers and colours were put out.

18. Thirdly, the fiery life awakened a thorny and hostile lust that was envy, as a hellish poison, the source of all devils, from which life became an enemy of God and all creatures. It raged and stormed in the covetous desire as a poison in the flesh. Whatever covetousness was not able to draw to itself, envy wished to murder. Because of this, the noble love of the soul was completely brought low.

19. Fourthly, there awoke in this fiery life a source like to fire. This was wrath that wished to murder and kill what did not wish to be subject to this pride.

20. Thus hell's foundation, a foundation called the wrath of God, was completely revealed in this soul and through it the soul lost God, Paradise and the kingdom of

heaven, and became a worm just like the fiery serpent that the devil had set before it in his image, and [the soul] began to rule on earth in a bestial manner, and did everything according to the will of the devil, lived in idle pride, covetousness, envy and wrath, and had no longer proper love for God; rather, in its place there rose up a false, bestial love for unchastity and vanity and there was no longer purity in [its] heart because it left Paradise and possessed the earth. It directed its mind only to art, subtlety, haughtiness and the multitude of natural things. Neither righteousness nor divine virtue remained in it. Whatever evil it was always doing, it covered with cunning by its domination and called it "justice."

21. When this had occurred the devil drew near to the soul and led it from one vice to another, for he held it captive in its essence (or, for it had imprisoned itself in his essence) and he placed before it joys and pleasure and said to it, "See you are now dominant, mighty, high and noble. See that you will become greater, richer and still more dominant. Use your art and subtlety so that everyone fears you and you will have respect and a great name in the world."

22. The soul did as the devil suggested and did not know thas he was the devil, but thought that it was guided by its own subtlety and reason and that it acted well and properly.

23. Now when it ran in this condition it was met by our Lord Jesus Christ, with God's love and wrath, who came into this world to bring to nothing the work of the devil, to bring judgement over all godless acts. He spoke into it as with great power out of his suffering, passion and death, and smashed the devil's work in it and opened the way for it to His grace, and He looked on it with His compassion and called it back again to be converted and repentant, because He wished to redeem it from such a spectre-like image, and to lead it back again into Paradise.

24. When it happened that the spark of divine light was

revealed in it, it saw itself both in its work and will and was aware that it stood in the hell of God's wrath and knew that it was a spectre and *monstrum* before God and the kingdom of heaven. It was so terrified at this that the greatest anguish awoke in it, because the Judgement of God was revealed in it.

25. When this occurred the Lord Jesus Christ spoke with His gracious voice into the soul, "Repent, and leave vanity and you will come to my grace."

26. The soul approached God in its spectre-like image, in its dirtied cloak of vanity, and prayed to Him for grace [that] God might forgive its sin. It considered the satisfaction and redemption of our Lord Jesus Christ.

27. But the evil characteristics of the serpent formed in the astral spirit did not wish to allow the soul's will [to remain] before God, but led its own lust and desire into it since it did not wish to die to its lust or leave the world because these were from the world. They also feared the world's scorn if they abandoned worldly honour and majesty. But the poor soul turned its face to God and desired grace from God so that God would give it his love.

28. When the devil saw that the soul prayed to God and wished to repent, he went to the soul and led the inclination toward earthly characteristics into its prayer and confused the good intentions that pressed toward God so that they might not come to God, and drew them back to earthly things. The soul's will groaned for God but the outgoing senses that were to press into God were scattered and were not able to reach the power of God.

29. This frightened the poor soul still more in that it could not bring its desire to God, [so it] began to pray more strongly. But the devil in his desire grasped the mercurially ignited fire-wheel of life and awakened the evil characteristics so that false inclinations rose up and went in where they had earlier found happiness.

30. The poor soul wished [to go] to God with its will,

and was in much anguish, but its thoughts all fled from God to earthly things, and did not want to go to God. The soul groaned and cried to God, but it [appeared] to it that it had been completely cast out from before God's face, [as if] it could not gain one glance of grace, and stood in vain anguish as well as in great fear and dread. It constantly felt that God's wrath and stern judgement would be revealed in it, and that the devil would grasp it. Thus it fell into great sadness and misery, so that the joy and temporal pleasure of things pursued earlier became troublesome and boring.

31. The earthly, natural will certainly desired these things, but the soul eagerly wished to forsake them and desired to die to all temporal lust and joys, yearned only to the first fatherland from which it originally came, yet it found itself far away from it, in great rejection and misery, and it did not know what it was to do. It thought that it would enter into itself to pray more fervently, but the devil came again to it and held it so that it[6] might not enter greater inclination and repentance.

32. The devil awoke earthly lust in its heart so that these inclinations upheld their false natural rights and defended themselves against the soul's will and desires because they did not wish to die to their own will and lust but to keep their temporal pleasure and they held the poor soul captive in their false desire so that it could not awaken itself no matter how much it groaned and sighed for God's grace.

33. When the soul prayed and pressed into God the fleshly lust took the beams that reached out from the soul into themselves and directed its thoughts to earthly matters and away from God so that the soul could not gain divine power. Then it appeared to the soul that it had been rejected by God and did not know that God thus drew it and was near to it.

34. The devil came to it in the fiery *mercurius*, or the fire-wheel of life, and mixed his own desire into the earthly lust of the flesh and he mocked the poor soul and spoke in

earthly thoughts to it: "Why do you pray? Do you think that God hears and wants you? Look at yourself. What kind of thoughts do you have before Him? You have vain evil thoughts and have no faith in God. How is God to hear you? He does not hear you. Bring it to an end. It is not good: You will lose your senses.

35. "What are you troubling yourself over? Look at the world how it lives in joy. It will also be holy. Has Christ not paid and made satisfaction for all men? You need only to comfort yourself [knowing] that this has happened, and you will be holy. You cannot come to divine perceptivity here in this world. Stop this, and enjoy your body and temporal majesty.

36. "What do you think would become of you if you became so melancholy and foolish? You would become everyone's fool, and live in vain sorrow that pleases neither God nor nature. Look at the beautiful world in which God placed you and made you lord over all creatures to rule them. Gather now temporal things for yourself so that you will not need the world anymore. Then when old age and the end arrive you can turn to repentance. God will soon make you holy and take you into heaven. It will not require such torment, arousal and grief as you now undergo."

37. In these and similar thoughts the soul was held by the devil in fleshly lust and earthly will, as if bound with great chains, and it did not know what to do. It thought back somewhat on the world and its pleasure, and yet found in itself great hunger for divine grace, and it would continually and eagerly have repented and come to God's clemency because the hand of God had stirred it and shattered it. Therefore it could find rest nowhere but groaned continually in itself because of regret for past sins and eagerly wished to be free of them, but it could not come to proper true regret, much less to a knowledge of sin, and stood in hunger and desire for regret and repentance.

38. Now when it stood in such sadness and could find no counsel or peace, it wondered where it could find a place free from the hindrances of the world and its works where it might repent properly and by what means it might gain God's grace. For this reason it decided to take itself to a private place and turn away from the [world's] work. It also thought that God would be gracious to it if it busied itself with good deeds to the poor and it sought every way to find its rest, whereby it might come to clemency and grace.

39. But it did not wish to bend everything and allow it to come to clemency since all its earthly works in the lust of the flesh followed it and it was just as before, caught in the devil's net and could not come to rest. Though it might be happy with earthly things for one hour, the next hour it was sad and miserable again, for it felt the aroused anger of God in it and did not understand what had come about or how it had happened. Often great anguish and temptation fell on it so that it could not receive any comfort, and was[7] ill because of anguish.

40. Thus the shattering beam of the first seizure of grace stirred it. It did not know that Christ stood in its hell in God's wrath and stern judgement and fought body and soul against the Satan and the false spirit. It did not understand that such a hunger and thirst for repentance and conversion came from Christ Himself, that it might be thus drawn [to Him]. Neither did it understand what was yet lacking so that it was not able to come to the reception of God. It did not understand that it was monstrous and carried the serpent-image of itself in which the devil had such domination over it and access to it, in which its good intentions were twisted and led away from God. Of this Christ said: The devil tears the word from their hearts lest they believe and be saved (Luke 8:12).

41. By the providence of God an enlightened and reborn soul met this poor, distressed soul, and said to it, "What is the matter, distressed soul? Why are you so restless and in such turmoil?"

42. The distressed soul said: "The Creator has hidden His face from me so that I cannot come to His rest. Therefore I am so miserable and do not know what I am to do to attain His clemency, for between me and His clemency lie mountains and great clefts so that I cannot come to Him, no matter how much I long for Him. I am still held so that I cannot reach His power, even though anxiously I wait for Him with passionate yearning."

43. The enlightened soul replied: "You bear the devil's spectre-like image that looks like a serpent. By it you are surrounded, and through it, as your characteristic, the devil has access to you and holds back your will so that it cannot press into God. Otherwise, if it were to happen that your will were to press into God, it would be anointed with the highest power of God in the resurrection of our Lord Jesus Christ. If this anointment were to break the *monstrum* in you, you and your first paradisaical image would be revealed in you, then the devil would lose his might in you. You would again be an angel. Since the devil does not wish you to have this, he holds the lust of your flesh captive in his desire. If you are not freed from this, you will be separated from God and never come into your own community."

44. The poor distressed soul was so frightened by this speech that it was unable to utter one word more when it heard that it carried the serpent's image in itself and that that separated it from God, and that the devil was so near it, and confused its will with false thoughts and that he had control over it. It understood that damnation was near, that it stood in the abyss of hell, imprisoned in God's wrath, and would have despaired of God's grace.

45. But the power of its shattering kept it from despair and it writhed within itself between hope and doubt. What hope raised up doubt tore down. [The soul] stood in constant restlessness so that finally the world and its beauty became vanity (loathsomeness)[8] and it did not wish to make use of the joys of the world and yet it could still not come to rest.

46. On another occasion the enlightened soul came again to it, and found it in such anguish and said to it: "What are you doing? Do you want to burst yourself in your anguish? Why torment yourself with your own abilities and will? You are but a worm and through this your torment only is greater. Yes, if you might sink to the depth of the sea, or might fly to the dawn and soar beyond the stars, you could not be free of it. The more you are anxious, the greater and more painful will be your nature, and you will not come to rest. Your ability is completely gone, even as a dry twig cannot gain sap and sprout by its own ability so that it might enjoy itself again among the trees, likewise you cannot reach God by your own abilities; you cannot change yourself into your first angelic form, for you are dry and dead to God as a twig without life or sap. You are only an anxious and dry hunger. Your characteristics are like heat and cold that always oppose one another and never are united."

47. The poor soul said, "What shall I do that I may sprout forth again and come to my first life which I had in peace before I became an image?"

48. The enlightened soul said: "You shall do nothing but leave your own will's possessiveness. Then your evil characteristics will weaken and begin to die, and you will sink your own will back into the One out of which you came in the beginning. You now lie captive in the creature. When your will forsakes this, the creatures that presently keep you from coming to God with their evil inclination will die in you.

49. "If you do this God will send you His highest love that He revealed to the humanity in Jesus Christ. This will give sap and life to you again, so that you can sprout forth again and rejoice again with the living things of God. You will also receive again the image of God and be free of this serpent image. Then you will join our angelic hosts and become my brother."

50. The poor soul said: "How am I to leave my own will

so that the creature dies in it? I live in the world and must have the world."

51. The enlightened soul said: "Now you look to worldly honour and goods, as well as to the pleasure of the flesh as your possessions, and you do not care what you do with them or how you draw them to yourself. If you see a wretched one suffer need, you do not help him even if he is your brother, but you put him in bonds and torment him. You make him work and suffer for you, and you even rejoice in this. In addition you are proud and haughty and hold yourself better than he and consider him small beside yourself.

52. "Thus the wretched one stands and sighs before God that his labour is forced from him and that, beside you, he must live in misery. With his sighs he thus awakens God's wrath in you which continually increases your flames and your unrest.

53. "These now are the creatures you love for whose sakes you have broken yourself off from God and directed your love to them. Thus they live in your love and you feed them with your desire and continual possessiveness. They live in your possessiveness and you bring your life's lust into them and they are only unclean, evil beasts who have formed themselves with you by your possessiveness.

54. "And that image is a beast with four inclinations: The first is pride; the second, covetousness; the third, envy; and the fourth, wrath. In these four characteristics the foundation of hell is based. They are pressed on you and in you and you carry them; you are completely captured by them. These characteristics live in your own life and by this you are separated from God and cannot come to Him unless you leave these evil creatures so that they die in you.

55. "But you say that I am to tell you how you are to leave your own creaturely, evil will so that such creatures might die, yet you still wish to live with them in the world. I

tell you that there is no more than one single way, a narrow and small one. In the beginning it will be very difficult for you to travel it. Later you will go on it with joy.

56. "You must consider properly that you are to go in the walk before the world in God's wrath and in the foundation of hell, that this is not your proper fatherland and that a Christian should and must live and move in Christ, and properly follow Christ; and that he cannot be a Christian unless the spirit and power of Christ live in him, so that he surrenders himself completely to Him.

57. "Now Christ's kingdom is not of this world, but in heaven. Therefore you must be in continual ascension if you wish to imitate Christ properly, even though your body must be among the creatures and must attend to them.

58. "The narrow way of such continual ascension and imitation of Christ is this: You must despair of all of your own capabilities and possibilities for by your own power you cannot reach the gateway of God. You must clearly decide to give yourself up completely to the mercy of God and firmly form in yourself the suffering and death of our Lord Jesus Christ. With all your reason and senses you must sink yourself down into Him, persevere in Him, and desire to die therein to your creatures.

59. "Moreover, you must very clearly intend to turn your longing and mind from every false possessiveness, and not allow yourself to be held by temporal honour and goods. You must cast all unrighteousness that might hinder you out of your way. Your will must be completely pure and directed to such an earnest resolution that never again will you enter into your false creatures but will leave them instantly and separate your mind from them: also[9] that you will immediately walk on the pure paths of truth and righteousness and follow the teachings of Christ.

60. "And even as you are now considering how to abandon the enemies of your own nature, you yourself must also

forgive your own external enemies and endeavour to lead them to your love so that no creature anywhere exists that might seize and hold your will, but that [your will] will be pure of every creature.

61. "Moreover, so that this might take place, you must eagerly leave your temporal honour and goods for Christ's sake, and not take to yourself[10] an earthly thing to love it but consider yourself in your position and worldly honour and goods only to be the servant of God and of your fellow Christians, a householder of God in your office. The haughty eyes of one's own love must be broken and bled so that no creature might be in them that can lead the senses into images.

62. "In addition, you must firmly consider that you will certainly receive the promised grace in the merit of Jesus Christ as His outflowing love, which will redeem you from the creatures and enlighten your mind, and ignite it with love's fires by means of which you will have victory over the devil.

63. "Not that you can or wish to do anything, but you are to consider the suffering and resurrection of Christ and see it as your own. By this means the devil's kingdom in you will be stormed and broken and your creatures will be killed. You are to resolve to enter this hour into Christ's passion and never more turn from it, but to give your will in all beginnings and acts to God so that He might work and do within you whatever He will.

64. "If your will and resolution are thus prepared it has broken through your creatures and stands purely before God, wrapped in the merits of Christ. Now it can come before the Father with the prodigal son, fall down before His face, pour out its repentance before Him, give all its strength to this work, and not with empty words confess its sin, disobedience and its turning from God, but [repent] with all its might. This is nothing more than a firm resolution, however, for the soul can do nothing by itself.

65. "When you are thus prepared so that the eternal Father can see your arrival, that you are coming to Him again in such humility, then He will speak into you and say: 'Behold. This is my son whom I had lost, who was dead, and is living again.' And He will come to you with the grace and love of Jesus Christ, embrace you with the beam of love, kiss you with His spirit of power. Then you will receive power to pour out your confession before Him and to pray powerfully.

66. "Here now is the right place for you to wrestle before the divine face. If you remain firm, if you do not bend, you shall see and perceive great wonders. You will discover how Christ will storm the hell in you and will break your beasts, what a great tumult and misery will arise within you, and how at first your unknown sin will rise up in you, and will wish to separate you and hold you back from God. Then you will properly discover how life and death strive with one another and also you will discover what heaven and hell are.

67. "In this you must not harm yourself, but remain firm, without deviation. Then all your evil beasts will become feeble and weak, and begin to die. Then your will will become more powerful and be able to overcome evil inclinations. Then will your will and mind daily go to heaven, and your creatures daily die and you will be changed into the image of God and lose the spectre-image of the bestial manner. Thus you will come to rest again and be redeemed from your anguish."

68. Now, as the poor soul began this way and custom and gained such earnestness, it believed that it would quickly triumph. But the heavenly gates were closed to its powers and abilities just as if it had been held back by God; and it did not gain a glimpse of grace. Then it thought to itself, "You have not given yourself wholly to God. You must not desire or wish for anything from God, but only to give yourself to His judgement so that He may kill your evil possessiveness. You must sink yourself into Him to the ground outside of nature

and creature and give yourself to Him to do with as He wills, for you are not worthy of speaking to Him." Thus it boldly decided to sink to Him and to leave its own will completely.

69. And when it did this, the greatest regret came to it for past sins and it bitterly wailed over its disfigurement and the fact that creatures lived in it and that it might not speak before God unless it saw in such regret the bitter suffering and death of our Lord Jesus Christ, who has suffered such great anguish and torment for its sake so that He might redeem it from such anguish and torment and need and change it back into the image of God. In this it sank wholly and completely and began to cry out over its ignorance and negligence in that it had not thanked Him for it, and never considered such great love, and had passed its time evilly and had not perceived how it might have partaken in such grace, but, with its vain lust of this world, had formed itself in earthly things out of which it received bestial inclinations and now lay captive in misery. It dared not lift its eyes for shame to God who hid His face of power from it and would not look on it.

70. And as it stood in such groans and tears it was drawn to the abyss of horror as if it stood before hell's gates and was to perish immediately. It was as if it went without any sense and was now completely forsaken, had forgotten all its acts and beings, and were to give itself wholly to death and no longer be a creature. Thus, it gave itself to death and wished for nothing else than to die and enter into the death of its Redeemer Jesus Christ, who had suffered such great torment for it, and even died for it. However in such concern it began to sigh inwardly and to cry to the mercy of God. And then it began to sink itself into the purest mercy of God.

71. When this occurred the friendly face of the love of God appeared to it and penetrated through it like a great light. Because of this it trembled and was joyous and began to pray properly and to thank the Highest God for such grace and to

rejoice inwardly because it was redeemed from the death and anguish of hell.

72. Then it tasted the sweetness of God and His promised truth and all evil spirits that had earlier plagued it and kept it from God's grace had to cease and turn from it. The marriage of the lamb took place and the betrothal of the noble Sophia with the soul and the signet ring of the victory of Christ was pressed in its essence and it was taken again as a child and heir of God.

73. When this occurred the soul was joyous and began to work in such power and to praise the wonders of God and believed that it now would continually go in such power and joy. But from the world it received scorn and reproach externally and great temptations internally so that it began to doubt whether its ground was from God and whether it really had gained the grace of God.

74. Then the slanderer came to it and wanted to destroy this way for it and lead it into doubt and said to it: "It is not from God. It was only your idea."

75. The divine light also grew faint and only glimmered in the internal ground as a mould-fire so that reason saw itself as foolish and abandoned. It did not know how this happened, or if it was really true that it had tasted of the divine light of grace; yet it could not stop from [thinking] this.

76. The fire-burning love of God was sown in it out of which there stood forth in it a great hunger and thirst for God's divine sweetness and it began to pray in earnest, to humble itself before God, and to test its evil inclinations in thoughts and cast them out.

77. In this way the reason of its will was broken and the evil inherited inclinations were more and more killed and this caused much pain to the nature of the body making it weak and sick, yet [this was] not a natural illness but a melancholy of the earthly nature of the body. Thus the false lusts were broken.

78. When earthly reason found itself thus abandoned and the poor soul saw that it was outwardly despised by the scorn of the world that it no longer wanted to walk in a godless way, and that it was inwardly grasped by the slanderer who mocked it and continually set before it the world's wealth, beauty and majesty and counted it a fool, it thought: "O eternal God, what shall I do to gain rest?"

79. In the midst of such thoughts the enlightened soul met it and said to it: "What is the matter, my brother, that you are so sad?"

80. The[11] soul said, "I have followed your counsel and received a glimpse of divine sweetness but it has gone from me again and now I am abandoned and in great temptation. Externally before[12] the world all my fine friends abandon me and scorn me. Inwardly also I am attacked with anguish and doubt and do not know what I am to do."

81. The enlightened soul said, "You are now most pleasing to me. Our dear Lord Christ goes with you on your pilgrim's path on earth, as He did when He was in this world. He too was continually reviled and He had nothing of His own. Now you bear His mark. Do not wonder at this for it must be so if you are to be protected and purified.

82. "In such sorrow you will often have reason to pray and hunger for redemption. By such hunger and thirst you will draw grace to yourself, both within and without.

83. "You must grow again into the image of God both from above and from below, as a young tree is moved by the wind and must stand in heat and cold, and in such turmoil draws its power to itself above and below and must endure many wind storms and stand in great danger before it can become a tree that bears fruit. In such turmoil the sun's power moves in it, the wild characteristics of the tree are pressed through and tinctured by the sun's power and by this the tree grows.

84. "Now you must first test your knightly struggle in

the spirit of Christ and work with Him. Then at once the eternal Father will beget His Son in you by His fire-might, who in you changes His fire into a flame of love, so that the fire and light become only one being that is a true temple of God.

85. "Now you are to sprout forth in the vineyard of Christ on the vine of Christ and bear fruit with doctrine and life, and as a good fruit-bearing tree demonstrate your love fruitfully. Thus Paradise must sprout again in you against God's wrath, and change hell to heaven in you.

86. "Therefore do not let the temptations of the devil cause you to err for he strives for the kingdom he once had within you. If he loses he will stand in shame and then must altogether leave you. Therefore he covers you eternally with the world's scorn so that his shame is not known and that you might remain hidden from the world.

87. "With your new birth you stand in heaven in the divine harmony. Be patient, therefore, and wait on the Lord. Whatever happens to you, think only that it comes from the Lord for your improvement." Then the enlightened soul departed from it.

88. This distressed soul now began its walk under the patience of Christ and entered into hope in divine trust. Day by day it grew mightier and more powerful and died more and more to its evil inclinations until finally it was placed in a great kingdom of grace and the gate of divine revelation was opened and the kingdom of heaven revealed to it.

89. Thus it came again to proper rest and was again a child of God. To this God help us all. Amen.

THE NINTH TREATISE
CONSOLATION TREATISE
ON
THE FOUR HUMOURS
(Written on request in March 1624)

That is, a guide in time of temptation for a heart continually attacked by melancholy; on the natural origin and cause of melancholy; how the temptation occurs. Including his words of consolation, [which are] very useful for hearts and souls under attack.

On the Cause of Fear or Melancholy, and What Terror or Anguish Is

1. All melancholy and fear under which man is terrorized and frightened is from the soul. The external spirit is not terrorized by the constellations and elements, since it lives in its mother who bore it. The poor soul, however, entered with Adam into a strange lodging, namely into the spirit of this world. There the beautiful creature is covered over and held in a dark prison.

2. The spirit of this world has four lodgings, in which the noble treasure is trapped. Each of these four and not all four [at once] is especially revealed in a man according to the four elements that each man has in him; and he is himself that same being. The soul is not the same being although it has been trapped in the same being. Yet only one lodging or form among the four has chief dominion over life. These four are called (1) choleric, (2) sanguine, (3) phlegmatic and (4) melancholic.

3. Firstly [the] choleric [humour] is the fire's nature and characteristic. It gives great courage, sudden anger, ascent of pride, self-centeredness [and] the refusal to seek advice. This form appears externally in a fiery light. It works according to

the power of the sun and always wishes eagerly to be lord.

4. Secondly, [the] sanguine [humour] is the air, subtle, friendly, joyous, yet not of great courage, changeable, easily turned from one thing to another; [it] naturally receives the characteristic and subtlety of the stars into its own essence, is chaste and pure and brings great secrecy in its knowledge.

5. Thirdly, [the] phlegmatic [humour] is according to the nature and characteristic of water, fleshly, gross and soft, of feminine will; [it] easily accepts, but holds fast what it receives. Art must be brought into it by shouting and teaching. It does not find itself in its root. It lets good be, does not make itself said, has a gleam of light, is not melancholy nor highly joyous but is light and the same [to all].

6. Fourthly, [the] melancholic [humour], the nature and characteristic of the earth [is] as the earth, cold, numb, dark, melancholy and hungry for light, ever in fear before God's wrath.

7. The earth and stones are grasped outside of eternal being, that is, in the ignited desire, in the *fiat* toward the wrath, also toward love's characteristic. Evil and good are mixed with one another. The good always has fear before the evil; it is a continual fleeing. The good always wishes to flee from the evil as is to be seen in metal whose *tinctur* is good but [the whole in which it is to be found] is completely earthly, evil and angry. The *tinctur* of metal always wishes to flee from the earthly, particularly if an evil constellation stirs it and wishes it [to go] out of the *centrum*. As a result metals grow, since their *tinctur* drives their desire out of themselves and desires to flee, but grasps in the desire such a lovely being as the spirit or the desire is; from this the metallic body arises.

8. Melancholic nature is dark and dry, gives little being, eats itself in itself, and always remains in a house of sadness. If the sun suddenly shines on it, it is still melancholy in itself although it receives from the sun's brightness some revival. However, in the darkness, it is always in fear and terror before God's judgement.

Here Note a Melancholy Mind

9. If one of these humours has the upper hand in man so that he is shaped in it, the poor soul, the noble treasure, stands in this house and must help itself with the sun's glance at this time (if it does not completely reach God's light in it), since the divine light's eye was locked from it in Adam in earthly torment (into which it went). In Adam the soul abandoned the external humour in itself as the spirit of the great world, of the stars and of the elements.

10. At this time one thing dwells in the other, the soul in the humours and they in the soul, but one thing does not grasp the other in essence. The soul is deeper than the external spirit but at this time they hang onto one another as the internal and external world, although neither is the other there. So also the external spirit is not the soul.

11. Know further: In its substance the soul is a magical fire-source, out of God the Father's nature, a great desire for light, even as God the Father desires his heart, as the light's *centrum*, in great desire from eternity, and brings [it] forth in his desiring will out of the fire's characteristic as light is born out of the fire.

12. However, there cannot be any fire unless the root for fire is also present as the *centrum* or form for nature that the soul also has in itself and burns out of the forms for nature as out of the dark world. This [world] drives itself in the source of its desire to the fire since it desires its freedom as light, as is explained in the book *On the Threefold Life*.

13. Since the soul is now a hungering magical spirit fire, it desires spiritual being as power by which it can keep its fire-life and soften the fire-source.

14. Now, it knows well how it lost itself in Adam by disobedience in the spirit of this world and ate from the spirit of the external world. For this reason, then, Christ became a man in our essence so that He might turn it again by the *centrum* and by the fire of God into the light as into the world

of meekness. This has now thus occurred in the person of Christ.

15. However, since our soul stands thus turned from the mother body in the spirit of the great world, in the humours, it eats immediately from the mother body (indeed in the mother) from the spirit of this world.

16. The soul eats spiritual food, namely from the spirit of the form of the humours, not wholly of the same essence but magically. It is its fire-ignition. The humour becomes in the soul's fire soul. It is as wood and fire against each other (understand by "wood" humour and by "fire" the soul) where the fire must still have the wood, that is, either the external humour or a divine being from God's being. From the one it must eat or die for no death is possible in it since it is a desire. Where desire now is, there also is being. Desire for itself makes being.

17. Now we understand why there is such a difference between men in willing and acting. What the soul eats, in which its fire-life is ignited, the soul-life brings its dominion over. If the soul turns out of its humour into God's love-fire in heavenly being, which is Christ's corporeality according to the angelic light-world, it eats of Christ's flesh, understood: heavenly, as His eternal being from the meekness, from the light of majesty in which the fire of God makes a *tinctur* in the brightness, in the same being as in the water-source of eternal life. Concerning this Christ said that He wishes to give us such water to drink [John 4:10-11]. From it the soul-fire eats as from divine heavenly being that is changed in the *tinctur* into heavenly blood, understood spiritually. From this the soul receives divine will and leads the body into compulsion to do what it does not eagerly wish to do according to its own form and [according to] the spirit of this world. The humours must not rule in the soul but only stand in the being of flesh and direct the fleshly dominion as regards the external body. Man seeks for God's Word and always has a continual desire

for God. His desire is always to speak about God. He always eagerly wishes to taste more of God's sweetness but he is hindered and covered by the humour so that a continual strife remains in him.

18. The soul strives against the humour since they [soul and humour] are now in one bond. The humour strives against the soul. It always eagerly wishes [to go] into the soul-fire and to ignite itself so that it might live properly. For when the soul eats of God's Word, the humour for the external life is as if impotent and captive where it still lives in itself.

19. The soul is so faithful to God's love, however, which alone comes into its being for help, and often (if it eats of God's love-being) brings a triumph and divine taste into the humour from which it becomes trembling and highly joyous. It awakens the whole body as if Paradise were at hand but it does not always have stability. The soul is immediately covered with something else (which falls in the humour and leads the external *imagination* from the spirit of the great world into the humour). From this it receives a mirror and raises it to reflect in it. Thus it goes out from the Spirit of God and is often dirtied in mire, if the Virgin of divine wisdom does not call it to turn again. This is set before in a mirror.

Further Concerning the Humours

20. If the soul makes an image in the humour and eats from it, and turns itself from God's word and will, it acts according to the humour's characteristic. It takes in everything that was thrown into the humour by the constellation, everything that the spirit of the great world brought into the humour with its *imagination*. It falls in love through the desire in the humour with all external being with all that the world does in words and works. This leads the desire of the humour into the soul-fire. In it the soul-fire burns.

21. Here one discovers how all evil deeds and works

burn in the fire of God the Father (in which the soul stands). Whatever is now not similar to the love of God cannot now receive the love. Here one discovers what and how sin is, how God is angered if such abomination as man does is brought before Him with the soul's burning or life. This holds the soul from God's love and the soul's fire stands blind before God's wisdom and light.

22. God's Spirit does not go into the fire's burning or [into] the life of abomination. When the soul goes out again and bathes itself again in the water of external life which occurs through earnest repentance, it is renewed again in the fire of the meekness of God and in the Holy Spirit as a new child, and begins again to drink from the same water and live with God.

Now Concerning the Four Humours with Their Characteristics

What does the soul and the whole man do, if the soul ignites its fire-life naked before the humours and naked before the constellations?

I. *Choleric Humour according to the Fire*

23. If the soul is wrapped with the choleric humour it is fiery, angry, pompous and destructive [and] gives itself such a body that is lean, evil, angry and wrathful. If the soul images [itself] in it, [and] ignites the humour yet more since it is also fiery, then wrath, pride, the desire for position in might and splendor enter the man to subject all to itself. Scorn of the wretched, domination over the bended knee, not noting whether it remains dead in wrath—[all these] enter man then, unless it happens that the constellation hinders it. With the union of the humour this often makes opposition and hinders much.

24. There is great danger in [this] humour if the soul lives in external *imagination*. It has a strong band if the one fire-source is bound to the other.

25. The angry devil has a powerful entrance to it for the fire's characteristic serves him. He is also proud and envious; so is the humour. O how difficult [it is for] the soul [to become] free, if it is properly ignited in this characteristic. Then the devil need not tempt it [for] it goes completely willingly according to his fiddle. It is not easily melancholy for it has a fire-light in the humour and it always thinks it is God's light, that it is on the good way. Yet it is a proud, envious, wrathful, dominant, low will and spirit as long as the soul alone helps the humour. O, it gives gladly a glittering appearance in its splendour out of its fire's humour and appearance. In its great pride and pompousness, it wishes also to be considered holy. O devil in angel's form, how dark you are, when the humour breaks in death.

II. *Sanguine Humour according to the Air*

26. [The] sanguine humour is soft, light and joyous. According to the air's characteristic it is sensual, soft and loving; it likens itself to life.

27. If the soul is wrapped with this humour and images [itself] in it and wishes to live accordingly, it shows itself friendly, artful, wishes to experience much, receives much. Everything that the constellation makes, it receives in the humour. It is joyous, yet quickly also before the fire's dominion (as before a great Hans [giant]) dejected. However, in itself it is mighty in its own thought, without counsel, a sharp reason in the humour according to the external spirit. It does not easily do evil in wrath. It is soon lifted up and haughty, falling again quickly as well, as the air. If it defends itself the devil is afflicted [and] cannot begin much in it in the humour.

He eagerly leads it astray so that it has many thoughts with which it is not able to make images according to God's kingdom. He throws unusual things before it, to use up its time. It eagerly studies many things for the stars cast their *imagination* in the air from which it receives many unusual wide-sweeping thoughts.

28. The man [in this humour] leads a weak, common with each man, pious, simple life, but regularly the devil raises his enemies' anger against him. He must suffer much, but goes through it lightly as the air goes through something. Seldom is he very melancholy since he does not have a fiery heart. Thus fear does not burn strongly in him. He can defend himself from unchastity and idolatry, so that the devil has [no] entrance into the humour.

III. *Phlegmatic Humour according to the Water*

29. If the soul is wrapped with this humour, and expands its life from it, it is a thick swelling life, clumsy, very vile and simple, of gross body, poor understanding, yet brought to all general being by teachers. The moon's governance does not reach it. Thus it is completely a gross dullard and therefore completely unhelped by the moon's governance.

30. One cannot portray this humour in general. It follows the water-spirit in all ways, sometimes bad, sometimes good. It would eagerly give itself to a holy hypocrite. It would reject a pious upright life although it would intermingle [with it]. Water is glistening. The soul too would not lightly be in God's wrath or in the dark world (which is in its *centrum*). It bites bravely on the abomination of the world and covers it under the water's shine, considering it as God's brightness.

31. The devil can lead all vices (which he knows in hell) into this humour, if the constellation does not hinder it and the soul permits it. He gains here as much as in the fire, in the

fire-humour, since sin is so lightly viewed as a water stream [that] runs by. He also has strength to attack it here with melancholy if it wishes to oppose him. He darkens the water's brightness with sins that he introduces and surrounds the soul with so that it remains away from God. In the storm of the soul, if it wishes to leave his control out of the house of melancholy, he does not prevail. The humour is too weak; he can hold [his position] better in fire.

IV. *Melancholy Humour according to the Earth*

32. [The] melancholy humour is like the melancholy earth that always stands in fear before the anger of God, who came into it in creation, gave it average understanding yet somewhat deep in consideration.

33. The humour's room stands open; it can grasp much if depression does not hinder it. If the soul is wrapped with this humour so that it eats of it, its fire's burning becomes very dark and highly melancholy. It does not view any worldly pomp as great. By this humour it is always depressed and frightened as the earth. The devil sifts it with force always wishing eagerly to bring it into the darkness, to trip it into his kingdom.

34. For where it is dark, there it eagerly enters. He makes an example for the soul and frightens it with his wiliness so that it might despair of God's grace. Since into this room of melancholy the soul brings nothing much useful and unless it be that it has bent from God's grace and has become completely light-minded, the body can be given to murders and robbers, [and the humour] will see a man, God and the devil in the same way. For, if it has bent aside and surrendered itself to the humour that it does with it, then, this man does everything that the constellation works in the humour and the devil mixes his *imagination* into it.

35. However, since it [the *imagination*] always remains in

strife, none of these four humours contains fewer vices for it is always in strife against the devil; it knows that it has him as a very near neighbour, for the darkness is his dwelling place in which he sifts the melancholy ones so eagerly. He wishes either to have them in the darkness or to trip them so that they despair and turn themselves away.

36. He knows well what the soul can do. If God's light ignites itself in it [the soul], it ignites his robber's castle. Then he stands in great shame and his malice is revealed.

37. In no humour is the devil's will more evident (if the soul in God's light [love] is ignited) than in the melancholy. This the tempted know well, if they break his robber's castle for him. They know immediately in the humour, in the nature, what a nasty unashamed bird he is. Thereafter he does not eagerly come near to them. When he sees that the soul is certain[ly his], and that it goes into the house of sin as a guest, he comes as a friendly dog so that the soul does not recognize him, sets sugar around, casts out piety to the soul until he can lead it once again into such a humour that it can eat the melancholy food.

38. O how craftily does he act with it; how like a bird-catcher he acts. He frightens it in its prayer (especially at night when it is dark), casts its *imagination* into it so that it thinks God's wrath is on it, and wishes to trip it. He always acts as if he had might over the soul, as if it were his, yet he has no hair of strength over it, unless it despairs itself and gives itself to him. He dare neither possess nor stir it spiritually. He encircles it with the *imagination* by the humour in it.

39. This is the reason why he looks at the soul as he does. The room of the humour is dark. In the light his *imagination* cannot shove in. He can only do it with the sin of men. In the humour, however, he can do it, for it is near to his desire because this desire makes darkness. Fear is in it because of the harsh earth. Otherwise he would not have a spark more right to be in or near it than in another. He can direct nothing

more with the *imagination* so he frightens man and makes him fainthearted. Insofar as the soul does not despair of itself and gives itself to him, he directs it so that it trips itself. He dare not trip it; it must do it itself.

40. The soul has a free will. If it stands before the devil and wills not what he wills, then he does not have so much might [as] to touch it in the external sinful body. He builds himself up well for his [own] might but is a liar. If he had might, he would soon show it. But no, by His entrance into death Christ unlocked the gates for all souls in the dark chamber of death and in hell. Each may enter to tear on the cross the devil's cord that bound the soul in Adam. O how uneagerly does he hear tell of the cross. It is a pestilence for him if it is done so earnestly.

41. The devil always eagerly casts the melancholy man's sin before him. He suggests that he might not reach God's grace, is only to despair, kill, drown, hang himself or murder someone else. [He does this] so as to get a little entrance into the soul; otherwise he may and can not touch it.

42. If he does bring it to the point that it wills to do such [for him], he is as a hangman who binds the trapped man and leads him to judgement. Yet he may not order or trip [the soul]; it does it itself.

Prescription against the Black Devil

43. If he [a man] sees the poor soul, that it is [about] to despair, let him give to it (if it comes) this prescription to take. The devil is a proud, arrogant spirit. One can do him no more harm, so that he turns away sooner, than to take fresh courage against him, [become] completely bold and high-minded, not be frightened before him (since he does not have the authority of a straw man) and to mock him, to cast his fall before him, [to point out] how he was so beautiful an angel and now has become a black devil.

44. In the first place, when he comes, do not dispute with him in any way if he brings the register of sins and brings his governance along with his approach to you. First give him no answer, but when he comes and beats on the soul with his *imagination*, casts evil thoughts before you and your sins and acts as if he wishes to lead you away in a frightening moment, uphold a defiant mind against him saying:

45. "Look, what's this, Black Jack? I thought you were in heaven among the angels. Now you come here and drag God's register of wrath with you. I thought you were a prince with God. How did you then become his jailer? Has a hangman's servant been made from such a beautiful angel? Fie on you, you insolent servant of a hangman. What do you want with me? Go to heaven with the angels. You are God's servant. Fie on you. Pack yourself away, you hangman's servant. Go to your angels. You have nothing to do here."

46. If he takes this prescription eagerly it will bring him health. If he weakens and reads the sin-register [which is] always there, stand before him and say, "Listen, read what comes before: The woman's seed is to tread the head of the serpent. Can you not find it? Wait a bit. I will light a light for you to find it. It stands at the beginning of the Bible. Where Adam fell into sin, God's wrath was first written, for the woman's seed was to tread on your head (Genesis 3:15)." This is the other prescription that he might eagerly take.

47. He may still not soften but may say: "You are a great sinner. You have intentionally committed this or that sin and knew well that it was wrong; do you yet now wish to beautify yourself with God's grace when God's wrath is now ignited in you and you are now the devil's fat [possession]?"

48. Then because of the devil's *imagination* the poor soul is frightened and thinks, "You are a great sinner. God has abandoned you because of your sins. Now the devil will trip you and strike the death blow." As a result the soul begins to be terrified before him.

49. If he thus comes, take up in yourself courage against him in Christ [and] say, "I have something else for you, devil. You cannot again be an angel. Take this in and say: The blood of Jesus Christ makes us clean of all our sins (I John 1:7). Again: The Son of Man is come to seek and to make holy that which is lost (Matthew 18:11).

50. "What would you do, devil, that God might be made man in you? I always have an open door of grace. You have not. You are a liar. Pack yourself off. You have nothing on me. If I am like a sinner, then you are responsible. You brought sins into me by your deception. Take it now as your own; the sin is yours. The suffering and death (of our Lord) Jesus Christ is mine. He became a man since He wished to save us from sin. You have worked sin in me. Keep it for yourself. My Lord Jesus Christ has worked in me the righteousness, which is valid before God. I keep this in myself. His suffering and death for sin is mine. He died for my sins that I did and He arose in His righteousness, and grasped my soul in His satisfaction. Christ is in me and I am in Him, and my sins are in you and you are in hell."

51. Mock him: "Ah beautiful angel, who could not remain a day in heaven. He was a prince and now drags himself with his register of sins, with his slimy sack. You hangman's servant, take my sins away in your beggar's sack. You are only a servant of sin. Bring them to your lord and I will be free of them. Then Christ's merit will remain in me. Christ said (John 10:28-29): My sheep are in my hands, and no one can tear them away from me. The Father who gave them to me is greater than all. How did you, a beautiful angel, become a bearer of a sack of sin; a prince, become a jailer's servant? Get out of here now with your sack of sin and take mine also with you. You need nothing other than sin. You have no part of my soul. If you can, eat me. Here I stand. But listen. I have a mark in me that is the mark of the cross on which Jesus overcame sin and death and destroyed hell for the devil and

bound him in God's wrath. Eat this in me and you will again be an angel."

52. Do not let the thoughts dispute with him, but do not be afraid of him. Only be prepared, be it day or night. He can do nothing to you if you mock him in the harshest manner. [Do so] if he gives cause. Otherwise do not mock him.

53. If he does not come with the terror of fear, he is not there. It is the soul's fear before the dark abyss that is terrorized before God's wrath. It often thinks, if the melancholy humour is attached to the anger of the constellation, that the devil is there but he is not. If he comes, he either comes with fierce terror or as an angel as friendly as a flattering dog.

54. If he comes in darkness and you are in a dark place and he frightens you, do not turn from him in that location. Do not flee from him. He is not worth a man's flight from him. Mock him in the darkness. Say, "Look. Are you there? I thought you were an angel of light, but you stand in the darkness lying in ambush like a thief. There is really another place for you where there is more stink than here since you only go around after the stink of sin." Yet do not call him to you so that he does not have cause [to come].

55. A defiant man, who does not weaken before him, he does not easily frighten, especially if the man makes up his mind and mocks him, for he is proud and wishes always to be lord. Thus the man who does not weaken before him irritates him. He does not wait there very long.

56. If he leaves there in a stink, leave immediately, saying, "Fie, you stinking hangman's servant, how you stink in your lodging. *Cloaca* smells the same as you do." He will not soon come again in terror.

57. Let your mind hold no disputation with him. It is not worth it. Only use a few small words [and] you have done enough. You need no more consolation in fear. The blood of Jesus Christ, the Son of God, makes us pure from all our sins (I John 1:7). Wrap all your thoughts in this. Let no others

leave you. The devil may shove what he will into you with his *imagination*. Think only that all that the devil says is lies. The verse is true. Keep the verse for yourself. Let him shove in what he will.

58. Seek not many words in event of terror. He is too cunning for you. He tears the first and the best from your heart so that you forget him or have doubts. Wrap your soul in itself alone. It is enough to stand against him. You can (if your soul is wrapped therein) fully mock him. He cannot disturb you, nor will he wait for long. If you do not weaken before him, he becomes a mockery before his other servants among men and before the holy angels. This he flees before all else before you mock him.

59. Repeat the verse. Grasp it in [your] heart and present yourself as defiant courage. The spirit which stays in the verse will stand by you well. If the soul trembles before him stand against him in anger, as if your life depended on it. Nothing will come against you. He dare bring no strength; he has none. Because man lives in this time, he dare do nothing to him, for Christ has opened the doors of grace. They stand open to the poor sinner when he lives on earth. The same doors of grace are open in man's soul.

60. Christ has broken the strong castle (which was locked in God's wrath) in his soul. Now all souls are of one quality. They all come from one, are all together in one tree with many branches. His breaking has gone to all souls from Adam to the last man. The doors of grace stand open to all. God has locked out none except those who do not themselves wish [to enter]. The mark of His entrance into humanity is revealed in all souls. This is also a witness to the godless on the Day of Judgement that they have despised it. Even if our sins were blood-red (as Isaiah [1:18] says) the doors of grace would stand open to it, for if he converts he will be as white as snow. Isaiah further says (49:15-16): Can a mother forget her child, so that she does not have mercy on the son of her body?

Even if she does forget, I will not forget. For see, in my hand I have marked you, namely in His hands cut through with nails, and in His open side He has marked the soul for all souls.

61. If one [soul] does not come and lay it in this, despise the mark of Christ, or allow the devil to cover it, it is itself guilty. If it covers it, it stands engraved in the greatest sinner in the world, for Isaiah says in the spirit of Christ: Even if a mother forgets her child (which happens with great pain) yet His love and grace is not to be forgotten. He has not forgotten the soul even if its sins are blood-red for He has marked it in His blood and death, not only singly but the tree with its root and branches. As the sins of one come to all so righteousness comes to all through Christ, says the Apostle [Romans 5:18]. As the sins brought death from one to all, so the righteousness from Christ brought life from one to all.

62. It is their fault that they do not all wish [to have it]. They have free will. God wills that all men be helped as in Psalm 5:5 [it is written:] You are not a God who wishes evil; (Ezekiel 33:11): As true as I live (says the Lord) I do not wish the death of the sinner but that he turn and live.

63. Therefore the soul is not to think, "The weight of my sins is complete; God has forgotten me. I cannot be holy." No. He has it in His hands marked in the nail prints. He is a small branch in a great tree of all souls and shares like qualities with all as a branch with the tree. As he lives in this world, he stands in the tree as long as the soul is clothed with flesh and blood.

On the Temptation [Rising] out of the Humour and the Constellation

64. Temptation does not all come from the devil (especially in melancholy men). Most melancholy comes from the thought of the soul. When it must stand in a melancholy

lodging, it is very easily sad and thinks that God has forgotten it or does not wish [to have] it. The melancholy humour is dark, has no light of its own as the others [do], but does not belong to the being of the soul. At this time of external life it is only the dwelling place of the soul. So also the soul's holiness and righteousness does not stand in the humour but in heaven with God. Saint Paul says (Philippians 3:20): Our walk is in heaven. This heaven, in which God dwells, is not revealed in the humour, but in itself in another *principium*.

65. It often happens that the holiest souls become thus covered and melancholy. God often allows this to happen so that they might be tested and strive for the noble conqueror's crown.

66. If the soul gains the crown of the Holy Spirit with storm and great firmness, it is much nobler and more beautiful than when it is only placed upon the soul after the body's death. The Revelation of Jesus Christ says: To him who conquers I will give the right to sit with me on my throne as I have conquered and been sat with my Father on His throne (Revelation 3:21). Again: To him who conquers I will give to eat of the hidden manna and will give to him a good witness and with the witness write a new name that no one knows who does not receive it (Revelation 2:17).

67. Often the constellation has an evil *conjunction* or coming together; often [there is] darkness in sun and moon. If *Mars* casts in his poisonous beams and the *conjunction* comes into an earthly sign, in the melancholy room it greatly frightens the same souls which are surrounded by a melancholy humour. They always think it is the angry wrath of God, or the devil, that he comes and wishes to take the soul. If it feels in the humour the poisonous beams of *Mars*, it sees that it is in a dark lodging. Then it thinks God has rejected it, that He does not wish it and, especially if it makes images and searches in the humour, so that it eats of the poison of *Mars* and expands its fire-life with it. Thus great bitter dread and

fear of the devil and God's wrath are in it. Then it speculates and thinks that God has not accepted it in Christ for eternal life. It is thus frightened [and] does not lift up its face eagerly before God. It always thinks that it is one of the greatest sinners, that the gates of grace are closed to it.

68. In truth, however, this is nothing other than a fantasy from the *constellation* in the humour by which the soul inwardly torments itself. If it is now in the spirit of the great world with the *constellation* of the stars, it forces its illusory game into it, brings in a marvellous fantasy, so that the soul is in torment, and the external spirit finally completely ignites itself in the earthly source by which the wheel in the *centrum* of nature is turned. Thus the spirit cannot grasp and hold its thoughts, is mad, and is heard of often among the melancholy.

69. If the devil sees this, he shoots his *imagination* into it [and] torments the poor soul yet more. However, he has no governance. The source of dread alone is his life-source. He is therefore eager for he is, without this, an enemy of the human race.

70. Therefore no one tempted by melancholy is to think to himself, when this tests him through the humour, that it is from God's gracelessness and wrath. It is a fantasy of the humour and constellation. One sees well how the wretched devil's filthy pigs that bake themselves every day and hour in sin are not sad and tempted. [The] reason [is that] they have an external light in the humour in which they dance with the devil in angel's form. As long as there is a spark in man that desires only God's grace and wishes eagerly to be holy, God's door of grace is open.

71. He who is forsaken by God, whose measure of sin is full, asks nothing either from God nor man nor the devil. He is blind, goes lightly in without fear, [and] has an external habit in his worship of God. A beast goes out again, where

there is no divine knowledge, only trinket and custom that he holds to be holiness.

72. In this the melancholy mind is to know that God does not thus reveal His wrath in this life, for if the godless [man] was similarly punished by God in this life, he would hold it only to be a thing that happens occasionally. Isaiah says in the person and Spirit of Christ: He will not break the beaten reed nor put out the glowing wick (42:3).

73. Again Matthew 11:28: Come to me all who are weary and heavy-laden. His yoke is also this that nature places on the poor soul. Be it temptation, persecution or sickness one is to bear it with patience and cast himself into His love and mercy. They do no harm to the soul; [the soul] is in truth better for them, for since it stands in a house of melancholy, it is neither in a house of sin nor in a [house of] pride and pleasure of the world. God holds it by this in reins away from the world's sinful pleasure. If it must be sad for a time, what [does] it [matter]? How quickly is it freed of the house of melancholy and the conqueror's crown of eternal joy set on it? O eternity, how long you are. Why is it that the soul must be melancholy for a short while and thereafter have eternal joy? He will wash away all tears from their eyes [Revelation 7:17]. As long as there is only a spark in the soul that longs for God, God's Spirit is in the same spark.

74. If a man desires God and groans for Him, it does not come from the man. It is the pull of the Father in His Son Jesus Christ to Himself.

75. The Holy Spirit is the divine desire itself. No man can desire God without His Spirit, which is in the desire and holds the will of the desire in God so that the poor soul is supported. Saint Paul says: We do not know what we ought to speak before God when we pray. The Spirit of God represents us mightily with unspeakable groans that are pleasing to God (Romans 8:26).

76. Why should we any longer be small-minded before His grace, [since] He takes us more readily to His grace than we would come to Him. Look how He acted with the prodigal son who wasted his father's inheritance with the devil's fatted pigs and became a naked stinking swineherd. When He looked on him, and [saw] that he had turned again to Him, He fell on his neck and kissed him saying: This is my dear son whom I have lost [and] who is come again. He was dead and now is alive. How He did call to order [others to come] and rejoice with Him over His son who had once been evil. Christ further teaches that there is more joy in heaven for the angels of God over one sinner who repents than over the ninety-nine righteous who do not need to repent.

77. The prodigal son is the poor sinful man. If he knows himself that he was a great sinner and thinks [he will] turn to God's mercy, our dear Father meets him in Christ, takes him in again with great joy and the angels and the holy souls in heaven rejoice greatly that again, a dear soul, a dear brother has come to them out of the house of sin, out of death.

78. The melancholy soul is troubled because of this, because it cannot in its desire awaken great joy in its heart. It groans and complains and thinks [that] God does not wish [to have] it, if it cannot feel anything. It looks at other men who are happy (they stand with it similarly in the scales, in God's fear) and they think their joy stands in God's power, but they are not pleasing before God. God does not wish [to have] them. They will feel little of God in their hearts.

79. So it was with me before the time of my knowledge. I lay in great strife until I received my noble crown. Then I first learned to know how God does not dwell in the external fleshly heart, but in the soul's *centrum*, in itself. Then I first realized that God had thus drawn me in the desire and [that] earlier I had understood nothing. I thought the desire was my possession, [that] God was distant from us. Hereafter I saw and rejoiced in this, [that] God is thus gracious. I wrote for

the example of others, to contend with no one, of consolation continued according to David's Psalm: And if it lasted into the night and again to the morning, etc. (Psalm 130:6).

80. So it went with the great saints. Many times they had to struggle for the noble conqueror's crown. None were crowned with it, unless they struggled for it. It is set beside the soul, but it lies in the second *principium*. The soul stands in the first. If it wishes to set [it on itself] in this time, it must battle for it.

81. If it does not receive it in this world, it will receive it after this time, in the laying down of the earthly hut. Christ says: Be consoled, I have overcome the world. Again: In me you have peace, in the world dread (John 16:33).

82. The noble pearl lies very much nearer in many tempted troubled minds, than in those who think they have grasped it. It hides itself however, for with whom He is at the best, He will not uncover it, and it seems to be as if He does not wish to be seen. Let no soul be frightened by this.

83. He hides it so that the soul will knock and find [it]. Christ says: Ask and you will receive; seek and you will find; knock and it will be opened unto you (Matthew 7:7). My Father will give the Holy Spirit to those who ask Him for it (Luke 11:13).

84. God's promise allows you to be more secure, and if your heart speaks a pure "No," let it not trouble you. One is not to believe that one receives joy in a fleshly heart in an external humour so that the mind might be joyous in the spirit, so that the heart and inners tremble alike for joy. This is not yet faith. It is only the Holy Spirit's love beams, a divine glance that is unstable. God does not dwell in the external heart nor in the humour but in Himself, in another *centrum*, in the treasure of the noble image of the likeness of God. This is hidden in the external world.

85. Proper faith is that the soul-spirit with its will desires and enters into that with the desire so that it does not see nor

feel anything. Understand: The soul, which it comes to purely [and] alone, does not stand in this time nor does it send the subtle willing spirit (which arises out of its fire-life) into it. In the same willing spirit the pearl is received so that the soul's fire always remains in the desire. So long as the pearl remains in the willing-spirit, so long is the desire in the soul, for the same pearl is a spark of divine love. It is a pull of the Father in His love.

86. The soul is to stand in its desire even if the external reason speaks a pure "No" out of the dark humour. If God is not there, no desire or will for Him is there. Where God is not in the willing-spirit, it is as blind and dead to God. It does not desire God, lives in its meanings, does not groan to desire God, [has] only a subtle knowledge of Him before the other beasts, so that the soul is graded higher [than they are].

87. Therefore a melancholy heart is not to allow the humour to form anything in the heart. If God is not there, not present, He does not wish this of him. Otherwise the soul eats such an image and is melancholy. It is a great sin for the mind to press such a fantasy into the heart, for the soul (it is a noble creature out of God's nature) is brought into dread in this. Fantasy ignites the soul's fire so that it burns in such painful torment.

88. Dear mind, do not think otherwise if the dread of the humour (ignited by the constellation) comes here. You stand in God's vineyard. You are to work, not to stand idle. In this you do God a great service. Your work is to conquer in faith. If no consolation soon appears to you in the external heart, it is not an error.

89. That is not faith in that I see, it is faith in that I trust the hidden Spirit and believe His word, that I would sooner lose my life than wish not to believe on His promise. He battles correctly with God, as Jacob of old [battled] the whole night [Genesis 33:24-30], who sees or feels nothing, but trusts on the promised word. He conquers God as it was said

to Jacob: You have wrestled with God and man and have prevailed (Genesis 32:28). You say, "Which word is that?" Answer: It is this: My Father will give the Holy Spirit to those who ask him for it (Luke 11:13). It is what Christ Himself said with His lips: He who will come will lead you into all truth, for He will receive [it] from one and make [it] known to you (John 16:13-14).

90. So that you will not be in doubt, know for certain that temptation and dread only come out of the humour. I place an example before you (which relates much more to a fire's humour, also to a melancholy [humour]). Go at night into a dark room. Frighten yourself and think always [that] there is something in the darkness that ought to frighten you. What kind of fright is this? Does the flesh fear itself? No, otherwise it would not go in. The poor soul captured in the flesh fears itself in the darkness, [and] always fears that the devil reaches for it. It knows that he dwells in the darkness. The fear is therefore that he will reach for it. In this it is clearly to be seen that the fear comes from fantasy. Thus it happens to the poor soul in a continually dark room of humour. It is afraid that it must live in the dark and is always frightened of the devil and God's wrath.

91. A soul in a melancholy chamber is therefore not to speculate about God's wrath, nor be eager to be alone or with people who speak [about it]. Thus the soul will build up the fantasy of speech and not speculate for no speculation is useful to it. If this cannot turn it to its salvation, it leaves it aside.

92. Such a man is not to read writings that teach about such an election. They all teach with misunderstanding and explain nothing correctly as the high tongue of the Holy Spirit has set it down and explained it and [as] is explained enough in our other writings.

93. He is not to use many such writings but to remain simply with the Scripture, where he can find a continual consolation.

94. However, if he is given a deep sense of God, [and] if the soul does not become slothful in research, let him lay himself in the fear of God with continual prayer on the *centrum* of nature so that he may study it (if he studies it). Thus, the soul sets itself in peace, for it sees its ground and all fear and melancholy disappear from it.

95. Of this, I know [something] to say what kind of light and stability there is for him who finds the *centrum naturae*. No self-reason reaches it. God indeed keeps no one from it, but it must be found in the fear of God with continual devotion and prayer. It is the greatest treasure in this world. He who finds it comes out of Babel.

96. A melancholy mind is to defend itself with great earnestness from drunkenness so that the soul might not be too greatly weighted down with earthly power. When the body thus loads itself with drink, it takes the earthly power of the drink completely [into] the chamber of the humour. Then the soul makes images in it, it eats the earthly source, it ignites its fire with it, and rejoices somewhat in it. However, if the power sinks again and recedes, that is, if the man becomes temperate in drinking again, the poor soul is, as it were, cursed, for it loses the divine *imagination* or desire in the overflowing earthly source. God's spirit will not dwell in earthly *imagination*. Then sorrow rises in the soul and it is, as it were, cursed.

97. Thus God's wrath is set against it as if it wished it to be cast into the root, into the *centrum*, into the darkness. Then the soul is frightened, [and] yearns again for a good drinking fountain so that it might once again have a fool's joy. From this arise drinking brothers who bind one day to the next and trip their souls into God's wrath and withdrawal of grace. I tell you faithfully what I have come to know high in the *centrum naturae* and in the *principium* of life.

98. The melancholy soul is to protect itself from wrath. Wrath is its greatest poison and brings madness, as is very

clearly to be understood in the *centrum*. The melancholy chamber is crude, like the wild earth, and is almost waste. It has a very weak hold on the wheel of nature. If anything now happens that the anger's fire moves it too greatly the wheel of nature moves in sound, as one then sees that the body trembles.

99. Because the humour's chamber is so waste, without being, the wheel cannot easily be held again and the thoughts are also not able to be grasped, but everything proceeds in a completely fiery and angry [way], as is to be seen among the mad so that the mind is not able to grasp the thoughts. It [the mind] does not know what it says and does or how the wheel goes. The devil also eagerly leads his *imagination* in [to it] so that often great evil occurs. This wheel truly stands in the external spirit but the poor soul also eats of it with a frightening result. One is not to damn any soul in this time, for the mark of the cross still stands in it with the open doors of grace.

100. The melancholy chamber is to protect itself from covetousness and must leave it in earnest, for it is as harmful to it as wrath. Covetousness is an earthly desire; its humour is also earthly and the proper chamber almost desolate. When the desire draws the earthly being into the desolate chamber and fills it with such dark *materia*, vain anger and God's wrath stick fast in it with falsehood and unrighteousness and evil being for the earth's characteristic that makes the humour, since, without it, it is an earthly desire, completely and fully earth.

101. From it the poor soul eats with its *imagination*, and feels then in its burning fire God's strong judgement that is ignited over falsehood and unrighteousness as if many such vile *materia* were brought along into covetousness. If the poor soul now finds itself in God, it begins to doubt and be dejected, for it sees nothing in itself but vain evil, earthiness, falsehood and injustice by which it only ignites God's wrath.

102. Let this be faithfully revealed. For a melancholy

mind nothing is better than to lead a simple solitary life without pride, in a common vocation wherever it may, indeed a moderate, temperate life, not loaded with great troubles. If it must indeed be [that it cannot have such a life, it] is to begin everything in the fear of God and prayer. Thus it will be successful in any position. In the melancholy chamber no greater counsel may be found. It is open insofar as it remains calm. It goes as deep as the sanguine chamber but without the fear of God it only attains external reason. It brings the greatest evil into the world. If it is open and in the sign of Saturn that is its lord, it builds Babel and all deception, [and] is almost as high and mighty as it is melancholy.

103. Therefore if one knows he is under this humour, he should never begin without prayer. Let him first commend to the Highest his heart, thoughts and mind, will and acts into His holy hands and ask Him that He be the ruler in all his willing and acting, so [that] he might bring forth much good. Outside of this no one sitting in his office and standing in the lodging of his chamber can bring forth anything good and pleasing to God.

Concerning the Other Three Humours

A common mirror in which each may see himself. Very briefly written as it was presented to me out of the grace of God.

On the Choleric Humour

104. If man has his best treasure as it were, the noble soul in a choleric house, he is before all things to practice humility or he will be in great danger. He might indeed pour water on the fire so that his noble image is not ignited in him. [Choleric] gives great pride, harshness, sudden wrath, and is raised high, feared and set forward but never deeply loved. When the water of God comes as noble humility into the fire, it is worthy of being loved and gives its first appearance.

105. This chamber has its own appearance in external nature. Indeed, it is not generally humble unless it has *Jupiter* as its life sign or *Venus*. Under *Venus* it has its devil that day and night plagues it with unchastity.

106. [I] state as a warning that great danger is in this humour, much greater than in melancholy. From it the devil comes in the form of an angel of light into the fire's brightness. He tickles the poor soul so that it helps itself to the fire's appearance and becomes high-minded. It places everything easily before itself. It bites lightly on sin; swearing, cursing, light conversation run against the Name of God, and bring unholiness into the soul. It is not seldom in this chamber. The fire's angry essence holds the mind away so that it enters with great difficulty into God's love and meekness (especially into proper abstinence and repentance). It always rises up eagerly in wrath. [It expects that] one is only to fear it. It happens that it enters into an earthly sign; it does not do it much good from its own form, which serves the honour of God.

107. Therefore, if one's best treasure lies in it, let him indeed look to what he does and how he lives. The poor soul sets its *imagination* in it and is ignited by it. It does not easily realize that it sits in God's wrath in hellish fire until it awakens or until it is robbed of the external fire's brightness in the humour with the death of the body. Then it is a proud angry devil and must even sit in the darkness.

108. Therefore it is good that such a person does not strive after might and honour. If, however, they are set on him, he is not indeed to allow his mind to look into them, for it is a proud evil fire's eye. Avid prayer is of much use here.

109. In this [humour] the soul is eagerly ignited so that it receives joy but generally from the fire's humour in the firelight. Thus it thinks it is God's Spirit. But no. God's Spirit comes only with great meekness and humility, if He reveals Himself in the soul. O what a triumph He brings into the fire's humour in the soul, if it appears. However it has now become

precious in man. The humour always remains lord. Therefore be warned. Be humble; busy yourself with meekness in words and works. Thus the humour can not easily ignite your soul, for a humble heart loves God. You are not further from God because of this humour. See [to it] only that you do not misuse it. Allow all to happen for God's honour. Thus nothing will harm you; break its will.

On the Sanguine Humour

110. You can so direct your life after this and in this noble humour you will not make yourself a hypocrite. With your prolixity you will discover much. See to it that you do not bring stubble and straw into the sanguine chamber and think it is the Holy Spirit. You have in the humour a shining light. It is indeed human but see to it that you do not bring it into earthliness.

111. Moderate living is good for you. Protect yourself from drunkenness. Otherwise you will soon fall into the enemies' arms. Since you love much protect yourself that you do not love unchastity and pride.

112. As you are humble by nature, pride can very easily be brought into you, for you carry a house of all stars, as light and the upper water.

113. If you walk in the fear of God, and help yourself properly in it, you can indeed truly find the *Mysterium Magnum* in yourself, but not by yourself. Only through God have you an open chamber to it. Therefore take care what you give your soul as food.

114. For if it is not so good, it may become evil, if an evil enters into it. If one despises you, ignore it and trust in God. Much will come to you because of your simple form. Keep what you have and do not use foreign subtlety. Thus you will not lead into your noble house a foreign spirit. Better to suffer mockery here than need after this life.

115. If you torment yourself with drunkenness, the devil will bring much evil and misfortune for you into your weak house for it is a grievous [place] to him; he has no seat of his own in it, except only in the introduction of sins. A solitary quiet life would be good for you, but you are too prolix, and find much. You also disperse it elsewhere as the air. See to what you take in and give out so that it be not the discovery of the stars but be born out of God. Otherwise you will be betrayed and led astray.

On the Phlegmatic Humour

116. Truth and righteousness would be a noble medicine in you, for otherwise you will be stuck full of lies and heed little what you give out and take in. You, poor soul, have here a dangerous way to go in this humour through the sorrowful sea. You are always dirtied with the vices of words and works.

117. Water has a bright hue in itself and gives a counter appearance but is nevertheless a false mirror. Thus in this humour the poor soul has an almost unjust mirror. The water takes all into itself. Be it evil or good, it holds it and darkens itself with it.

118. It is the same way with this humour. It takes the poisonous beams of all the stars into itself, and places them as a mirror before the poor trapped soul on which it bites, and it directs what is only a magical mirror in the humour into the body to work.

119. O how good sweet words, like to sweet water, are without payment but mixed full of bitter gall from the stars. There is almost no deception. Lies are the mantle of hypocrisy, letting it see itself with a mirror's hue where good Christians are in Babel; it is and wishes to be counted as to worship [but do not do it].

120. You do not discover that you act unjustly, but if

one comes too near to you with a spark, it is already in your mirror. It would be good to counsel you so that you might know how you are in your inner sinful man. You can truly enter into proper repentance and ask God for the dominion of His Holy Spirit so that the evil effects of the stars are broken and held in rein so that the poor soul might not grasp them and thus become a fool.

121. A temperate life will also be healthy for you. Always watch and pray and be continually in the fear of God so that all evil from the constellation will be turned away. He who lives in the constellation lives like all animals. If one thinks in his heart on the fear of God, the soul becomes a lord over the external life and compels that to obedience. If it does not happen the humour becomes the master and guide of the soul. If it cannot quickly direct the soul in its own might, it sets its elemental and starry mirror before the soul in which the soul lets itself be caught and trapped.

122. Therefore a man is to be a man and not an animal. He is to direct his soul humanly and not with the desire of the humour. Thus he can achieve the highest and external good, be under whatever humour he will.

123. There is no humour so noble, [so] that if a man desires simply to live according to its stars [influence], that the devil [would not] have his pleasure in it.

124. Therefore Saint Peter's writing says correctly (I Peter 5:8): Be temperate and watch for your adversary the devil goes about like a roaring lion and seeks whom he can swallow. Stand against him in the fear of God and never be at ease before him.

Lord, You are our refuge.
End

NOTES

Introduction

1. On the Boehmist tradition see Rufus M. Jones, *Spiritual Reformers in the 16th and 17th Centuries* (New York, 1914); Nils Thune, *The Behmenists and the Philadelphians* (Uppsala, 1948); Serge Hutin, *Les disciples anglais de Jacob Boehme* (Paris, 1960); Arlene A. Miller, *Jacob Boehme: From Orthodoxy to Enlightenment* (unpublished Ph.D., Stanford, 1971); and relevant sections in Gerhard Wehr, *Jakob Böhme* (Hamburg, 1971) and Hans Tesch, *Jakob Böhme* (München, 1976).

2. On the textual tradition of Boehme's works see in particular: Werner Buddecke, *Die Jakob Böhme Ausgaben* (2 Bde.; Göttingen, 1937, 1957).

3. For biographies of Boehme note particularly: Will-Erich Peuckert, *Das Leben Jacob Böhmes* (2. Aufl.; Stuttgart, 1961) in Jacob Böhme, *Sämtliche Schriften*, hrsg. Will-Erich Peuckert (Stuttgart, 1955-1960), Bd. 10/2. The Franckenberg biography and ancillary material are printed in *ibid.*, 10/1. See also John Joseph Stoudt, *Sunrise to Eternity* (Philadelphia, 1957), and Wehr, *Böhme*.

4. On Schwenckfeld see Selina Gerhard Schultz, *Caspar Schwenckfeld von Ossig* (Norristown, Pa., 1946; reprint with Introduction by Peter C. Erb, Pennsburg, Pa., 1977). No full history of the Schwenckfelders exists. See however, Horst Weigelt, *Die spiritualistische Tradition im Protestantismus* (Berlin, 1973) for an excellent guide to Schwenckfelder history, thought and influence in Silesia.

5. On Paracelsus and Weigel see Alexandre Koyré, *Mystiques, spirituels, alchimistes* (Paris, 1955).

6. No detailed study of Boehme's use of Schwenckfeld has yet been done. On his use of Paracelsus see Peuckert, *Leben*, 218ff., and note the parallels between sections of *The Way to Christ* and Weigel cited in Böhme, *Schriften*, IV, Einleitung, 12-16. Note as well Heinrich Bornkamm, *Das Jahrhundert der Reformation* (2. Aufl.; Göttingen, 1966), 340-345, and his detailed study of similarities and differences between Boehme and Renaissance Neoplatonism in his "Renaissance-mystik, Luther und Böhme," *Luther Jahrbuch* 9 (1927) 156-197. See also Wilhelm August Schulze, "Jakob Boehme und die Kabbala," *Zeitschrift für Philosophische Forschung* 9 (1955) 447-460; R.T. Llewellyn, "Jacob Boehmes Kosmogonie in ihrer Beziehung zur Kabbala," *Antaios* 5 (1963/64), 237-250, and extensive discussion in Miller, *Boehme*.

7. On the history of Scholasticism within Protestantism see Isaac A. Dorner, *History of Protestant Theology*, trans. George Robson and Sylvia Taylor (2 vols.; Edinburgh, 1871) and Peter Petersen, *Geschichte der aristotelischen Philosophie im protestantischen Deutschland* (Leipzig, 1921). A more

recent but less useful work despite its bulk is Robert D. Preuss, *The Theology of Post Reformation Lutheranism* (2 vols.; St. Louis, Mo., 1970-   ).

8. In this its opponents were mistaken. See Herman A. Preuss and Edmund Smits, eds., *The Doctrine of Man in Classical Lutheran Theology* (Minneapolis, Minn., 1962) xix-xxii.

9. On this movement see above all Max Goebel, *Geschichte des Christlichen Lebens in der rheinisch-westphalischen evangelischen Kirche* (Coblenz, 1852-1860) and relevant sections in F. Ernest Stoeffler, *The Rise of Evangelical Pietism* (Leiden, 1970). Cf. as well Heinrich Bornkamm, *Mystik, Spiritualismus und die Anfange des Pietismus* (Giessen, 1926).

10. On Arndt see Wilhelm Koepp, *Johann Arndt: Eine Untersuchung über die Mystik in Luthertum* (Berlin, 1959).

11. On this theme see Ernst Benz, *Der Prophet Jacob Boehme* (Mainz, 1959).

12. On Boehme's thought see particularly Alexandre Koyré, *La philosophie de Jacob Boehme* (Paris, 1929); Hans Grunsky, *Jacob Boehme* (Stuttgart, 1956); Nicolas Berdyaev, "Underground and Freedom" in Jacob Boehme, *Six Theosophic Points and other Writing* (Ann Arbor, Mich., 1958); Paul Bommersheim, "Die Welt Jacob Bohmes," *Deutsche Vierteljahrsschrift* 20 (1942) 340-550; and Ernst Benz, "Die Geschichtmetaphysik Jacob Böhmes," *ibid.*, 13 (1935) 421-455. Valuable studies are also Herbert Deinert, "Die Entfaltung des Bosen in Böhmes *Mysterium Magnum*," *Publication of the Modern Language Association* 79 (1964) 401-410. With respect to this study note as well Gerhard Wehr's introductory material and notes in his abridged edition of Boehme's *Christosophia* (Freiburg im Breisgau, 1976).

13. Böhme, *Schriften*, 2, *Von den drey Principien*, 24:1.

14. *Ibid.*, 9, *Theosophische Send-Briefe* 10:48.

15. *Ibid.*, 44.

16. Cf. Jacob Böhme, *Die Urschriften* (Stuttgart, 1966) II, 476.

17. In spite of Boehme's insistence to the contrary, he was clearly influenced much by earlier material. See studies cited above n. 5. Boehme's statement that he did not take his material "from any other masters" (Böhme *Schriften*, I, *Aurora*. 3:48) is not a denial of his own indebtedness to the many ideas that he must have learned in Görlitz' circles of Paracelsians and others, but an insistence that what he had used was used only under the Spirit's guidance. Earlier Boehmists who emphasized too strongly his "inspiration" did not take seriously enough his learning.

18. Cf. Boehme, *Schriften*, 3, *Vom dreyfachen Leben* 6:10 and cf. *ibid.*, 2, *Von den drey Principien*, 24:2.

19. Bohme, *Schriften*, 1, *Aurora* 9:11.

20. *Ibid.*, 19:13.

21. See Tesch, 25f. Further study must be done to determine the influence of Marian imagery on Boehme's portrayal of Sophia.

22. Bohme, *Schriften*, 5, *Antistiefelius*, II, 253.

23. *Ibid.*, 3, *Viertzig Fragen* 1:205.

24. *Ibid.*, 5, *Libri Apologetica* II, 64.

25. *Ibid.*, 64-66.

26. *Ibid.*, *Von der Menschwerdung*, I, 1:12.

27. Martin Luther, *Werke* (Weimar, 1883-   ), 5:163.

28. *Ibid.*, *Tischreden* 1:26.

29. *Ibid.*, 3:111-112; cf. 3:124.

30. See Bengt Hoffman, "Luther and the Mystical," *The Lutheran Quarterly*, 26 (1974), 321, 323.

31. See W. Philipp, "Unio Mystica," *Die Religion in Geschichte und Gegenwart* (3 Aufl.; Tübingen, 1957-1965), VI, 1334-1338. Cf. M. Schmidt, "Prot. Mystik," *ibid.*, IV, 1252ff.

32. See Heiko A. Obermann, *The Harvest of Medieval Theology* (Cambridge, Mass. 1963), 341-343, and cf. his *"Simul gemitus et raptus*. Luther und die Mystik" in Ivar Asheim, hrst., *Kirche, Mystik, Heiligung und das Natürliche bei Luther* (Göttingen, 1967), 20-59.

33. On this matter note the comments of R. Newton Flew, *The Idea of Perfection in Christian Theology* (Oxford, 1934), 244ff., 275ff. Modern Protestant antagonism to mysticism is rooted in the thought of late 19th-century liberalism and the dialectical theologians of this century. See Bengt Hägglund, *The Background of Luther's Doctrine of Justification in Late Medieval Theology* (Philadelphia, Pa. 1971), 2-3.

34. Luther, *Werke* 5:119.

35. *Ibid.*, 5:176.

36. See Gordon Rupp, *The Righteousness of God* (London, 1953), 143-144.

37. Luther, *Werke*, 4. 265. cf. 4. 267:9, 97.

38. *Ibid.*, 4:519.

39. Note especially, Werner Elert, *The Structure of Lutheranism*, trans., Walter A. Hanson (St. Louis, Mo., 1962), 173-174, n. 26.

40. For citations see Erich Vogelsang, "Luther und die Mystik," *Luther Jahrbuch* 19 (1937), 48-50.

41. See Elert, *Structure*, 168, on Luther's use of *quasi*.

42. Luther, *Werke*, 7:54.

43. *Ibid.*, 101:74.

44. *Ibid.*

45. *Ibid.*, 20:229-231.

46. On the young Luther's concern with progressive improvement in the Christian life, see Jared Wicks, *Man Yearning for Grace: Luther's Early Spiritual Teaching* (Washington, 1968).

47. Luther, *Werke*, 103:157-158.

48. For the best comparison of Boehme and Luther see Arlene A. Miller, "The Theologies of Luther and Boehme in the Light of their *Genesis* Commentaries," *Harvard Theological Review* 63 (1970), 261-303.

49. On Luther's doctrine of baptism see Paul Althaus, *The Theology of Martin Luther*, trans. Robert C. Schultz (Philadelphia, Pa., 1966), 353ff.

50. *Ibid.*, 251ff.

51. Cf. *ibid.*, 25ff.

52. The work is available in English translation. See Johann Arndt, *True Christianity*, trans. Charles F. Schaeffer (Philadelphia, Pa., 1869).

53. Tesch, 82.

54. Böhme, *Schriften*, 4, *Theosophische Puncten*, 1.

55. *Ibid.*

56. *Ibid.*, 4, *Von der Menschwerdung*, I, 2:14.

57. *Ibid.*, 6, *Von der Gnadenwahl* 5:10.

58. See Heinrich Schmid, *Doctrinal Theology of the Evangelical Lutheran Church*, trans. Charles A. Hay and Henry Jacobs (Philadelphia, Pa., 1899), 480f.

59. Cf. Armand A. Maurer, Introduction to Master Eckhart, *Parisian Questions and Prologues* (Toronto, Ont., 1974), 38.

60. On Boehme's view of language see above all Ernst Benz, "Zur metaphysischen Begründung der Sprache bei Jacob Boehme," *Euphorion* 37 (1936), 340-357. Note also Peter Schäublin, *Zur Sprache Jacob Boehmes* (Winterthur, 1963), and Wolfgang Kayser, "Boehmes Natursprachenlehre und ihre Grundlagen," *Euphorion* 31 (1930) 521-562.

61. Boehme, *Schriften* 9, *Clavis*, 1:6-8.

62. *Ibid.*, p. 116.

63. See Schäublin, 108f.

64. See Werner Elert, *Die voluntaristische Mystik Jacob Böhmes* (Berlin, 1913), 67f.

65. Böhme, *Schriften*, 4, *Von sechs Mystichen Puncten* 5:23.

66. *Ibid.*, 4, *Mÿsterium Pansophicum*, 1.

67. *Ibid.*

Text

All extant manuscripts copied by Boehme himself are edited in Jacob Bohme, *Die Urschriften*, hrsg. Werner Buddecke (2 Bde.; Stuttgart-Bad Cannstatt: Friedrich Fromann Verlag [Gunther Holzboog], 1963-1966). The most significant alternate readings in the manuscript are listed below.

II

1. MS. adds: *De poenitentiam* with *m* stroked out by later hand.
2. In MS date appears at end of treatise.
3. MS: *despair of.*
4. MS: *his own.*
5. MS: *leading.*
6. All editions except 1730 and MS read: *heavenly.*
7. MS: *loves and honours.*
8. MS omits: *and still holds.*
9. MS: *these images, images* added by later hand.
10. MS: *images.*
11. MS adds: *in the soul as in the corrupted image of God.*
12. MS adds: *and the soul.*

III

1. MS: *Prayer Book for each day in the week.*
2. MS: *my.*
3. MS omits: *heart- and.*
4. MS omits: *God-loving.*
5. MS omits: *On the . . . to pray.*
6. MS: *lay.*
7. MS: *with.*
8. MS: *His gifts.*
9. MS omits: *Himself.*
10. MS: *He the Holy Spirit.*
11. MS section 9 reads: *For this reason we are not only to come before God with bare breath and words if we wish to pray correctly and be lifted up, but with proper earnest repentance and conversion from our false way of life.*
12. MS omits: *which . . . bought.*
13. MS adds: *since we are the publican and prodigal son.*
14. MS: *with His power of the Spirit.*
15. MS *sic* but second hand notes change of order to read *to hear God actually speaking.*

16. MS: *or*.

17. MS omits: *Many words are not needed . . . encourage him* and reads: *Since one groan works with God, if the will stands purely before God and has cast off from itself the earthly cloak, that is, false passion*.

18. MS: *your*.

19. MS: *the*.

20. MS omits: *poor man*.

21. MS omits: *almighty*.

22. MS referent: *God*.

23. MS: *they*.

24. MS: *does not sin*.

25. MS omits: *by . . . grace*.

26. MS: *immoveable*.

27. MS adds: *so that I never more bend from You*.

28. MS: *love it*.

29. MS adds: *also*.

30. MS: *prayer*.

31. MS: *clothe over*.

32. MS: *weakness*.

33. MS omits: *daily*.

34. MS: *in*.

35. MS omits: *lust*.

36. MS: *beam*.

37. MS: *the*.

38. MS: *word and work visible*.

39. MS: *never*.

40. MS: *majesty*.

41. MS: *turn*.

42. MS omits this heading and section 51 that follows, neither of which appear to have been Boehme's work.

43. MS: *prayer*.

44. MS: *Prayer*.

45. MS: *the form of lies* for *lies, anger*.

46. MS adds: *to form [it]*.

47. MS omits: *to serve*.

48. MS: *it*.

49. MS: *of*.

50. MS omits: *Amen*.

51. MS reads: *so that your servant maid, ox, and ass may rest from their work*.

52. MS: *lust*.

53. MS: *the*.

54. MS: *or*.

55. MS: *and*.

56. MS: *in vain sorrow, need, attack, plunder*.
57. MS: *us*.
58. MS: *with*.
59. MS: *before*.
60. MS ends here.

IV

1. MS omits: *men*.
2. MS: *wrath*.
3. MS omits: *and evil*.
4. MS: *by*.
5. MS omits: *of God*.
6. MS: *forces itself*.
7. From here to end of section 11, MS reads: *He seeks through dry places, seeks rest . . . than he is and turns again into the same house and when he comes he finds it cleaned with brooms and decorated and he goes in and he lives there himself and hereafter it is worse with the same man than at first*.
8. MS: *and finds*.
9. MS omits: *and consider*.
10. MS: *as then*.
11. MS: *knowing*.
12. MS omits: *part*.
13. MS: *since it must*.
14. MS: *or*.
15. MS: *teach*.
16. MS: *teach*.
17. MS: *highest*.
18. MS omits: *It is*.
19. MS: *said*.
20. MS: *before*.
21. MS: *which*.
22. MS: *he*.
23. MS: *and in each there is a play*.
24. MS omits: *from the darkness*.
25. MS omits: *and becomes . . . essence*.
26. MS omits: *and had . . . Ens*.
27. MS: *it cannot endure Him in itself*.
28. MS omits: *not revealed*.
29. MS omits: *(and its being)*.
30. MS omits: *(no more being)*.
31. MS: *stands*.
32. MS omits: *newly*.
33. MS omits: *and is*.

34. MS: *in*.
35. MS omits: *(with Christ's death)*.
36. MS: *him*.
37. MS: *as he brought the covenant of promise again in the flesh*.
38. MS omits: *is*.
39. MS omits: *in*.
40. MS omits: *deception*.
41. MS: *thus*.
42. MS omits: *only*.
43. MS: *yet*.
44. MS omits: *but*.
45. MS omits: *become or*.
46. MS omits: *and to break self*.
47. MS: *when he was*.
48. MS: *all which is earthly*.
49. MS omits: *only*.
50. MS omits: *but*.
51. MS omits: *then he . . . Jesus*.
52. MS: *proper*.
53. MS omits: *out of you*.
54. MS omits: *Christ's children* and reads: *we*.
55. MS: *but upon* for *upon your*.
56. MS omits: *Halleluja. Amen. Rejoice . . . Halleluja*.

VIII

1. MS omits: *Conversation* and reads: *Epistle or open letter*.
2. MS places: *to a soul . . . Christ* after *Epistle or open letter*.
3. Most editions (including this one) place a sketch of serpent with tail in mouth at this point.
4. MS omits: *(into the fire wheel . . . mind)*.
5. MS omits: *and possessiveness*.
6. MS adds: *itself*.
7. MS: *became*.
8. MS omits: (loathsomeness) which appears in 1682 and 1715 editions. Editions of 1649-1663 read *loathsomeness* and omit *vanity*.
9. MS: *but*.
10. MS: *itself*.
11. MS: *This*.
12. MS: *by*.

INDEX TO PREFACE AND INTRODUCTION

Revelation, Boehme's, 6, 8; as light, 21; and wisdom, 9
Richter, Gregory, 6, 7
Righteousness, and baptism, 14
Robson, George, trans., *History of Protestant Theology*, 275
Runge, Phillip, xii
Rupp, Gordon, *The Righteousness of God*, 277

Sacraments, images of, 16; inner and outer aspects of, 15
Salvation, and new birth, xiv; order of, 16, 22
Sanctification, of fallen man, 15
Saviour, and faith, 14
Schaeffer, Charles F., trans., *True Christianity*, 278
Schäublin, Peter, *Zur Sprache Jacob Boehme*, 278
Scheffler, Johann, 1
Schleiermacher, xv
Schmid, Heinrich, *Doctrinal Theology of the Evangelical Lutheran Church*, 278
Schmidt, M., "Prot. Mystik," 277
Schultz, Robert C., trans., *The Theology of Martin Luther*, 278
Schultz, Selina Gerhard, *Caspar Schwenckfeld von Ossig*, 275
Schulze, Wilhelm August, "Jakob Boehme und die Kabbala," 275
Schwenkfeld, 4, 275
Scripture, 16
Self-reflection, xiii
Semi-Pelagianism, 15
Separator, definition of, 23
Signatur, definition of, 23
Silesian Angel, 1
Sinn, translation of, 25
Sinner, is justified, 11
Six Mystical Points, 7
Six Theosophical Points, 7
Smits, Edmund, ed., *The Doctrine of*

Man in Classical Lutheran Theology, 276
Sophia, cf. Wisdom; bride of soul, xviii; and creation of Adam, 20; and desire, 9, 10; difficulty of understanding term, 9; leads man, 17; man's unity with, 9, 10, 14, 17, 21, 24; and Marian imagery, 277; and Trinity, 9
Son, begotten in the will, 18; and Trinity, 18, 22; and Word, 18
Song of Songs, 12. 2:1; 41.
Sorrow, for past sins, 15
Soul, cf. Man; began in eternal nature, 21; bridegroom of Sophia, xviii; and new birth, 2; unrest of, xv
Sparrow, John, 1, 2
Spiritual, as internal, 15
Spiritus mundi, definition of, 23
Stahlschmidt, Johann Christian, xi
Stoeffler, F. Ernest, *The Rise of Evangelical Pietism*, 276
Stoicism, xiii
Stoudt, John Joseph, 25; *Sunrise to Eternity*, 275

Taylor, Sylvia, trans., *History of Protestant Theology*, 275
Temperamentum, definition of, 23
Tersteegan, Gerhard, xi
Tesch, Hans, *Jakob Böhme*, 275, 277
Thune, Nils, *The Behmenists and the Philadelphians*, 275
Theosophical Letters, 7
Theosophical Questions, 7
Tieck, Ludwig, xii
II Timothy, 3:17; xv.
Tinctur, definition of, 23
Trinity, xiii; as God, 15; image of in man, 15, 18; movement of, 18; is One, 22; revelation of, 22; and wisdom, 9, 18
True Christianity, 5, 15, 278

INDEX TO TEXTS

and life, 117, 143; material, 187; and nature, 228, 229; origin of, 213, 214, 215, 217, 220; seven, 109; as spiritual, 185, 215; and *tinctures*, 147; and will, 65, 200, 216

Choleric, description of, 245, 250, 251, 270, 271; and Jupiter, 271; and Venus, 271

Christ, anger of, 37, 48; anguish of, 47, 54; became man, 34, 47, 52, 142, 207, 208, 247, 257; calls man, 42, 43, 55, 111, 136, 161; calls sinners, 33, 69, 230; cleanses us, 48; desire for man, 139, 241; dies for man, 33, 35, 47, 51, 139, 241; as Fountain-source, 36, 49, 52, 72, 85, 131, 154, 207, 212; as God, 54; hidden from man, 37; imitation of, 44, 176, 183, 227; innocence of, 89; and judgement, 29; leads man, 84, 98, 234; is love, 78, 84, 85; majesty of, 85; as man, 54; in man, 65, 73, 84, 93, 98, 104, 107, 164, 167, 190, 192, 238, 257; merits of, 45, 86, 133, 158, 239, 257; as new Adam, 54; praise of, 85, 96; promises of, 31, 32, 37; protects man, 54; and redemption, 38, 234; satisfaction of, 89, 231; son of God, 42, 48, 63; son of man, 42, 151; takes man's place, 47, 54, 133, 139, 151; temptation of, 41, 44; union of God and man, 52; way to, 36, 46, 93; wounds of, 42, 46, 47

Christ's love, and faithfulness, 33; and God, 47, 85; indescribable, 175; man with, 159, 192; overcame hell, 42, 48; and wrath, 50, 52, 84, 90

Christ's Spirit, as judge, 188; leads man to repentance, 31; man enters, 140, 191; man puts on, 132; man reborn in, 137, 163; man's work in, 32, 130, 133, 169, 188, 244; in preacher, 161; renews man, 32, 54, 56, 74

Christian, born of Christ, 138; bride of Christ, 46; called fool, 46; and church, 163, 164; given to Christ, 190; and knowledge, 156, 159; lives in Christ, 238; and mother, 140; righteousness of, 139, 157; titular, 156, 157, 164; true, 156, 161; way of, 118, 156, 157

Christianity, 153, 155, 164; religion of, 165

Church, and Babel, 118, 162, 164; as body of Christ, 16; not Christ's temple, 160, 163; and Christian, 163; and saint, 162

Clavis, 226

Cold, and heat, 228

Colossians, 3:17; 27.

Commandments, fulfilled, 104; lead man, 135; to man, 102, 103, 105, 106, 108, 109, 112, 146; Ten, 66; 1st, 101–105; 2nd, 105–108; 3rd, 108–111; 4th 111–113

Conception, of Christ, 41

Confession, difficulty of, 38; of faith, 220; form of, 34, 80, 81; and Holy Spirit, 81; of sin, 34, 37, 239, 240; of unworthiness, 81

Conjunction, and constellation, 261

Conscience, anguish of, 47, 82; false, 183; and God's wrath, 46; and injustice, 195; and lack of faith, 136; and Sabbath, 110; and sin, 37; and work, 90

Constellations, of creature, 120; and deception, 117, 118, 123;

external, 121, 124, 144, 148, 217; and *humour*, 261, 262; and *spiritus mundi*, 211, 217; of three worlds, 144

Contemplation, of the divine, 65, 70, 95, 171, 194; way to, 65

Contrarium, cf. Fire, Light, Time; creatures and human life, 208; and darkness, 207; of darkness and light, 126, 198; of formed and nonformed, 208; good and evil, 197, 200, 206; of heat and cold, 228; human life and divine will, 208, 214, 216; and mind, 198, 200; and *Mysterium magnum*, 211–212; nature and divine knowledge, 213, 214; necessity of, 196, 197; of power, 222; of sharp and dull, 222; visible and spiritual world, 221; of will, 196, 197, 200, 223; of wisdom and folly, 202, 203

Contrition, awakened, 82

Conversion, God desires in man, 33; in man, 56, 77, 83, 124, 134, 188, 230; man's desire for, 36, 66, 67, 234; need for, 81, 132, 138; in order of salvation, 16; of persecutors, 54, 77

I Corinthians, 2:14; 154. 6:19; 65, 138, 174. 11:29; 160. 12:6; 95. 15:41; 188. 15:45; 208.

II Corinthians, 6:16; 153. 13:14; 193.

Corpus, external, 219; internal, 219; origin of, 201, 217; and spirit, 144, 217

Corruption, cf. Image; of flesh, 28, 60, 130, 149, 152, 153; of man, 97, 112, 151, 169; of man's heavenly part, 33, 52, 116, 153; of man's image, 43

Covenant, cf. Promise; and Abraham, 131; of baptism, 14, 28, 34; of Christ, 28, 85, 86, 111,

160; Christ fulfills, 44, 52; of God, 75, 149, 150; man has forsaken, 34; and Mary, 150; and preaching, 161; and Sophia, 44

Covetousness, avoidance of, 90, 157, 269; as false image, 66, 69, 92; man's, 136, 182, 211, 229, 230; as vanity, 28

Creation, and divine outflow, 200, 201; of elements, 221; man's place in, 96; revealing God, 210; and separation, 221, 222; use for good, 92

Crown, of Christ, 39; of Holy Spirit, 261; of pearls, 58, 61; of Sophia, 44, 61; of thorns, 47; of victory, 40, 45, 61, 261, 263, 264, 265

David, 121, 150, 265

Death, awaits man, 29, 35, 36, 98; brought by Adam's fall, 21, 28; of Christ, 35, 36, 42, 44, 46, 47, 48, 49, 55, 73, 74, 79, 81, 84, 85, 87, 91, 100, 131, 132, 152, 157, 230; conquered by Christ, 36, 38, 41, 81, 85, 86, 151, 179, 255, 257; and Sophia, 59; turned to life, 57

Desire, cf. Man's Desire, Self-will, Soul's Desire, Soul's Will; for contemplation, 65; for conversion, 66; of devil, 51; evil, 28, 63, 127; false, 52, 74, 90, 99, 115; of flesh, 61, 149; and God, 51, 72; sinner's for Sophia, 44; and vanity, 48

Despair, and devil, 126; and godless man, 182; and God's anger, 47; and hope, 235; and hypocrisy, 68; and judgement, 29; and reason, 204; and soul, 254, 255

De tribus principiis, 137

Devil, attacks man, 35, 44, 46, 52,

60, 61, 63, 87, 88, 90, 92, 99, 100, 110, 116, 117, 146, 154, 167, 183, 205, 227, 228, 230, 235, 254; bonds of, 47, 54, 82, 133, 233; and *centrum*, 117, 118; created in heaven, 126; death of, 68; desire against soul, 28, 48, 51, 54, 77, 139, 148; envy of, 56, 91; leads man to death, 37; overcome, 117; place of, 188, 189; has robber castle, 45, 47, 48, 58, 121, 254; rule of, 127, 145, 228, 256; scorn for, 255, 256, 257; strive against, 39, 49, 77, 111, 256; and vanity, 38, 45, 99; and will, 207

Deuteronomy, 5:6–7; 101. 6:5; 101. 27:26; 106. 38:14; 105.

Divinity, energy of, 202, 205; ground of, 201; and harmony, 152; and knowledge, 185, 205; and nature, 202, 205; and outflow, 199, 200, 201, 202, 219

Earth, 221; hardness, 223; and melancholy humour, 253, 254

Ego, cf. Self, I

Elements, 211; end of, 186; and evil, 99; and external, 144, 217; and fifth essence, 217; hidden spirit of, 219; and *limus*, 102; and man's work, 78; origin of, 141, 143, 206, 221; and Paradise, 109, 131, 228; and *spiritus mundi*, 211, 217; and wisdom, 95; and world, 140, 245, 247

Enemies, cf. Devil, Godless Man; creatures as, 175; flesh as, 131; forgiveness of, 239; of God, 126; rule over, 94; of sin, 133

Ens, divine, 126, 204, 206, 207; and divine love, 212; internal, 207; and man's essence, 211

Envy, of devil, 56, 91; as false

image, 66, 67, 69; and man, 182, 211, 229, 230; man must leave, 74, 90, 157; as vanity, 28

Ephesians, 3:12; 76.

Esau, 156

The Eternal, "in" and "out", 225; and law, 130; One, 178, 185, 192, 197, 207, 208, 211, 213, 214, 215, 222; and soul, 127

Eve, 100; creation of, 147; fall of, 148; and Mary, 150

Evil, and anger, 127; avoidance of, 157; inclination to, 166; man turns to, 182; protection from, 91, 99; redemption from, 194; speaking of, 67

Exodus, 20:2–3; 101. 20:7; 105. 20:8–11; 108. 20:12; 111.

Ezekiel, 33:11; 31, 33, 37, 260.

Faith, appears as foolishness, 203; and Christ, 190; is a desire for God, 164, 199, 265; and gift, 168, 169; and grace, 74; ground, 190, 220; and Holy Spirit, 266; and hope, 169; and knowledge, 152, 220; lack of, 66, 68, 82, 104, 112, 135, 136, 191; and new birth of man, 154; and mystical union with Christ, 89; pray for, 112; promised in baptism, 28; in resurrection, 88; and saints, 183; and Sophia, 59, 60, 62; strengthening of, 32, 82, 85; and works, 78, 168

Fall, of Adam/man, 42, 44, 81, 90, 93, 94, 102, 146, 149, 218, 229; of Eve, 148, 149; image of God lost by, 44; of Lucifer, 44

Father, 90, 92, 99; and Christ, 91, 153; as creator, 111; draws man, 37, 65, 66, 67, 263, 266; gives Holy Spirit, 42, 50, 68, 76, 83, 265, 267; gives man to Christ,

42, 159, 257; gives Son, 244;
man comes to, 89, 239, 240; man
returns to, 74; and mercy, 76;
nature of, 247; parents an image
of, 111; pray to, 73, 76, 87; and
Trinity, 63, 95; will of, 72; his
wrath, 35, 52; his wrath changed
to love, 33

Fiat, creation of woman, 147; and
desire, 246; external, 146

Fire, and anger, 102, 115, 271;
breath, 144, 153, 154; and
centrum, 247; and choleric
humour, 250, 271; and darkness,
143; and devil, 207; divine, 133;
external, 216; essence of, 141;
and God, 52, 60, 96, 103, 126,
143, 186, 247; hardness, 223; and
hell, 191; internal, 217; and
judgement, 187; and light, 192,
211, 216, 217, 218, 221, 244,
247, 271; and love, 93, 99, 107,
120, 142, 153, 180, 181, 186,
244; and nature, 114; of
Pentecost, 86; and soul, 57, 58,
59, 60, 62, 248, 249, 250; spiritual,
218; and suffering, 142, 153; and
water, 141, 145, 147; and world,
143, 217; as wrath, 143, 212

Flesh, and Adam, 99; Christ is life
of, 42; Christ's, 86, 138; as
corrupted, 28, 60, 130, 149, 152,
153; as earthly, 51, 98, 99, 128,
138, 169, 187, 203; not eternal,
187; eternal, 144; and humours,
248; and lust, 30, 77, 81, 82,
138, 157, 188; must die, 140;
pleasures of, 134, 135; as prison
of soul, 50; spiritual, 187; strive
against, 39, 131, 155; tempts
soul, 31, 39, 61, 76, 132, 155;
and vanity, 34, 43, 48, 52, 55,
77, 82, 152; wrath in, 47

Forgiveness, and absolution, 160,
161; desire to ask for, 27; false,
160; of God, 91, 161; of other
men, 91; and sacraments, 162;
true, 132, 160

Forty Questions on the Soul, 137

Galatians, 2:17; 139. 2:20; 95. 4:6;
76. 4:19; 138. 4:30; 131, 156,
157. 6:8; 204.

Garden of Eden, 149

Genesis, and *Mysterium Magnum*,
70. 1:27; 65, 142. 1:28; 208. 2:17;
146. 2:18; 146. 2:21; 146. 3:5;
148. 3:15; 149, 256. 21:10; 131.
22; 157. 32:26; 77. 32:28; 267.
33:24–30; 266.

Glorification, of man after death,
188

God, cf. Honour; as the abyss,
209, 215; anger of, 47, 57, 82,
85, 97, 98, 99, 102, 104, 106,
112, 145, 149, 151, 234, 250;
became man, 44, 148, 149;
blessings of, 63, 72, 83, 91;
breath of, 143, 144, 209, 210,
213, 216; calls man, 81, 85, 129;
in Christ, 33, 57, 65, 81; comes
to man, 75; as creator, 29, 87,
90, 92, 94, 101, 105, 108, 112,
128, 171, 194, 209; cursed earth,
149; draws man, 82, 112, 133,
134, 157, 233, 264; dwells in
world, 141, 142; enmity against,
28; as Fountain-source, 51, 63,
71, 83, 84; gifts of, 73, 92; gives
Himself, 100; glory of, 57, 94,
175; His goodness, 87; hidden,
95, 96, 98, 179, 189, 194, 195,
196, 213, 235, 241; jealous, 60,
143; as Judge, 47; knowledge of,
96, 194; majesty of, 57, 58, 86,
88, 94, 95, 99, 103, 111, 136;
man rests in, 109, 175, 235; as
merciful, 27; and nature, 171,

195; necessity of, 195; not wish death of sinner, 31, 33, 37; order of, 109, 123, 124; patience of, 35, 56; permits evil, 192, 195, 196, 202; praise of, 57, 63, 84, 86, 90, 92, 95, 96, 100, 106, 107, 108, 202, 212, 242; present in man, 33, 49, 110, 203, 205; protector, 63, 87, 88, 99; revealed in our humanity, 34; not seen, 194, 202; Spirit of, 122, 123, 124, 146, 165, 166, 167, 168, 169, 204, 220, 250, 263; sustainer, 194; thanks to, 57, 63, 76, 84, 87, 92, 99, 100, 101, 104, 108, 241; and Trinity, 19; and truth, 57; way to, 132, 158; wills only Himself, 198; wisdom of, 30, 52, 96, 105, 122, 165, 166, 178, 206, 210, 250

God's judgement, and Christ's love, 47; of sin, 32, 108, 125; on sinner, 29, 35, 43, 47, 82, 107, 231, 232, 234, 246; and useless work, 124

God's love, absent, 183; and Christ, 91, 100, 152, 207, 208, 212; as desire, 51; and grace, 51, 63, 104; and man, 31, 33, 49, 55, 56, 75, 77, 85, 86, 91, 99, 101, 107, 112, 149, 185, 207, 230, 241; man rejects, 28, 34; and man's blindness, 54; man's desire for, 116, 119, 152; man's rest in, 108, 199; and nothing, 180; prayer to, 85; preserves man, 35, 37, 47, 48, 107, 249; and service, 63; and wrath, 115, 149; and His will, 130, 185, 192

God's mercy, 100; accept, 172, 175, 238, 241; desire for, 30, 35, 54, 63, 72, 74, 75, 79, 82, 120, 132, 235, 264; faith in, 41, 57, 68, 81; given, 104; and grace, 80, 81, 90, 100, 113, 234; intends

good for man, 55; and love, 143; man prays to, 46, 88, 241; nourishes man, 79; and self, 128; wasted, 28

Godless man, cf. Man, Sinner; beast, 149; believer seen as, 54; and church, 160, 162; death of, 30, 182, 212; as enemy, 51, 53, 55, 63, 88, 128, 138, 177, 191; and false images, 106, 107; and free will, 260; and grace, 66, 67, 158, 159; and hell, 183, 191; and judgement, 161, 189, 190, 191, 192; loses heaven, 30, 182; loses image of God, 29; needs law, 165; place of, 188, 189; pray for, 55, 91; scoffs at Christian, 46; and sin, 164, 260; unworthy, 40; works of, 169, 191

Godly man, appears as fool, 32, 39, 46, 53, 69, 202, 203, 233, 243; God is his blessing, 176; mocked, 54, 155, 190, 202, 242, 243; and mortal life, 204; not need law, 165; persecuted, 134, 166, 169, 176, 191, 203; tempted, 134, 135, 242, 243

Gods, false, 107

Good works, cf. Service; and Christian, 164; and divine power, 78; and Father, 95; and grace, 234; and love, 133

Grace, acceptance of, 90, 110; active, 75; availability of, 33, 66, 68, 69, 75, 78, 80, 94, 104, 128, 155, 208, 210, 234, 243, 259, 262; and Christ, 69, 90, 230, 240, 259; Christ is, 65, 70, 75, 93, 113, 131, 208, 209, 210, 225; desire for, 36, 77, 82, 83, 119, 232, 233, 262; as gift, 16, 28, 81, 101; from God, 83, 256; and godless man, 66, 67, 158, 159; hope in, 74, 183; and love, 51,

63, 104; man disloyal to, 34, 69; man doubts, 242, 255, 262; man kept from, 241, 242; man received in, 33, 100, 231, 264; man's search for, 27, 75, 234; man unworthy of, 34, 35, 68, 81, 119; as outflowing, 225; power of, 79, 89, 99; as saving, 36; and Sophia, 60, 154; way of, 47; and worthiness of man, 65

Greed, cf. Covetousness; of devil, 91; and willing spirit, 117

Ground, of all things, 179, 208, 223; creaturely, 225; divine, 178, 201, 206, 225; and doctrine, 79; as eternal, 185, 206; external, 220; of faith, 190; and God, 182, 195, 216, 223, 226, 242; internal, 226, 242; and love, 178–179; of man, 56, 76, 92, 209, 228, 242; and *materia*, 222; and mercy, 172; and mind, 198; and *Mysterium Magnum*, 70; and nature, 196, 199, 212, 213; and new birth, 137; and pain, 192; and prayer, 71; and soul, 93, 268; spiritual, 200, 203; supernatural, 172, 194, 195; and *tinctur*, 218; and will, 197, 207

Heat, and cold, 228

Heaven, Christ is, 159; is everywhere, 182, 185; hope for, 32; joy in, 56, 70, 77; kingdom of, 30, 43, 53, 80; in man, 60, 139, 141, 149, 151, 159, 182; man an enemy of, 29; man put on, 134; power of, 75; and Sophia, 60; and soul, 182; striving against hell, 45

Heavens, tell of God, 95

Heavenly corporeality, 40, 52, 99; and Christ, 151, 152, 153, 248; and saints, 161

Heavenly part (being), 33, 45, 52, 150, 152, 154; and light, 144

Hebrews, 3:7–8; 66. 6:4–6; 155. 11:6; 68.

Hell, 211; changed to heaven, 183, 244; conquered by Christ, 38, 41, 42, 76, 84, 85, 255, 257; and darkness, 186, 189; is everywhere, 182, 185; God preserves man from, 37, 47, 48; in man, 42, 57, 139, 141, 151, 182, 183, 229, 234; man captive of, 28; man deserving of, 29, 35, 98; man redeemed from, 57; *matrix* of, 126; place of, 188, 189; and Sophia, 59; soul in, 159, 235; striving against heaven, 45

Herod, 134

Holiness, of Christ, 42, 104, 112; desire for, 65, 137, 262; and *Ens*, 206; false, 168; of God, 81, 86, 93, 96, 98, 100, 106, 107, 116, 118; and man, 52, 69, 73, 86, 91, 108, 111, 161, 171, 181; and Names of God, 27; restored, 207; of spiritual world, 142, 144

Holy Spirit, baptism of, 135; as breath of life, 144; and Christ, 75; and confession, 81; dwells in man, 43, 138, 174; gifts of, 78; given by Father, 42, 50, 68, 76, 83; in God, 74; govern man, 63; and joy, 53; leads man, 88, 89, 92, 120, 121, 263; and mind, 94; presents Himself to God, 73; and prayer, 41; renews soul, 250; sent by Christ, 42; sent by God, 32; as teacher, 34, 37, 162; and Trinity, 63, 95; and will, 174; and wisdom, 95

Honour, desire for, 168; of God, 57, 61, 67, 73, 95, 112, 120, 122, 126, 202, 271, 272; of man, 145; for parents, 111, 112; and reason,

117, 118; of Sophia, 40; of
world, 32, 39, 40, 66, 67, 72, 92,
135, 231, 238, 239, 271

Hope, and despair, 235; and faith,
169; in God, 122, 209; in grace,
74, 183; and love, 168; for
redemption, 32, 130, 199; in
resurrection, 88; as sure, 85, 164;
and *temperamentum*, 224; and
trust, 244

Humanity, of Christ, 32, 33, 34,
36, 41, 42, 47, 49, 51, 70, 81,
85, 89, 93, 100, 104, 112, 132,
142, 149, 159, 179; Christ's in
us, 40; as corrupted, 52, 60, 63,
150, 151, 153; external, 141; and
grace, 79, 128; internal, 141;
reconciled to God, 28, 110; and
Word, 153

Humility, and grace, 120; in
heaven, 192; and hope, 224; lack
of, 118, 191; of man, 96, 114,
120, 121, 122; and reason, 122;
of Sophia, 39, 58; of soul in
repentance, 34, 40, 74, 80, 83,
85, 134, 174, 242; of soul seeking
Sophia, 45; of Word, 150

Humours, 245; characteristics of,
250; and *Mars*, 261; shape man,
247; and soul, 248, 249, 265,
266, 267

I, cf. Self, Ego; break, 178, 207;
and faith, 152; and will, 185; and
reason, 204

Illumination, and Holy Spirit, 73;
and light, 96, 182; and man's
spirit, 86

Image, angelic, 148; and
characteristics, 221; of Christ,
156, 176, 208; created, 205;
destroyed, 102, 203; and devil,
66, 67, 106, 228, 230, 234, 235,
240; of divine power, 223; of

earth-spirit, 219; external, 146,
185, 205; of external Adam, 156;
of God, 29, 40, 51, 52, 65, 66,
90, 92, 93, 94, 96, 102, 104, 105,
111, 129, 142, 145, 203, 243,
265; heavenly, 44, 102, 148, 153,
155, 235; idolatrous, 106, 107;
and internal element, 143; lost by
Adam's fall, 44; man's corrupted,
43, 49, 52, 56, 69, 92, 147, 149,
152; and mind, 214; renewal of,
53, 54, 90, 104, 241, 243; of
reason, 204; of self, 191, 209; of
spiritual world, 216; of time and
eternity, 143, 145; way of, 173,
206

Imagination, definition of, 24; and
desire, 115, 128, 147, 180, 268;
and devil, 145, 151, 157, 163,
254, 255, 256, 259, 262, 269;
external, 249, 251; false, 117; and
God, 150; and humour, 249, 251,
252, 253, 269; and soul, 271; and
vanity, 148

Impression, and darkness, 199,
200; and nature, 202; and will,
212

Incantation, and *magia*, 127

Incarnation, Christ's, 41, 44, 54;
of God, 149; of new man, 134

**On the Incarnation and Birth of
Jesus Christ**, 137

Innocence, and Adam, 89; of
Christ, 89; and man, 89

Isaac, 156

Isaiah, 1:18; 83, 125, 259. 26:16;
167. 29:13; 72. 42:3; 263. 49:15;
46. 49:15 – 16; 259.

Ishmael, 156, 157, 158

Israel, 101

Jacob, 77, 83, 266, 267

James, 2:19; 156.

Jeremiah, 23:23; 33.

72, 73, 85, 91, 157, 168; for parents, 112; and power, 178; of Sophia, 58; and suffering, 178; and world, 67, 106; and wrath, 41

Lucifer, fall of, 44, 115, 128, 134; and pearl, 60; and self, 114, 121

Luke, 8:12; 77, 160, 234. 11:4; 128. 11:9; 67, 83. 11:9–13; 76. 11:13; 68, 83, 265, 267. 11:13–19, 134. 11:23; 124. 11:34; 133. 15:7; 31, 70, 77. 16:22; 29. 17:20–21; 182. 17:21; 33, 138. 17:31; 105. 19:10; 69.

Lust, death of, 85, 122, 157, 242; earthly, 210; of flesh, 35, 38, 46, 60, 77, 81, 99, 110, 138, 232, 233, 234, 235; in man, 28, 91, 92, 98, 100, 103, 110, 123, 180, 229, 232; man loses heaven by, 30, 102, 206; and unrighteousness, 88; and vanity, 146, 182; and world, 60, 81, 98, 99, 115, 129, 183

Magia, as false, 127

Man, cf. Godless Man, Godly Man, Image, Lust, Sinner, Soul; and action, 157; after mortal death, 187; as beast, 67, 102, 147, 155, 172, 230; and being, 151; belongs to God, 73, 74, 98, 101, 104; blindness of, 96, 109, 110, 262; bride of Christ, 89; can do nothing, 35, 43, 46, 50, 68, 72, 73, 83, 91, 92, 96, 103, 104, 110, 120, 172, 209, 238, 239; children of Christ, 53, 56, 66, 74, 82, 136, 137, 156, 158, 177; children of God, 112, 115, 121, 129, 130, 132, 134, 163, 165, 166, 167, 169, 170, 181, 192, 225, 241, 244; in Christ, 104, 107, 257; is Christ's payment,

158; consider what he asks for, 72; desires God, 249; enters God, 69; essence, 151, 152, 211; examine his state, 71, 139, 140, 142, 157, 167; external, 152, 154, 155, 185, 186, 210, 211; faithless, 47, 66; and false images, 66, 67; fears God, 164; not forsake Christ, 48; and gifts, 78, 92, 165, 166, 168, 169; gives himself to Christ, 173; gives self to God, 93; guilty, 47, 164; as image of God, 29, 40, 51, 52, 65, 66, 90, 92, 93, 94, 96, 102, 104, 105, 111, 129, 142, 145, 203, 243, 265; inheritance of, 34, 97, 157, 159, 189, 203, 225, 241; an instrument, 119, 120, 121, 122, 146; internal, 155, 159, 162, 210; internal strife, 155, 163, 167, 184; and knowledge, 164, 165, 166; like all things, 173; majesty of, 96; member of Christ, 65, 140, 153, 170, 177, 190; new birth of, 32, 52, 53, 54, 55, 56, 71, 74, 100, 107, 113, 133, 134, 136, 137, 138, 139, 140, 152, 154, 163, 218, 241, 244, 250, 264; nothingness of, 97; nourishment of, 65, 75, 79, 84, 98, 111, 138, 153, 162, 190, 212; as pilgrim, 53, 54, 61, 91, 98, 227, 243; prepared for prayer, 78, 79, 80; as prodigal son, 74, 104, 239, 264; purity of, 76; put on Christ's merit, 159; reveals God, 210; rule with Christ, 94, 96, 103; ruler of creation, 90, 94, 102, 104, 105, 144, 172, 173, 179, 208, 228, 233; is a sinner, 28, 38, 46, 47, 81, 90, 103, 139, 152, 164, 256, 262, 264; and Sophia, 40; and spiritual world, 187; stands before Christ, 33;

stands before God, 68; as swineherd, 28, 35, 68, 104, 264; temple of Christ, 139, 140, 153; temple of God, 140, 152, 162, 244; as temple of Holy Spirit, 43, 138, 139, 153, 174; tempted, 48, 87, 91, 146, 172, 175; tested, 44, 146, 176; turned from God, 98; turned to God, 82, 99; unclean, 49, 93, 155; unworthy, 29, 34, 35, 38, 41, 42, 49, 68, 74, 81, 84, 85, 103, 104, 120, 241; weakness of, 55; worker for Christ, 48, 62, 63, 73, 91

Man's desire (will), and *centrum*, 127, 199; and devil, 120; directed to Christ, 152; directed to God, 114, 116, 119, 120, 121, 199; must die, 140; turned from all things, 173

Manifold, 206, 207, 214

Mark, 7:24–30; 38.

Mars, 261

Mary, 41, 44, 49, 52, 150, 151

Materia, and anger, 269; external, 222; hard, 222; and resurrection, 186

Matrix, and fire, 114; and hell, 126; *venus matrix*, 147; of woman, 147; and world, 115

Matter, form of, 222; origin of, 222

Matthew, 2:16; 134. 5:23–24; 77. 6:12; 77. 7:6; 149. 7:7; 83, 193, 265. 7:21; 72. 10:37–39; 40. 11:12; 80. 11:28; 31, 33, 81, 111, 161, 263. 11:28–29; 130. 12:30; 210. 12:43–45; 116. 15:13; 124. 15:73; 168. 17:20; 45. 18:3; 132, 138, 173. 18:11; 257. 21:19; 220. 22:37; 101. 23:15; 170. 25:34–36; 190. 26:41; 87. 27:43; 203. 28:18; 174. 28:20; 33.

Melancholy, 242, 251, 263; and darkness, 261; description of,
245, 253, 254; and drunkenness, 268; and fear, 245, 255, 264, 266, 267, 268, 269; and madness, 262; origin, 245; and pride, 270; and temptation, 260

Mercurius, and covetousness, 229; and fire-wheel, 228, 231, 232; and metals, 219; and *tinctur*, 222; and *vulcanus*, 228

Mind, chasteness of, 40; created, 205; as faithless to God, 27; God revealed to, 195; and grace, 35; ground, 198; image of God, 94, 96, 111, 205; and *mysterium*, 200; origin of, 205, 210; outflow of, 198, 214; purification of, 89, 100; and repentance, 27, 40; and sin, 128; and Sophia, 40; strife in, 199; turned from God, 94; turned to God, 89, 94, 100, 105, 110, 129, 132, 238; will of, 130

Miracles, 92, 96, 126, 178, 216

Monstrum, broken, 104, 235; and serpent, 210; and soul, 231

Moses, 146

Mother, of body, 154; and *centrum*, 117; Christ as, 113, 140; and desire, 128; and devil, 126; of evil and good, 115; true, 118; Word as, 111, 112

Mount Moriah, 157

Mount Sinai, 101

Mysterium, and judgement, 124, 125; and mind, 200; and wisdom, 192, 199

Mysterium Magnum, as Creator, 214, 216; discover, 194, 213, 272; and outflow, 224; and power, 199, 211–212, 218, 224; and will, 221, 222

Mysterium Magnum, the work, 70, 137, 226

Mystery, dangerous, 122; of elements, 224; understanding of, 65

Names, Divine, of God, 27, 43,
52, 94, 102, 104, 105, 106;
Jehovah, 33, 52, 65, 150; of
Jesus, 33, 42, 43, 45, 51, 52, 79,
93, 94, 101, 105, 107, 108, 110,
150, 153, 161, 176; misuse of,
27, 43, 88, 105, 106, 107, 108,
109

Nature, and anger, 114, 149, 205;
and *centrum*, 114, 117, 118,
127, 128, 142, 200; of divinity,
202; dominion of, 124, 206;
eternal, 109, 114, 126, 128, 131,
142, 146, 184; external, 116, 118,
204, 210; and God, 171; ground
of, 196, 199, 212, 213; human of
Christ, 42, 44; human as
corrupted, 52, 60, 63, 150, 151,
153; human, as hidden, 55; man
stands in, 172; man's, 90, 96; and
revelation, 210; and self, 171; and
temperamentum, 208; temporal,
114, 205; will of, 200, 201, 223

Nicodemus, 138, 177

Nothing, The, incomprehensible,
179; and love, 178, 180; as search
for something, 180; and will,
121, 209

Nutrimentum, and external life,
211, 220; and plants, 218; and
spiritus, 217

Obedience, of Christ, 50; lack of,
41, 103, 112, 123, 146, 196, 239,
247; man's, 32, 50, 65, 74, 83,
102, 104, 105, 111, 112, 113,
129, 133, 135, 157, 165, 274; and
will, 130, 140

On the New Birth, 70

On the Three Worlds, 137

On True Repentance, 70

Paradise, 249; and Adam, 42, 90,
108, 149, 150; creation of, 126,
128, 143, 144; and earth, 109; as
garden, 56; and harmony, 218;
and *limus*, 101; man led to, 56,
230; and pearl, 39, 60; restored,
110, 244; return to, 88, 101, 111;
and sin, 33, 65, 126, 155; and
Sophia, 61; and will, 130, 205;
and wisdom, 10

Pearl, 159; and beasts, 149, 157;
and *centrum*, 223; gained in
Christ, 44; as gift, 57, 58; given
by Christ, 49; loss of, 154, 155;
and Sophia, 41, 45, 46, 59, 60,
61; and soul, 153, 265, 266;
swallowed by body, 39; and
unity, 224

Penance, delayed, 38

Pentecost, 86

Perceptivity, working of, 215, 218,
219, 223, 228

I Peter, 5:8; 274. 5:8–9; 87.

Pharisees, 169

Philippians, 3:20; 139, 159, 174,
182, 261.

Phlegmatic, 245; description of,
246, 252, 253, 273, 274

Pilate, 47

Polus, 222

Power, and body, 187; of Christ,
36, 50, 52, 53, 85, 89, 153, 161;
of death removed, 41; of devil,
48, 76, 149; divine, 29, 43, 49,
51, 78, 79, 120, 121, 144, 151,
161, 166, 187, 188, 197, 199,
200, 206, 223, 225, 226;
divisibility of, 200, 221; earthly,
206; eternal, 215, 223; external,
218; of Father, 112, 240; of God,
52, 56, 57, 77, 78, 86, 88, 93,
94, 95, 96, 99, 100, 101, 102,
106, 107, 112, 151, 152, 188; of
God as help, 39, 41, 51, 166; of
grace, 79, 89, 99; of heaven, 75;
hidden, 219; of Holy Spirit, 91,
92; internal, 219, 220; of man,
35, 42, 50, 51, 52, 73, 76, 82,
83, 110, 136, 166, 175; of man

after death, 188; material, 187;
and outflow, 200, 221; and
prayer, 74, 76; of reason, 143,
144; of Saviour, 92; of sonship,
133; and soul, 247; of world, 32
Prayer, for enemies, 77; God calls
us to, 71, 74, 76; for grace, 231;
for help, 46, 51, 55, 68, 75; and
Holy Spirit, 41; improper, 72,
73, 76; for love, 104; mouthed
only, 71, 72, 75, 78, 80;
necessity of, 169, 270; proper,
71, 72, 73, 74, 76, 77, 78, 79,
80, 81, 114, 241; for repentance,
27; and Sophia, 39, 49; of soul,
231, 232, 268; for strength, 42,
69, 134, 176; in temptation, 46,
53; for wisdom, 92
Prayer Book, 113
Preaching, 160, 161, 162
Pride, and darkness, 116; as false
image, 66, 69, 92; in man, 169,
182, 191, 230; turn from, 74, 90,
157, 270; as vanity, 28; and
willing spirit, 117; of world, 106,
114
Principium, and contrariety, 207;
and devil, 127; and divine
ground, 206; and division, 127,
201; earthly, 201; first, 205, 207,
209; heavenly, 201, 261; and life,
268; and mind, 205; second, 206,
265; third, 206; three, 205, 218
Promise, cf. Covenant; Christ is,
52, 89; of Christ, 31, 32, 37, 42,
43, 50, 58, 67, 68, 69, 83; of
Christianity, 156; and faith, 28;
of God, 41, 46, 47, 49, 69, 83,
84, 90, 131, 149, 150, 242, 265;
of grace, 239; of Holy Spirit,
266; land of, 101; of man, 28, 46;
tested, 164
Prophets, 121; testimony of, 72,
150
Proverbs, 24:16; 139.

Providence, of God, 63, 72, 234
Psalms, 5:5; 260. 6:2; 56.
18:26–27; 188. 19:7; 95. 23:4; 58,
84. 23:5; 63. 112:4; 212. 130:6;
265. 143:2; 139.
Purification, desire for, 89; of
man, 100; of mind, 89, 100; of
soul, 85, 243
Putrefaction, and works, 124

Reason, and contemplation, 65; die
to, 121, 122, 134, 203, 242;
dominion, 114, 119; earthly, 55,
76, 116, 203; external, 45, 116,
117, 118, 119, 122, 123, 155,
174, 270; forsaken, 242; as light,
117, 118; limits of, 194, 202,
203, 204; as mirror, 116, 119;
and pride, 114; not to be
rejected, 122; rest of, 195; and
self, 125, 135, 268; and suffering,
195, 202; turned to God, 238;
and understanding, 92, 118, 203;
unworthy, 122; and will, 117,
119, 195, 203, 204, 209, 242; and
wrath, 114
Reconciliation, of Christ, 28, 47,
160; of enemies, 77; and man, 91;
and work, 163
Redemption, through Christ, 39,
47, 49, 54, 57, 74, 82, 85, 87,
107, 183, 231, 241, 242; desire
for, 35, 36, 56, 86, 99, 243; and
foolishness, 203; hope of, 130,
199; pray for, 111, 128, 129, 243;
and self-will, 202; not seen, 194;
and Sophia, 62; and will, 86
Regeneration, and pretence, 131;
of will and desire, 36, 100
Repentance, and Christ, 38, 230,
231; constant, 174, 175, 181;
delayed, 233; desire for, 27, 31,
67, 82, 99, 101, 107, 231, 233,
234; and new birth of man, 56;

for past sins, 36, 40, 82; proper, 74, 80, 82, 234, 274; and righteous, 77; and Sophia, 154; way of, 31, 49, 65, 238

Resignation, to God, 115, 146; man called to, 129; man has left, 118, 121; path of, 122, 135; of soul, 179; of will, 43, 61, 120, 125

Resolution, earnest, 38, 39, 40; to gain love of God, 32; to new birth, 43, 134; and repentance, 27, 32, 37, 38, 49, 69, 238; and Sophia, 40

Resurrection, of body, 186; of Christ, 42, 49, 71, 82, 84, 86, 89, 100, 132, 158, 162, 235, 239; of heavenly part, 45, 153; man's through Christ's, 36, 50, 84, 88, 90, 188

Revelation, of eternal knowledge, 200; of Eternal One, 185; of God, 51, 53, 81, 94, 122, 144, 149, 150, 166, 179, 185, 194, 195, 197, 210; of God's love, 55, 85, 126; of God's wrath, 126; of good and evil, 145; of heaven, 185; and judgement, 125; and knowledge, 166; of Sophia, 56; of spiritual world, 186

Revelation, 118. 2:17; 261. 3:21; 261. 5:12; 120. 7:17; 263.

Righteousness, of Christian, 139; and God, 28, 32, 47, 55, 66, 103, 106, 109; lack of, 83, 103, 139, 167, 230, 235; man's, 74, 77, 140, 170, 190, 238, 257, 260; man's service in, 52, 86; pray for, 88; strive for, 165

Romans, 5:18; 208, 260. 7:20; 128. 7:23; 128. 8:1; 129, 138. 8:15; 76. 8:19–22; 201. 8:26; 73, 263. 10:8; 33, 105. 11:32; 139.

Sabbath, 108; Christ is, 110, 111; Paradise as, 110; profaned, 109, 110

Sacraments, man's use of, 160, 161, 163; and saints, 161–162

Saints, and church, 162; community of, 29; death of, 30, 192; and eternity, 29, 186, 192; and faith, 183; and holy works, 163; joy of, 192; and judgement, 161; path of, 121, 265; and Pentecost, 86; and sin, 161

Salvation, desire for, 36, 88; false idea of, 117, 203, 233; man united in, 73; merited by Christ, 158; through the Son, 33

Sanctification, and grace, 83; of man, 42, 110

Sanguine, 245, 270; description of, 246, 251, 252, 272, 273; and drunkenness, 272, 273

Satan, and Christ, 234; deceit of, 28, 91, 102; and soul, 117

Saturn, 270

Saviour, 87, 88, 99; in Christ, 37; death of, 55, 86; and grace, 75; helps man, 54, 63, 92, 96; man waits for, 139; promises of, 42; promises to in baptism, 28; not recognized, 35; not seen, 194, 203, 204

Scripture, 62, 65, 118

Self, cf. Ego, I; break, 49, 134, 208; capable only of sin, 35, 123; deceived, 116, 117, 121; despair for, 68; die to, 114, 125; and divine energy, 202; false seeking of, 35, 66, 115, 116, 119, 134; as fool, 35; given to God, 37, 95; and grace, 208; and knowledge, 91, 93, 115, 119, 166, 167; and pride, 114; and soul, 52, 56; turned from God, 119, 123, 135,

136, 184; and vanity, 34, 37; will
of, 36, 116; and work, 168, 169;
and wrath, 114

Self-desire, cf. Self-will, Soul's
Desire, Desire

Self-will, and characteristics, 216;
and darkness, 185, 200; death of,
123, 125, 179, 180, 192, 203,
208; desire for, 206; divisibility,
196, 199, 200, 202, 225; madness
of, 207; as material, 200, 201;
and perceptivity, 214; and
resigned will, 186; serves sin,
129, 130; turned from God, 122,
123, 129, 184; turned to God,
123, 203

Senses, and contemplative, 65;
dedicated, 88, 110, 238; and
divine order, 210; false, 206; and
lust, 102; outgoing of, 205, 214,
231; and wisdom, 205

Sensus, and divine love, 207, 211;
and good and evil, 197

Separator, and characteristic, 215,
216, 217, 221; as Creator, 216,
217, 220; and divisibility, 221;
external, 218; hidden, 220; made
visible, 216; and power, 216,
223; ruler of nature, 215;
spiritual, 217; and *tinctur*, 218,
221; and will, 214, 215, 216, 225

Servant, to Christians, 239; of
God, 94, 123, 239; faithfulness
of, 73; man is, 88, 91, 93, 103; as
obedient, 63; of sin, 129

Service, to all men, 91, 189, 190;
to Christ, 189, 190; and God,
52, 63, 106, 135, 165, 168,
192, 266; to godly men, 92, 190;
lack of, 190; to neighbour, 90,
168; to poor, 90, 135

Shame, 99; and devil, 48, 254;

man's, 35, 55, 98, 100, 103, 147,
149, 241; for sin, 35, 56, 85; for
will, 36

Signatur, and *Separator*, 217

Silence, and hearing God, 171, 209

Sin, cf. Forgiveness; cleansed by
Christ, 48, 82; conquered by
Christ, 41, 81, 86, 129, 131, 151,
240; die to, 36, 37, 131, 133,
139, 157; and flesh, 128, 129,
138, 151; forgiveness of, 27, 56,
57, 69, 73, 83, 85, 129, 160, 161,
162, 163, 231; and God's anger,
250; inherited, 55, 150; law of,
134; man guilty of, 46, 47; man
lives in, 28, 29; sorrow for, 30,
31, 82, 132; strive against, 39,
92, 158, 164, 240; man trapped
in, 35, 58, 82; and vanity, 54

Sinner, called to Christ, 33, 81;
God's love for, 33, 34; leaves sin,
130; as repentant, 33, 70, 83,
158; warned by Sophia, 44

Solomon, 121; Song of, 2:1; 41.
Wisdom of, 11:21; 143.

Sophia, cf. Wisdom; not abandon
man, 61; bride of Christ, 154;
bride of soul, 58, 60, 62, 70, 154;
and fountain, 62; hides herself,
154; honour of, 40; as humanity
of Christ, 70; leads man, 44, 154,
249; love of, 40, 49; love for soul,
58, 59, 62; man's unity with, 44,
45, 46, 57, 60, 61, 62, 69, 70,
242; and miracles, 58, 59; and
pearl, 41, 45, 46, 59, 60, 61;
Queen of heaven, 60; and
repentance, 56, 154

Son, 87, 88, 99; cleanses us, 48, 88;
death of, 42, 55, 74; given by
Father, 244; and God's love, 85,
91; and grace, 83; man calls on,
73; man heir to, 82; sent by God,

33, 63, 75, 81; and Trinity, 63, 95

Sonship, of Christ, 158; false, 133, 158; inherited, 159, 225; man not in, 134; tested, 135; true, 133, 158

Soul, cf. Man; bound to earthly life, 28, 38, 147, 153; bridegroom of Sophia, 56, 58, 59, 60, 62, 154; captive, 76, 132, 161, 230, 232, 233, 234, 235, 267; and *centrum*, 43, 103; Christ is life of, 42; cries to God, 63, 232; darkness in, 141; defiled, 34; enlightened, 227, 234, 243; eternal, 218; eternal part, 154, 155; and fear, 36, 77, 231, 235, 256, 258, 259, 261, 268; God speaks with, 79, 80, 81, 171, 209, 231; and grace, 27, 37; as guilty, 31; and heaven, 182; and joy, 57, 242; not know itself, 34; and light, 141; and love, 41, 49, 57, 229; messenger of God, 61; and new birth, 75, 230, 234; nourishment of, 36, 42, 43, 49, 50, 79, 80, 86, 119, 131, 153, 161, 248, 249; and pearl, 60; purity of, 76, 77, 230; remain firm, 45; and repentance, 56, 75, 81, 230, 231; rest of, 182, 234, 235, 240, 244; as robber castle, 45, 47, 48, 254, 259; and Sophia, 39, 58, 59, 61; substance of, 247; surrounded by sin, 40; temple of Holy Spirit, 182; tempted, 28, 31, 39, 45, 46, 77, 79, 158, 227, 228, 230, 231, 232, 233, 234, 243, 244, 254, 260, 263; tested, 79, 243; torments of, 99, 231, 232, 234, 241, 243; turned from God, 27, 34, 47, 60, 82; turned to God, 63, 87, 100, 110, 111, 232; union with Sophia, 9, 10,

14, 17, 45, 46, 57, 60, 61, 62, 69, 70, 242; unworthy, 56, 57; weakness of, 31; wounded, 56

Soul's desire, for Christ, 32, 36, 37, 48, 52; and Christ's death, 36, 71; dedicated, 88, 103; for God, 34, 41, 51; led to Christ's love, 42; and *limus*, 211; and Sophia, 45, 58; turned from God, 110, 127, 229; for vanity, 184; and Word, 41

Soul's will, to be broken, 36, 39, 179; directed to God, 121, 125, 152, 179, 231; eternal, 131; false, 212; free, 255; and heaven, 53; and humility, 121; to be obedient, 36, 41, 50; and purity, 77; shame for, 36; turned from God, 28, 228

Sorrow, for past sins, 30, 31, 37, 241

Spirit, astral, 231; and Christ, 85; deceived, 117; enlightenment of, 37, 92; external, 217, 245, 247, 262; of the flesh, 39; of God, 55; of grace, 69; and Holy Spirit, 42, 53, 122; and love, 86; of soul, 42, 50, 52, 79; and *tinctur*, 218, 219

Spiritual, being, 187; flesh, 187; life, 187; as internal, 142, 148; working, 186; world, 92, 142, 144, 145, 185, 186, 187, 211, 215, 216, 217

Spiritus, and *centrum*, 217; of earth, 218; external, 217; and medicine, 224

Spiritus mundi, power of, 217; and sun, 211

Stars, and chaos, 221; and light, 95, 117; and prayer, 71; and sanguine humour, 272; source of, 206, 221; and world, 140, 247

Suffering, and darkness, 141, 142;

and desire, 195; and evil, 194; and light, 141, 142; and love, 178; reason for, 202

Sufferings of Christ, as comfort, 133; and grace, 82; man enters in, 32, 54, 71, 84, 131, 152, 158, 175, 238, 239, 241; and man's impurity, 42, 89, 230; as protection, 31, 36, 47, 50, 54, 257; and soul, 42

Supernatural, ground of, 194, 195; knowledge, 213; life, 171, 172; and love, 179

Temperamentum, and divine knowledge, 205; and divisibility, 196, 224; and Eternal One, 207; as eternal rest, 206, 208; and hope, 224; and nature, 208; and understanding, 199, 200; and unity, 224

Temptation, cf. Man, Soul; of Christ, 41, 44; and judgement, 48, 49; prayer in, 46, 53; of soul, 28, 31, 39, 45, 46

Testament, 161; of Christ, 167

Three Kinds of Lives of Man, The, 137

Time, and eternity, 140, 141, 143, 144, 145, 178

Tinctur, and characteristics, 147, 150; and Christ, 248; as fiery, 222; forms itself, 221; and ground, 219, 220; and love, 151; material, 187; and medicine, 220, 224; and metal, 246; *Mysterium magnum*, 218; as noble, 222, 223; and perceptivity, 219; and power, 219, 220; and *Separator*, 218, 221; and Sophia, 57

Trinity, dwelling in man, 153; man in presence of, 33, 79; is One, 87, 95, 222

Trust, in God, 83, 122, 203; lack of, 82, 97, 229; and neighbour, 123; and self, 117; and soul, 103, 244

Turba magna, and anger, 127; of man, 136; and sin, 164

Ungodly, cf. Godless Man, Sinner

Un-ground, and will, 198, 206

Union, of all men, 78, 91, 165; of believer and Christ, 32; of Christians, 177, 190; divine, 207; eternal, 215, 223; in God, 94, 104, 110, 123, 222, 223, 225; of God and man, 52, 167; lack of, 167, 169, 170; in man, 167, 206; of man and Sophia, 44, 45, 46, 60, 61, 62, 69, 70, 242; and movement, 223; outflow of, 215; and separation, 214

Vanity, death to, 36, 37, 44, 54, 74, 77, 99, 147, 157; and flesh, 34, 48, 51, 52, 148, 149; and hell, 191; of lost time, 31; and man, 98; man bound in, 44, 81, 103, 153, 154; and misery, 30, 60; put aside, 40, 148, 152, 154, 155, 167, 201; and self, 37; and soul, 28, 48, 51, 58, 75, 77, 147, 182, 230; and will, 140, 154; will of, 55; of world, 34, 38, 82, 138, 155, 183

Venus, 271

Verbo fiat, and creation, 143, 145; of eternal nature, 146

Virtues, and divine power, 78; divisibility, 200; lack of, 230; of love, 178; and power, 214; and wisdom, 213

Vulcanus, and fire-wheel, 228, 229

Water, 221; in all things, 223; and external life, 250; and phlegmatic humour, 252, 273; as source, 248; thinness, 223

Will, break, 62, 83, 93, 100, 101, 119, 120, 122, 172, 195, 207, 242; blinded, 81; captured, 208; changed, 212, 225; of Christ, 47, 130; and *contrarium*, 196, 197, 200; created, 201; of devil, 50, 83, 254; directed to God, 79, 80, 86, 92, 102, 106, 108, 110, 119, 120, 122, 165, 172, 174, 182, 197, 203, 209, 210, 239, 240; divine, 216, 218, 223, 226, 248; divisibility of, 196, 197, 199, 201, 214; eternal, 201, 213, 214, 215, 225; as evil, 83, 134; false, 183, 184, 185, 210, 211; of Father, 72; of flesh, 61; and God; 37, 50, 65, 74, 76, 199; and grace, 35, 63, 119; of God, 51, 65, 90, 91, 93, 94, 102, 104, 108, 116, 122, 123, 124, 126, 128, 130, 164, 166, 184, 185, 196, 197, 203, 205, 206, 209, 213, 214, 216, 221, 225; and Holy Spirit, 79; image of God, 205; and law, 130; natural, 232; origin of, 205; outflow of, 197, 199, 205, 214, 216, 218, 225; perceptivity, 206, 225; purity of, 80, 81; as resigned, 122, 125, 128, 129, 130, 172, 182, 186, 208; resoluteness of, 39, 69, 76, 77, 133, 134; and sin, 132, 140; supernatural, 195; turned from creatures, 174; turned from God, 80, 92, 102, 103, 104, 106, 109, 110, 116, 172, 174, 182, 209, 235; ungrounded, 198; weakness of, 79

Wisdom, cf. Sophia; and creation, 213; divine, 94, 205, 249; earthly, 177; and folly, 202, 203; of God, 30, 52, 96, 105, 122,

165, 166, 178, 206, 210, 250; and godly man, 181; heavenly, 177; as *Mysterium*, 192, 199; pray for, 92; and Spirit, 10, 95

Wisdom of Solomon, 11:21; 143.

The Word, 108, 249; became man, 41, 42, 43, 107, 188; calls man, 111; and creation, 105, 150, 185, 213; essence of, 98; given to man, 88, 105; and God's power, 152; hidden, 225; and judgement, 189; man's seeking for, 248; is Mother, 111, 112; outflow of, 215, 225; resurrection, 88; revealed, 95; reveals God, 213; and will of God, 65, 199, 213, 214, 221

Words, of Christ, 42, 45, 46, 69, 83, 86, 174, 189; and devil, 77; of God, 67, 110, 171, 210; not heard, 160, 161, 163; instrument, 168; many not needed, 80; mouthing of, 39, 43, 71, 72; must be kept, 44; and slander, 67; and the Word, 225

Work, belongs to God, 73, 102; in Christ's spirit, 32, 130, 133, 169, 188, 244; and Christ's vineyard, 32, 48, 62, 63, 73, 74, 266; of creation, 92; divine, 188; external, 78, 133, 163; of God, 90, 105, 109, 124, 178, 179; and grace, 93; and Holy Spirit, 41, 63; internal, 78, 163; and man, 96, 157, 168; place in God, 69, 71, 90, 92, 99, 102, 135, 168, 170, 210; of repentance, 38, 69, 74, 99; and self, 123, 124, 125; working of God, 51, 63, 71, 77, 79, 91, 92, 93, 95, 99, 102, 109, 111, 125, 152, 165, 180, 188, 205, 220

World, cf. Spiritual; as dark, 142, 148; detachment from, 32, 172,

173, 181; eternal, 142, 216; external, 142, 143, 145, 148, 153, 186, 187, 216, 247, 265; false love for, 67; not grasp God, 140; internal, 142, 143, 148, 154, 186, 211, 247; and light, 95, 140, 142; man in three worlds, 142, 151; pleasures of, 60, 233, 235; reason why created, 225; scorns godly man, 32, 40, 53, 69, 131, 176, 177, 181, 202, 242, 243; spirit of, 245, 247, 248, 249; spiritual, 92, 142, 144, 145, 185, 186, 187, 211, 216, 217, 221; strive against, 39, 45, 80; tempt man, 183, 233; visible, 185, 187, 200, 210, 215, 216, 217, 221

Wrath, changed to love, 33, 42, 50, 84, 91; of Christ, 33, 46, 54, 55; of God, 27, 28, 31, 36, 39, 42, 46, 47, 48, 50, 51, 55, 56, 58, 59, 61, 67, 76, 83, 86, 90, 97, 98, 100, 102, 103, 104, 109, 110, 112, 114, 117, 123, 124, 125, 126, 130, 132, 139, 141, 143, 150, 158, 159, 161, 169, 176, 183, 191, 229, 230, 232, 234, 244, 254, 258, 262, 267, 268, 269, 271; and guilt, 91; man must leave, 74, 90; and soul, 47, 50, 67, 88, 182, 229, 230; and strife, 224; and vanity, 28, 182

Zion, 53, 56, 136